W9-CNA-508

W. Clarence & Stephen Schilt

A Life
TO DIE FOR

Discover the Secret of Christ's Transforming Power

Pacific Press® Publishing Association
Nampa, Idaho
Oshawa, Ontario, Canada
www.pacificpress.com

Cover design by Steve Lanto
Cover design resources from iStockphoto.com
Inside design by Aaron Troia

Copyright © 2009 by Pacific Press® Publishing Association
Printed in the United States of America
All rights reserved

You can obtain additional copies of this book by calling toll-free 1-800-765-6955 or by visiting http://www.adventistbookcenter.com.

Scripture quotations marked NLT are taken from the Holy Bible, New Living Translation, copyright © 1996. Used by permission of Tyndale House Publishers, Inc., Wheaton, Illinois 60189. All rights reserved.

Scriptures quoted from NKJV are from The New King James Version, copyright © 1979, 1980, 1982, Thomas Nelson, Inc., Publishers.

Scripture quotations marked ESV are from The Holy Bible, English Standard Version®, copyright © 2001 by Crossway Bibles, a publishing ministry of Good News Publishers. Used by permission. All rights reserved.

Scripture quotations marked NIV are taken from the HOLY BIBLE, NEW INTERNATIONAL VERSION®. Copyright © 1973, 1978, 1984 by International Bible Society. Used by permission of Zondervan. All rights reserved.

Scriptures quoted from TEV are from the *Good News Bible*—Old Testament: Copyright © American Bible Society 1976, 1992; New Testament: Copyright © American Bible Society 1966, 1971, 1976, 1992.

Scriptures marked NCV are quoted from *The Holy Bible, New Century Version,* copyright © 1987, 1988, 1991 by Word Publishing, a division of Thomas Nelson, Inc. Used by permission.

Scripture texts credited to NRSV are from the New Revised Standard Version of the Bible, copyright © 1989 by the Division of Christian Education of the National Council of the Churches of Christ in the USA. Used by permission. All rights reserved.

Library of Congress Cataloging-in-Publication Data

Schilt, W. Clarence, 1942-
 A life to die for : discover the secret of Christ's transforming power /
W. Clarence Schilt, Stephen Schilt.
  p. cm.
 ISBN 13: 978-0-8163-2308-1 (pbk.)
 ISBN 10: 0-8163-2308-9 (pbk.)
 1. Christian life—Seventh-day Adventist authors. 2. Self-denial. I. Schilt, Stephen. II. Title.
 BV4647.S4S33 2009
 248.4'86732—dc22

                                                                                        2008049586

09 10 11 12 13 • 5 4 3 2 1

Dedication

To our wives, Dianna and Dee Dee, for their patience with this project, their willingness to be a part of our stories here, their valuable feedback, and most important, their love, which provides us daily opportunities to learn and more effectively live a life to die for.

Acknowledgments

This book went through considerable editing and refining before it was completed. Many of the improvements depended on the invaluable feedback provided by several who read the early drafts. We would like to express our heartfelt thanks to all those involved and in particular, those recognized here:

- Jeannie Andrews, for her ongoing editorial coaching throughout the writing process;
- Mike Jones, Clarence's dear friend, who was a constant source of encouragement and support from the inception to the completion of this project;
- Edna Maye Loveless, for her advice to "show" rather than "tell," which made for a more engaging read;
- Nathan Schilt, our brother, who shared critical input on the potential for misunderstanding this life to die for, which led to important modifications;
- David Jarnes, for supporting the editing process after the manuscript was submitted to Pacific Press®;
- and members of Clarence's church, for their willingness to engage in and experiment with the journey of a life to die for, which provided invaluable experiences that influenced the applications shared in this book.

Table of Contents

Preface

"To die for" is an expression that describes the absolute best, which is exactly the life you will learn about in this book—the very best! But our title is more than an expression. We mean it quite literally. The life described here is so extraordinary that we are willing to die for it—it's that good. Indeed, to have the life we are talking about, *you have to die*—something that will become evident later. In the meantime, we welcome the chance to tell you what this life is, and, almost as important, what it is not.

It might be easier to tell you first what this life is not. Our title is not meant to suggest another self-improvement formula for success. Although this life to die for ultimately provides immense rewards and comfort, it challenges the conventional wisdom in ways that make for anything but a typical self-help book. If that is what you are looking for—another pat formula providing a "leg up" that is never quite enough—don't bother reading further; this is not the book for you.

No, this book is for those of us who are burned out on self-help. It is for the many who can no longer accept the elusive lie that suggests our golden opportunity is just around the corner—one that requires just a little more effort or luck on our part. It is for those who are sick of the daily grind, of attempting to survive merely to eke out a few more moments of pleasure—moments all too fleeting. It is for those who are missing the self-fulfillment that seems to be working for everyone else. It is for those who have fallen victim to the myth of self-improvement, an unwitting deception that has become evident in an age when self is accorded such undeserved esteem. In short, this might best be described as the definitive *unself-help* book.

In contrast to self-help, which is ultimately a vain endeavor, this book provides hope beyond belief. It conveys a crucial message that is as old as the Bible, yet as new as this modern age that has all but erased it; a message that has the potential to radically alter your life as it has so many others, including our own. This book is about overcoming the losing battle of self-gratification, about ending enslavement to mere survival as you discover the freedom to really live. It is about life that is liberated from the frenzied struggle to satisfy our insatiable wants. This will become evident as we share our experiences, describing our failed attempts at taking care of ourselves before we discovered the only alternative: ending self-improvement efforts to allow self to be replaced. We share this not only to provide a rationale, a description, and a vision of this life to die for, but also to present specific strategies that successfully embrace this new paradigm. (If you think this is just a twist on self-help, keep reading.)

This book has been written from the unique perspectives of two brothers—one a pastor and the other a psychiatrist. From both personal and professional viewpoints, we address the bankruptcy of the widely held secular solutions to the question of how we should live, while also noting the equally inadequate answers provided by today's mainstream Christianity.

And now a little about ourselves.

Clarence: I have been a pastor for forty years in churches that range in size from less than a hundred people to membership in the thousands. Despite a rewarding ministry, I experienced significant struggles in learning to live the life of faith I preached—that is, until recently, when I was blessed with some profound insights. Recognizing and removing the barriers to my spiritual walk has radically changed my life. Since then, I've had the opportunity of presenting these discoveries in seminars held around the country. The strong positive response I've received inspired this book. While I am responsible for the spiritual conceptual framework of the book, my brother Steve has put it down in written form, including the chapters bearing my name.

Steve: I've been a practicing child, adolescent, and adult psychiatrist during the past twenty-five years, working in hospitals, military clinics, community mental health centers, and private practice. My life has been dominated by a secular, humanistic agenda that accorded spirituality little relevance. Only recently have I discovered the truths contained in Clarence's message, but with this discovery, I've come to a life of faith that would previously have been unthinkable. I welcome this opportunity to join Clarence in sharing with you our struggles and perspectives on pursuing this totally new life—a life to die for!

Section I

Dead Living

The two of us were just surviving—one seeking the good life, blissfully ignorant that it was an illusion, while the other pursued spiritual reality yet was frustrated by the failure of his own efforts. Our endeavors were useless, serving only to distract us from the ultimate reality. Although we were coming from radically different perspectives, in terms of the abundant life Christ offers, we were both merely surviving through our own futile efforts—an existence we call "dead living."

Chapter 1

The Good Life

(Steve)

"All is meaningless . . . utterly meaningless."
—*Ecclesiastes 12:8, NLT*

"Kidney failure."

The doctor's simple statement shattered our world, his stark pronouncement on my wife's condition reverberating over and over, gradually obliterating my desperate refusal to believe it. This just couldn't be. Things like this happened to other people—not us! I listened numbly, hearing little as I withdrew into my own world. Panic threatened to overwhelm me, while I fought to regain some sense of control. Suddenly, I felt Dee Dee clutching my hand, commanding my attention as she sobbed quietly.

I was vaguely aware of the doctor's attempt at reassurance; he was suggesting that Dee Dee could still have a normal life. But I had stopped listening. As a physician, I knew better. It was the end of my world, the end of our world, obliterating our plans, our hopes, and our dreams. Life as we knew it was over. Nothing the doctor could say would change this.

Kidney failure. In one fell swoop, those two words laid waste to all the years of effort I had expended to assure us a comfortable, rewarding life. I was in my prime, with everything going according to plan. A fulfilling marriage and family, increasing wealth and professional status—I was experiencing all that life had to offer.

And our plans promised even greater pleasure in the future. Without doubt, I was living the good life—until the day our world came crashing down.

Not that I hadn't had problems in my life or faced other struggles. But I usually took these on as challenges that always had solutions. With patience, understanding, and discipline, I could eventually work through any problem. I used this optimistic, can-do approach in my psychiatric practice, and it had worked in my personal life as well. But kidney failure? The challenge felt insurmountable.

Dee Dee and I returned home still in shock, trying to absorb the implications. We had to tell the children something, but what? I was still trying to process the whole thing myself. Can you imagine the challenge of trying to inform five children, ages nine to fifteen, that their mother's kidneys were no longer working? We could barely grasp this ourselves, let alone describe it to anyone else.

How could we explain that their mother was going to change in ways they couldn't possibly imagine? How could we tell them that she would no longer have the boundless time and energy they counted on, that they would no longer be the center of her life as she became increasingly preoccupied with the struggle to live—dealing with countless medical appointments and procedures? How could we tell them that in spite of these efforts, she would suffer from frequent pain and physical setbacks? And how could we explain that after all this, the devastating disease would insidiously sap her strength and ravage her body with new twists and turns until it finally claimed her life?

The questions were a blur that would have to wait. Our own pain took precedence, leaving us paralyzed as we dropped down onto our winding stairway, which was simply too difficult to climb. We stared at each other as the impact of what we were facing began to register. Suddenly, we broke down sobbing while we held one another. We were grieving for ourselves and for each other; we saw the life we knew and had thought would continue into the future slipping away.

We had been positioned to weather just about any storm that might threaten the good life. Any, that is, other than our health, which was something we had always taken for granted. This peril was one that we could barely comprehend, with complications that few can understand. But with my medical background, I knew all too well what Dee Dee would be facing—what we would have to endure together. It was a crushing blow, making a mockery of everything I had planned and anticipated. I was crying inside, wanting to protest the unfairness of it all to someone—anyone. But there was no need to tell Dee Dee; she was suffering enough already. Why upset her with the reality, which would be far worse than anything she could possibly imagine? She would learn soon enough. In the meantime, let her enjoy every moment of blissful ignorance. I was left to my own thoughts—a kind of private hell—as I waited, anticipating the coming storm.

Reprieve for the good life

Two years. According to her doctor, that was the time that remained before she would have to begin the dreaded dialysis. Two precious years.

Although the news was devastating, we took comfort in knowing we had time to prepare—time for more of the good life before reality hit. You know the feeling; we wanted to have some pleasure before we

Our dream of the good life was abruptly replaced with an unending nightmare!

had to deal with the pain. After all, that's what our lives had been about—living for the good times, anticipating and planning so that we could experience life to the fullest during our remaining years.

I was soon in recovery mode, attempting to focus on the positive, knowing we had a little more time. There would be opportunity to learn more about what we would be facing; in the meantime, we could hide from the impending loss a while longer. I was determined to make the most of what time we had left—time to experience a few more moments of pleasure, time to create some special memories. Just a little more time for the good life.

Once again, I was setting goals and solving problems, and the familiar, reassuring sense of control began to take hold once again. I immediately booked a romantic getaway to Jamaica while exploring options for a family Caribbean cruise. But it was not to be. The doctors were wrong. All my plans were for naught. Dee Dee became weaker by the day, barely able to climb the stairs as the number of her oxygen-rich blood cells dropped precipitously. Just two months after first hearing the devastating news, she underwent her first dialysis treatment.

Our dream of the good life was abruptly replaced with an unending nightmare! We were on constant information overload as our entire focus suddenly centered on learning everything necessary for Dee Dee's survival. The nutritionist advised us of her dietary restrictions. Since her kidneys could no longer clear potassium (and dialysis only helps intermittently), eating too many fruits and vegetables could produce a lethal heart arrhythmia. Almost no cheese or ice cream was allowed because the phosphorus in dairy products would cause her bones to dissolve. And Dee Dee had to limit fluids regardless of her thirst, in order to avoid excess swelling, fluid on her lungs, and increased blood pressure. *What had happened to the good life?*

The first six months of Dee Dee's treatment were a blur. She dreaded the lengthy dialysis procedure at the hospital three days a week, and after three months, we chose to provide her treatments at home. A medical team had to teach me all that was involved in cleaning her blood. They told me how to insert the large-bore needles into her fistula—a large vessel in the arm that is created surgically to allow access to the blood. I learned to set up the dialysis equipment for each treatment and what all the alarms on the machine meant. Then I needed to know all the potential complications that could occur, along with interventions needed, since we were not in a hospital facility with emergency backup. Finally, our bedroom had to be gutted to accommodate the dialysis equipment and supplies.

In the early months, my despair and hopelessness formed a pervasive cloud that seemed to cast a constant shadow upon me. Previously, I had always been able to plan and enjoy pleasurable experiences. But now, I simply had no interest, and I was dismayed by the absence of my usual optimism. Eventually, I resigned myself to the expectation that despair would haunt me for the rest of my life.

Hope for the good life

But the cliché that time heals all wounds proved true. After six months, I was surprised to notice glimmers of pleasure and hope once again. While many people in renal failure are rather debilitated, others experience a reasonable quality of life. Hope indeed springs eternal, and I chose to focus on the positive, determined that we would tackle any obstacles in order to recover the good life.

So, Dee Dee's kidney failure became the central challenge of my life, and overcoming its effects my obsession. Often during her dialysis, I searched the Internet, reading about the experiences of patients and professionals and looking for clues on how to improve Dee Dee's health and her ability to function. I believed that determination, knowledge, and patience were virtues that could overcome any obstacle, and so my competitive side kicked in. We were going to beat this thing. With renewed confidence, I determined to find answers that would ensure a normal life. Finally, I was back in control, sure that my efforts would once again bring meaning to all our plans.

Initially, we were able to experience some periods of normalcy, such as it was. We took some Caribbean cruises, and she dialyzed in ports. Once she even joined our annual five-mile backpack and campout on the Washington coast. But as much as we wanted to recapture the good times, we knew it could never be the same. That became evident when Dee Dee joined the rest of the family on the beach in St. Thomas following a grueling dialysis treatment. The children were playing gleefully in Caribbean waves that broke over the powdery white sand as I stood on a bluff taking home movies of the gorgeous scene below. It was picture perfect—except for one thing: all Dee Dee could do was sit and watch wistfully as she reminisced about the times when she had been able to play with them. She was simply too exhausted to do anything else.

Still, I refused to give up. I attempted to discover different techniques or accommodations that would bring some quality to her life. You've probably had struggles in your own life when you just couldn't admit defeat. We've all had them. When it comes to our own efforts, we just can't seem to give up. I certainly couldn't; I knew there had to be a way around this.

Unfortunately, Dee Dee encountered far more than the usual complications. Each time I searched for answers; but with each new discovery, hope was soon dashed as her illness took twists and turns that made a mockery of my attempts. Her petite, eighty-pound body proved to be a curse, as her tiny vessels clotted frequently, requiring multiple vascular surgeries and procedures to maintain a fistula. She began to experience chest pain, and the doctors discovered that she was in danger of a massive heart attack, requiring emergency bypass surgery. Her heart disease was caused by extremely high blood pressure, which various medications failed to control.

I *had* to find a solution. After further research, I learned that rather than the United States standard of three- to four-hour treatments, some other countries did overnight dialysis. This not only lowered the patients' blood pressure but also significantly improved the quality of life for many of them. The medical team we were working with had never done this, so we began the extended treatments on our own, being one of the first in the Northwest to undertake this procedure. This improved Dee Dee's blood pressure dramatically, but the hoped-for improvement in the quality of her life never materialized.

After six years of dialysis, Dee Dee's fistula failed to heal.

Dee Dee was placed on the transplant list, but her five pregnancies had increased her antibodies, dramatically reducing the likelihood of making a successful match. Still, a call at 3:00 A.M. telling of a possible match gave us renewed hope, but it was all too quickly dashed as the cross-match revealed incompatibility.

After six years of dialysis, Dee Dee's fistula failed to heal, which resulted in multiple hemorrhages. One almost claimed her life, as blood pooled in a parking lot while she waited for paramedics to arrive. The required transfusions increased her antibodies still more, reducing the chances of finding a kidney to less than one in a hundred. With her fifth fistula surgery, the implanted synthetic vessel became infected. The infection spread to her blood and then to her heart valves. Tiny blood clots broke off and lodged in her brain, causing ministrokes. Though, miraculously, she recovered, the ordeal left her with impaired thinking and memory, poor concentration, and complete loss of equilibrium. The latter resulted in falls, which, in turn, occasionally produced fractures due to the osteoporosis she also suffered. In addition, she struggled with chronic severe nausea and vomiting. What had become of my plans for the good life?

Hope is truly an amazing thing as it grabs hold with each setback, always wooing with the expectation of a positive outcome no matter how improbable. Hope continued to pull me along on the roller-coaster ride of Dee Dee's illness. With each downward spiral, I was driven to find new answers, expecting to regain control, which would bring us the good life once again. Hope became a cruel hoax, seducing us as it mocked us with each new twist in her disease.

You'd think by that point, I'd have been ready to throw in the towel. But when it comes to self, our misplaced confidence knows no bounds. I refused to give up, insisting that we could still get our life back. Attempting to regain the good times, we hauled the dialysis machines to Canada for a family cruise to Alaska. However, Dee Dee was sick much of the time, making the vacation more of an accomplishment than a joy. Still, I was determined not to let this stop us, even if it meant pretending normalcy. So, for our twenty-fifth anniversary, we flew to Tahiti with four hundred pounds of supplies and medical equipment. The first few days were beautiful. But when the portable dialysis machine failed during Dee Dee's initial treatments, she became increasingly ill. Toxins built up in her blood, and we were told to fly home immediately for treatment. I stayed up all night, desperately attempting to provide the dialysis she needed. Eventually, the equipment functioned, successfully cleansing her blood, and we were blessed with two more beautiful days together. Still, the impact of her disease was inescapable, tracking us relentlessly like a starving wolf that was ever ready to attack.

The following year, I booked another cruise. This one would last two weeks, giving us plenty of opportunity for pleasurable moments, even with the occasional down days. I had worked out all the kinks in the portable dialysis equipment and was sure that this time, it would function properly. By now, Dee Dee was ill most of the time, with chronic nausea and vomiting. But I thought that if we could simply get away for a time, things would improve, allowing us to recapture some of what we had experienced in our early years together. Unfortunately, changing the scene didn't change her illness, which continued to take its toll, leaving her cabin-bound most of the time. I finally realized she preferred her own bed, and we left the cruise early. *What had happened to the good life?*

Reality of the good life

Following this ordeal, I began to entertain the notion that the good life—all that I had wished for, hoped for, worked for, and planned for—was not to be. I still wasn't quite ready to capitulate fully, but Dee Dee was, and what she shared after our last failed vacation forced me to reexamine all of my assumptions. Despite all my efforts, she was bedridden, physically miserable, and felt totally useless most of the time. She reflected on the reality of her condition, and then she shared the unthinkable—she wanted to stop dialysis. We both knew that without dialysis, she would die in ten to fourteen days.

I panicked. This was something I couldn't control. My problem-solving mode had no place for this option. The notion was unimaginable. Never had I felt so totally helpless.

As we discussed her death, Dee Dee spoke with sadness about all she would miss—as though she would somehow retain some awareness of what she was missing after her death. You've probably had similar thoughts when you reflect on your own death or that of a loved one. Of course, when we really consider this, it's a rather absurd notion, since, obviously, after we die, we miss nothing. But these thoughts also forced me to see the absurdity of my own frantic attempts to gain a few more fleeting moments of pleasure. Why was I so driven to have the good life when, inevitably, it would end sooner or later? In the overall scheme of things, what was the point of having a few more pleasurable experiences and creating a few more memories?

However, even as Dee Dee's physical health continued to deteriorate, she began to experience spiritual recovery. As she counseled with my brother Clarence, she discovered a new faith. I was pleased for her, since my own efforts had failed to provide much relief from her suffering. At least now, she had something that gave her a positive outlook.

I had always supported people's faith—it seemed like a good coping tool. But I had decided long ago that religion was not reality. It was the opiate of the masses—far less destructive than other pleasurable pursuits; yet, nonetheless, just a comforting illusion with little basis in reality. Sooner or later, science was destined to solve most of our problems. When we're involved in handling life ourselves, it's hard to see any other possibilities. I had managed quite well on my own and certainly wasn't about to question the pragmatic approach to life that had served me well thus far.

Still, as Dee Dee considered ending her treatment, I began to have some nagging doubts. I was quite certain that when life ended, that was it. But if so, why was I so obsessed with gaining as much as possible of the good life, when I believed that it would simply be erased with my death? I knew that our planet was a speck of dust in the endless universe, which meant that our individual lives were infinitesimally insignificant. The sun would burn out in a few billion years, and—if we didn't destroy ourselves before that time—all the pleasures and horrors of earth would be obliterated.

It all seemed so futile. What was the point of being responsible, of creating treasured memories, of making a difference in the world, or even of worrying about our legacy for future generations, for that matter? If you think about it, what difference does it make whether the planet dies in ten thousand years or ten billion years? But if life has no meaning, why did I find it so terribly meaningful, and why was I addicted to the illusion of making it more meaningful?

My assumptions about life were wrong. The rock-solid life I thought I had built turned out to be a sand castle that the tides of life washed away. The reliable, good life I worked for, the life of abundance and self-fulfillment I had counted on, had morphed into a desperate struggle for survival. As I saw my life and plans caving in, I wondered what I had missed and how I could have been so terribly wrong.

Chapter 2

The Abundant Life

(Clarence)

"I have come that they may have life, and that they may have it more abundantly."
—John 10:10, NKJV

It was a typical Northwest afternoon—gray and socked in with a heavy drizzle, pervasive and unrelenting. My mood was even darker than the oppressive weather as I stood at Dee Dee's bedside, praying silently. It was a familiar experience; previous setbacks in her illness had brought me here before. But this was different. From what Steve had shared, I knew this was a bullet she might not dodge as she had others during her six years on dialysis.

She was suffering from a massive infection throughout her body. The four attending physicians—a nephrologist, a thoracic surgeon, a cardiologist, and an infectious disease specialist—had indicated that she had barely a fifty-fifty chance of survival. The infection, which threatened to overwhelm her, had spread to her heart valves and had the potential of damaging her heart permanently, or, worse yet, causing extensive brain damage. The cardiologist likened the large bacterial growths on her heart valves to a basketball caught in the net, swinging wildly and threatening to break free with each heartbeat. If the growths broke off, in all likelihood, she would suffer a massive stroke.

You can imagine how helpless I felt, standing there looking down at her. Alone with my thoughts, I did the only thing I could do—I prayed. Dee Dee and I had often prayed together, but this time she was semiconscious, and I knew I was the only one who was talking to God. I thought back over my feeble attempts to provide spiritual support as she struggled to survive, and I wondered whether she had ever experienced the abundant life in Christ I so often preached about. Would she become another of the many I had ministered to who would die before ever truly living in Christ?

Like the oppressive weather, that question hung heavily over me as I realized that I had only recently begun to experience this life myself. During the past forty years, as I ministered to thousands in various congregations, I had confidently told the good news of this joyful life. But incredibly, I had been missing it myself. For years I had awakened each morning, lying in a fetal position, gripped with fear. As the all-too-familiar waves of anxiety coursed through me, I knew with certainty that I wasn't living the life I believed was possible.

Learning of the abundant life

Religion had been a central part of life in the large family in which I grew up. Regular church attendance, religious schooling, and daily family worship at home ensured that I was fully ensconced in all the tenets and doctrines of the Christian faith. Sounds like the perfect background for a pastor, doesn't it? But when I graduated from high school, nothing was further from my mind.

I came from a professional family, so college enrollment was an assumption rather than a choice. My lack of investment in the process was evident when it came to choosing a major—I was clueless. But since my father was a physician and my mother a nurse, it seemed reasonable for me to sign up for courses in science.

I know what you're thinking, and you're right—it was a truly pathetic decision. As you would expect, my heart wasn't in my studies. I found myself floating around the campus in off hours, putting off my assignments as much as possible, searching aimlessly. You know that feeling you have when you're looking to escape? That's what I was feeling. I was looking for something—anything—that I could use to avoid what I was supposed to be doing.

Then I found it. There was a room in the basement of the men's dormitory where people played table tennis. The game intrigued me. I began playing, and within weeks, I was quite literally addicted to it, spending every spare moment in that basement room. When I wasn't playing, I was standing in front of a mirror, attempting to emulate the smooth strokes of an expert player I idolized.

For two years, I majored in table tennis while occasionally dabbling in studies on the side. My dedication was rewarded in two ways: First, I won the college table tennis tournament, for which I received a trophy that, after several moves, has joined other irrelevant items in storage. Second, I ended my sophomore year of college with the ignominious record of an overall D+ grade point average. Still, I basked in the glorious feeling of victory, knowing that nothing could top winning— or so I thought, until an unforgettable day just before the school year ended.

It was one of those splendid spring days in the Northeast when everything is vibrant and alive, hardly conducive to finals preparation. But then, I seldom needed excuses to avoid my studies, and, as usual, I was procrastinating. As I sat on a bench by a large oak tree in front of our library, a friend came over to join me, and we struck up a casual conversation.

Our talk soon progressed to a serious discussion about life. This was not what I was expecting, and, as you can imagine, I found it somewhat disconcerting. Suddenly, to my surprise, my friend began talking about God—not just in the abstract but in a way I had never heard before. Maybe I had never really been listening. It wasn't just what my friend was saying but the way he was saying it. He spoke with such joy and confidence about his faith that I was overcome, faced with the emptiness of my existence. What I had known stood in stark contrast to his life, which was full of meaning and purpose. It was a Holy Spirit moment, and I hungrily devoured all he had to say. As he shared the love of God and spoke of His plan for us, I felt a deep sense of longing. My friend sensed my desire and asked if I would like to receive Christ into my life. With an overwhelming sense of relief, I gratefully accepted, having little awareness of how radically my life would change.

I majored in table tennis . . . while dabbling in studies.

Seeking the abundant life

I would never be the same. My priorities changed, and without hesitation, I accepted the call to become a minister for Christ. But the excitement that accompanied my newfound faith began to dissipate over time. You've likely had similar experiences, feeling a spiritual high that soon evaporates. While I remained confident in Christ and His working in my life, the Christian walk often felt like a struggle to me, bringing pain that seemed incompatible with the life I had been told Christ offers.

Looking back on those early years, I realize that I was not experiencing the depth of spirituality possible from a personal, intimate relationship with Christ. Neither was I experiencing victory in areas of my life that I knew needed changing. Most notable in this regard was TV. I had transferred an addiction to western novels and movies that had dominated my teenage years to this medium. I knew my addiction was limiting my spiritual life by leaving little room for Christ, but my drive for escape left me seemingly helpless. Much of the time, I could hardly wait for the day to end; I was literally counting the minutes till I felt the relief my fix provided. Maybe you've felt a similar need yourself—an overpowering urge to gain solace.

From time to time, I wondered what I was missing—not only in my own life, but also in my ministry. I knew that despite my attempts, fellow Christians usually failed to experience the abundant life—that tantalizing promise that seemed more like some sort of cruel hoax. As I prayed desperately, agonizing over the lack of fulfillment in my life, I wondered if all this—the gnawing void, the worry, the lack of peace—was part of the Christian walk. Perhaps God meant the dissatisfaction I felt to help me guard against spiritual complacency. Still though, something felt terribly wrong.

Through the years, I continued to study and pray, trying in vain to experience the fullness I read about. But my spiritual life ebbed and flowed, and I failed to reach any depth of satisfaction. I thirsted for a more vibrant life with Christ. Would I ever drink the living waters, much less lead others to them that they might never thirst again?

The question gnawed at me as I stood at Dee Dee's bedside, watching helplessly while she lay near death. She was in and out of consciousness for several days. But amazingly, she didn't die. Still, despite her seemingly miraculous survival, the ordeal left her with devastating impairments. I was distressed to see her further robbed of the quality of life most of us take for granted. But I was far more concerned with her spiritual status, so I was relieved and hopeful when she continued to live. That meant I still had the opportunity to address what I knew was her ultimate need. Although I had provided extensive spiritual support and counseling for her in the past, this time would be different. I was determined to share new and exciting discoveries about the Christ-filled life that I was just beginning to experience myself.

After all the years we wandered in an often-barren spiritual wasteland, my wife, Dianna, and I had made some exciting discoveries recently. God had given us a whole new awareness of the obstacles blocking us from His abundant life. And what a life we had experienced since then! The anxieties that plagued me for years vanished. The defensiveness, irritability, resentment, and withdrawal so familiar in my marriage of thirty-nine years became a rarity. Dianna and I were truly living the abundant life! We had found good news that we *had* to tell.

As I began sharing these discoveries, my excitement over Christ's call grew. Other struggling believers began to experience this new life. Word spread and we began giving this message at various seminars across the country. As interest and enthusiasm multiplied, I was struck with the need to share these discoveries with a wider audience. This led to another of the seemingly miraculous events surrounding this message—the production of a DVD.

Sharing the abundant life

When the thought of producing a video first occurred to me, it was more than a little surprising. It had to be inspired, as it wasn't an idea that would have occurred to me naturally. Knowing that I was no risk taker, Dianna struggled to support what we both agreed was a rather improbable notion. We couldn't afford the production costs and were sure that sales would be unlikely to cover the expenses. Our only option was to seek financial backing from others. With tenuous faith in the outcome, we wrote, explaining the need, to some fifty friends and family members.

I will never forget the Wednesday afternoon we finished writing that e-mail, said a prayer, and hit the Send button. Following our usual prayer meeting at church, we returned home and checked our e-mail. The first message was a brief note from Steve and Dee Dee: "We're sending a check to cover all costs of the project." Dianna and I broke into tears of gratitude, totally overwhelmed. The support was especially moving because Steve was not a devoted believer at the time and had no idea that his gesture was an answer to prayer. Dee Dee did know the message on that DVD well. She had gone through some dramatic changes following our discussions together. It was inspiring to observe her engage in spiritual recovery, even though her physical condition continued to deteriorate. Unfortunately, Steve did not share her experience. He showed little interest in the message on the DVD, despite my suggestion that he take a look at what he was financing. I appreciated his support, but I knew God wanted more than his money.

Steve was . . . a psychiatrist who viewed life primarily from a . . . humanistic perspective.

Steve was a nominal believer, a psychiatrist who viewed life primarily from a pragmatic and humanistic perspective. I knew there was little in his training or experience that would lead him to seek spiritual answers. He lived in a world of science that either had the answers or needed only more time to discover them. Besides, caring for his critically ill wife left him little time for other explorations. The understandings he sought were certainly not spiritual; his search was for answers that would reverse Dee Dee's downhill course.

The stories people have told Dianna and me of lives transformed as a result of our sharing our journey in the DVD set has been gratifying and humbling. But none has been more thrilling than the following e-mail, which I received from Steve:

Unbelievable! Unbelievable! Simply unbelievably powerful and challenging! We just finished the first disk. I wasn't exactly in the mood for this tonight as I had much going on. But Dee Dee wanted to get started early, so I interrupted my office work to watch. I found that third session unbelievably challenging and exciting. So much of the time we—or I should say I—feel fairly right and deserving. But I could really see how very destructive this is and how much it seduces us subtly away from dying to self. I felt very challenged with the concept of sinning when we are so right. I think that some of what has kept me going, from a purely human perspective, is somewhat of a martyr mentality. Look at all I do, caring for the kids, Dee Dee, etc., so much more than others, never (or seldom) complaining . . . must not be all that bad, etc., and truly raising self to a whole new level! Then I have a ready-made platform for obviously well-justified demandingness and resentment when things don't go my way.

When we finished, Dee Dee and I prayed. I actually thanked God for the experience of her dialysis (not for her being on it, which I don't think He caused) that had brought me to my knees. I think that the selflessness that was forced on me, even when I wasn't a believer, prepared me for the excitement and joy I feel as I begin tentative, albeit feeble, attempts of dying to self. One more thing: I feel my life somewhat turned upside down as my priorities are so radically changing.

Anyway, brother, thanks for further confusing (though in an exciting way) my already confused life!

Love,
Steve

You can imagine how excited I was to see firsthand how God was using the message. Now I was even more committed to His leading in this work—that is until people suggested that I publish it in book form. Immediately, I felt fear and resistance. I knew God was leading, but while I was blessed with speaking skills, they were not accompanied by a similar ability to communicate in writing. As Moses needed a mouthpiece, I needed a writer. (And no, I'm not comparing myself to Moses!)

While I prayed and searched for assistance, I continued to correspond with Steve, who was sharing the struggles and triumphs of his early steps with Christ in e-mails. I looked forward to each one, enjoying his candor, insights, and captivating style of writing. Suddenly, it hit me—God had given me my writer!

I never cease to be amazed by the transformations God brings to a life fully committed to Him. My brother's experience is no exception. Although his circumstances have actually worsened, Christ's resurrection power has radically altered his perspective.

But I'm getting ahead of myself. I'll let him tell you about it in the next chapter, as he introduces a journey that leads to truly abundant living—escaping from pursuit of the good life to a whole new life.

Chapter 3

The New Life

(Steve)

"What profit is it to a man if he gains the whole world, and loses his own soul?
Or what will a man give in exchange for his soul?"
—*Matthew 16:26, NKJV*

It was 1:00 A.M., but I couldn't sleep. Things were simply happening too fast. My thoughts raced as I lay there listening to the rhythmic sounds of the pump that circulated Dee Dee's blood during her overnight dialysis.

Just six months prior, my entire focus had been on caring for Dee Dee, ensuring my children's success, maintaining my professional career, and building my savings. I planned for retirement, considering how I might enhance the quality of our lives as we looked forward to our golden years. It sounds like the typical American dream, doesn't it?

But during the past four months, a radical transformation had taken place. I had suddenly realized that there had to be more to life—much more. With a completely new perspective, I focused on inviting Christ to live in me and through me. My life turned upside down, and my priorities changed completely. I donated to several causes, emptying a savings account previously slated for further investments in the good life. Considering my usual focus on preparation for our golden years, this was so unnatural and bizarre that I wondered whether I was losing it. Then there were the changes in my thinking. Suddenly and strangely, I worried less about the myriad of concerns—including Dee Dee's survival—that had troubled me for years. Given that this had been such an obsessive focus, being free of it felt odd.

All that I had previously considered to be significant in life now seemed relatively unimportant. My time, my talents, my work, my money, all my plans—gone! It was all God's now. Nothing would ever be the same. Now I thought about how God wanted me to serve Him during the remainder of my life. The change was not only relieving and freeing but also in some ways disconcerting. I had morphed into someone I hardly knew, as though there had been some sort of alien takeover—which in some ways there had been.

A high-pitched beeping sound interrupted my thoughts as the dialysis machine signaled a problem, temporarily shutting down. After checking the pressure readings and resetting the alarms, I lay down once more and continued ruminating over my life and how it had come to this point.

I . . . had been managing life quite well on my own.

I had grown up in a conservative Christian home, where I learned about the way life should be lived. Throughout my Christian schooling, I was a believer, even majoring in theology before attending medical school. But I was what might be termed a cultural Christian, filled with beliefs and good principles for living, yet seldom experiencing the reality of Christ in my life.

I found the study of science, medicine, and eventually psychiatry very satisfying. The scientific principles that were knowable and predictable appealed to my need to have control. After psychiatric training, followed by a child psychiatry fellowship, I settled into a comfortable and fulfilling career.

I'd had an exciting marriage, five children, and increasing professional and financial success. I certainly was living the good life—that is, until Dee Dee's kidney failure shattered my complacent, self-assured world. We were devastated for a time but finally managed to recover to some extent. I recalled having had the vague thought (with some resentment) that caring believers were likely hopeful this would bring me to my knees. But I was independent, self-assured, and had been managing life quite well on my own, thank you. I certainly wasn't going to cave over this.

Assumptions questioned

However, when Dee Dee told me that her quality of life had deteriorated to the point that she wished to end the life-preserving dialysis treatments, I panicked, realizing that no amount of trying on my part could fix this. Losing her still seemed inconceivable, but being forced to consider the possibility made me reflect on things that for years I had considered irrelevant.

Eventually, I came to the painful awareness that, up to that point, life had been solely about increasing my pleasure and sense of security. In light of Dee Dee's impending death, all this felt rather futile. What difference would it make whether or not I had a few more years of pleasure with her? Sooner or later, it would all end anyway. Other than occupying time with pleasurable moments that would help us avoid thoughts of our ultimate demise, what was the point?

As I struggled with these questions, I began to read extensively. I'm a natural-born skeptic, which made taking a leap of faith seem impossible for me. But as I read and contemplated existential questions, I began to realize that I had already been living life based on a leap of faith. Given the numerous questions that are unknowable, any coherent paradigm of life must adopt certain presuppositions. As I came to understand my own assumptions, I began to realize how shaky they were. I was a borderline agnostic or nominal deist. Like most physicians—70 percent of whom believe in God—after studying the phenomenal intricacies of the body, I could never buy evolution as an explanation for our existence. I always believed in intelligent design. It seemed far more logical than the notion that even the simplest one-celled organisms—all of which are unbelievably complex—could suddenly appear spontaneously.

But my belief in humanism and the ultimate meaninglessness of existence seemed increasingly untenable. With growing discomfort, I realized that my secular explanations required a far greater leap of faith than did the Christian paradigm. I began to see that my avoidance of spirituality was not so much based on its improbability as on the uncomfortable obligations and changes I would face if I admitted its truth. I didn't experience a sudden light dawning, but gradually my reading and study brought me to an astonishing yet almost inescapable conclusion: as improbable as it seems, Jesus was—and is—indeed the Son of God!

Initially, things didn't change much other than that I spent more time reading and praying with my family. I was already living a conservative lifestyle. As Clarence used to tell me, I lived in far greater accordance with Christian principles than did most professed Christians. Then I began to view Clarence's DVD, *How to Die Right and Live to Tell About It*.[1] Suddenly, I glimpsed the possibility, as well as the challenge, of a full relationship with Christ—and everything changed. I was overwhelmed with Christ's invitation to have Him daily in my life in a whole new way. I was also humbled and frightened as I became aware of the numerous obstacles still in my life. All my efforts to preserve and improve my position suddenly seemed rather pathetic and futile. Yet strangely, it seemed unbelievably difficult to let go of them.

Up to that point, I had believed that living the Christian life involved accepting Christ and praying that He would help make one a better Christian. This was something I was good at, and I felt confident in my ability to embrace this understanding of faith. After all, I already knew all the Christian doctrines. I had a positive view of myself and even felt a smug complacency. I thought I needed only a little help to walk the Christian walk. Clearly, my recent conversion wouldn't require much change other than adding Christ to the life I was already living—or so I thought.

Beyond being good

However, after viewing Clarence's DVD, I suddenly realized how truly helpless and hopeless I was. I felt powerless as I faced the reality of my desperate and despicable condition. Conversely, I also felt a sense of empowerment as I glimpsed the possibilities of Christ living in me. With a mixture of fear and excitement, I realized that I didn't need Christ to *assist* me; I needed Him to *replace* me. There was room for Him only when there was none for me. And the way I lived my life, with all my control needs, made clear that there was a lot of me to clear out if there was to be any hope of Christ living in me.

I prayed for understanding—and sleep—as I reflected on my schedule of patients for the following day. Just then, I heard the familiar thud of the pump shutting down, followed by the repetitive beeping of the incessant alarm. I made the necessary adjustments and was soon back in bed, thinking once again of the incomprehensible turn my life had taken.

The dramatic changes had also influenced how I viewed my professional life. I had been a practicing psychiatrist for twenty-five years and had treated thousands with various traditional interventions. I considered myself a respected professional in the community and certainly believed in the effectiveness of various therapies, including medication. But having experienced the power of Christ in my life, I now realized that in the vast majority of cases, self was a major obstacle to heal-

I didn't need Christ to *assist* me; I needed Him to *replace* me.

ing. Clearly, the impact of my traditional treatments paled in comparison to Christ's power in a life that was emptied of self. Considering the radical changes in my own life, this was an inescapable conclusion.

I was just beginning to doze when I was startled—flashing on the thought that had begun my reflections that night. I felt torn as I recalled Clarence's request that I collaborate in writing a book with him. Initially, the idea seemed more than absurd—me, write a book? Clarence had to have connections with people far more qualified. *Why me, a total novice?* I wondered, thinking how improbable—even impossible—it seemed.

My thoughts returned to what I had just been reading in the book of Acts. Thinking of all the miracles that happened at that time, I was wondering if Dee Dee would have been healed if she lived back then. I asked Clarence why there were so few miracles in modern times. I'll never forget his response. He said, "The change [God] has brought in your life is His greatest miracle." As I reflected on the remarkable turn my life had taken, I knew he was right. If someone had suggested a year before that I could experience the transformation of attitudes and priorities that I had experienced, I would have insisted it was impossible. But the failure of my efforts had given me a glimpse of myself from Christ's eternal perspective.

Once again I reflected on Clarence's request, and then I prayed. I told God I really wasn't a writer. (Of course, He already knew that!) I told Him how challenged and inadequate I felt. I told Him that I'm a physician with lots of responsibilities, and if that weren't enough, I have my family: kids who haven't yet left the nest, and Dee Dee, who needs daily care. There was every reason not to write this book. So, I thought, it was settled.

But I still couldn't sleep, despite the soothing hum of the machines that were filtering Dee Dee's blood. God continued to call, and I was bursting inside, unable to contain myself over the power that came with dying to live in Christ. "You are the Word," I prayed. "Please give me the words that will present a vision of how our lives can become Yours."

I sighed, feeling a sense of resignation mixed with excitement as I knew where this was leading. Attempting to ease my sense of trepidation, I reminded myself that I risked nothing. Like the rest of me, the writing was His. Once again, forgetting self brought great peace. That was my last thought as I dozed off.

Called to abundant life

The call to Christ's abundant life that Clarence and I describe in this book offers both a tremendous challenge and a tremendous opportunity. But to be candid, I don't believe I could have heard this call a year earlier, while I was still in the middle of trying to fix things myself. I couldn't have heard it if I hadn't been brought to the place of futility, where I finally gave up on gaining success through my own attempts—attempts that He couldn't really support. The greatest difficulty we face seems to be the struggle to give up the belief that we can do what needs to be done with great effort on our part and a little help from God. Not so. We just get in the way. God can't help us unless we fully release the notion that we can help ourselves.

Please don't construe our attempt to share perspectives on this life as indications that we have any special expertise in living it. Like you, we continue to face numerous challenges. This endeavor is an outgrowth of the pain and struggles that drove us to seek a deeper understanding of what prevents Christ from filling our lives. As we share our perspectives and journeys, which are far from complete, we hope you gain a glimpse of the exciting life Christ is offering.

However, there are significant roadblocks that must be addressed and overcome if there is to be any hope of receiving the abundant life. Understanding this will be disconcerting at times, but meeting the challenge will provide immense rewards. In fact, the major reason we often fail to gain this life is because we short-circuit the process. We focus on what Christ offers and seek His presence in our lives, while neglecting to understand the corollary requirement: that we must continually recognize that self is unsalvageable and relinquish it.

This essential perspective will be the primary focus of the next section, in which we discuss the natural inclinations that Christians are so adept at hiding. This awareness leads us to engage in the difficult process of losing what is naturally our dearest and most cherished possession. The recognition of our terminal condition will elicit the typical responses that come with any major loss. But the loss of self—letting go of this precious entity that we so naturally defend, protect, and promote—is like no other loss.

As we fully explore our hopeless addiction to self in the following chapters, you will find the process arduous and even distressing at times. Like us, you will likely experience resistance and dismay and will want to skip to the more encouraging and hopeful aspects of our life in Christ. And as you struggle through the stages of grieving the loss of self, you will likely wonder why we are expending such an inordinate amount of energy and effort on what many would argue is the most negative and discouraging aspect of this journey. After all, focusing on such an overwhelming loss hardly seems like the abundant life Clarence discussed. But just as Christ could experience resurrection only after the devastating loss of His life, so we must endure our own shadow of death if we hope to experience a joyful resurrection in Him. Resurrection power comes only to the dead—to those who are dead to self.

An overwhelming despair inevitably follows our becoming aware of our terminal condition—a painful reality that C. S. Lewis pointed out. "Of course, I quite agree that the Christian religion is, in the long run, a thing of unspeakable comfort. But it does not begin in comfort; it begins in the dismay I have been describing, and it is no use at all trying to go on to that comfort without first going through that dismay."[2]

While dying this death is an unending and demanding process, it also offers tremendous hope. The more open we are to seeing and experiencing the hopelessness of self through the eyes of God, the greater our ability to access the astounding rewards of dying to self—daily resurrection to a new life in Christ! Our destiny, abundant living, is as radical as it is rewarding, assuring our ultimate survival while demanding nothing less than dying. It is a paradox we must learn, the conundrum we must live: a life to die for!

Section II

Condition: Terminal

News of a terminal condition is never easy to hear. Initially, it is always met with extreme resistance. The pain is excruciating. We cling to hope, especially when it comes to losing what is naturally our most precious possession: life. However, our eternal survival depends on accepting the inevitability of the demise of self. We cannot adopt a new life until we let go of the old, even though it means participating in the process that accompanies any devastating loss. We reach the mountaintop only by going through the valley—working through the stages of grief over the loss of self: denial, self-deception, protest, despair, and finally acceptance.

Chapter 4

Denial:
The Cover-up

(Steve)

People will be lovers of self, . . . lovers of pleasure rather than lovers of God, having the appearance of godliness, but denying its power.
—2 Timothy 3:2–5, ESV

"He was a good man."

The words jolted me from my reflection, shattering a reverie that couldn't escape reality. I stared at my father's casket.

"He was a good man," the pastor repeated, causing me to wince.

Did he even know this man? The words were anything but comforting, creating a painful dissonance with my own thoughts. I wondered what others were thinking, especially those who had lived with him. There was Clarence, in the row ahead. He had been much closer to Dad than I. What was he thinking about this "good man" eulogy? I realized that while I had heard Clarence speak many times, I had never heard him speak at a funeral. I hoped he did better than this—offering trite platitudes that had little basis in reality.

"He was a faithful member of this church, worshiping each week and leading out in Christian education classes. He was a good man."

If that made Dad good, then I must be in real trouble, I thought. The last time I had been in church was to get married, and this certainly wasn't tempting me to return. *Good* was hardly the adjective that came to mind when I thought of Dad.

But I had to admit he had believed far more than I did—in many ways, much more than the typical Christian.

Religion was a central focus of Dad's life. He was an ardent student of the Bible and Christian writings, relishing lively discussions on spiritual practices and doctrinal issues. You know the type—always able to quote Scripture and to be persuasive in a theological discussion. He ensured that each of his ten children from two marriages received a Christian education, both at home and in church schools. Financially, he supported the church with far more than most people gave. Indeed, to most, he appeared to be a pillar of the church.

But I knew there was another side to my father. I knew it from the family stories, even more than my own personal experience. Despite Dad's belief, those of us who lived with him saw little evidence of the message of love he claimed to espouse. This eulogy certainly added further support to the skeptical view I held at the time. I believed that religion was an illusion, reflecting human need rather than reality. To me, it was clear that even strongly held beliefs didn't result in a change of character. This was evident in my father's life—the life behind the facade. Looking back, it seems like such a puzzle. *Why the appearance without the power?*

The cover-up

"He was a good man," the pastor continued. "He was a pillar of this community; a dedicated, caring physician. He was a good man."

I cringed, looking over at my brothers and sisters. Those who knew him well would likely question this. As a physician, he was trained in and believed in the holistic Christian practice of medicine. But the disdain and denigration he often voiced toward others must have been evident in his psychiatric practice. I wondered whether any of his patients were present. Then I realized I knew one—my sister. Several years before, Dad chose to be her attending physician. He administered a series of electroconvulsive treatments to his own daughter! As I glanced over at her, I wondered whether she was recalling the ordeal. Whatever her thoughts on Dad's ethics, I knew from her pain that she had wanted his love far more than his medical treatment. It was a love she never received; a love that—despite his beliefs—he seemed incapable of giving. *Why the appearance without the power?*

"He was a good man" continued ringing in my ears as I reflected back on Dad's life. His dedication to the church went well beyond weekly attendance. When, thirty-three years ago, the call went out for a medical missionary, he had volunteered. Taking his wife and four children, he left a successful practice to become the medical director of a fledgling hospital in Baghdad, Iraq. But his ministry was cut short. His commitment to Christ's message of love didn't result in its power influencing his own life. The facade was shattered by his flagrant affair with a missionary nurse. For Mom, the voyage back home was lengthy and painful. Dad spent most of his

Why the appearance without the power?

time with another passenger—the nurse. After returning stateside, my parents had their sixth and last child—me.

God only knows how often Dad strayed as he vainly sought to compensate for his misery and feelings of inadequacy. Most of the relationships were brief—except one. That one tore our family apart, officially ending an eighteen-year marriage that was over long before. *Why the appearance without the power?*

As a five-year-old, I had little knowledge of how dramatically the divorce would affect my life for the better. It was only in retrospect, hearing from others and observing him in later years, that I realized my good fortune. Within months of the divorce, Dad called Mom, expressing regret and wondering about getting back together. But his fiancée had become pregnant prior to the separation, and there was no turning back.

In spite of Dad's infidelity and the resulting church discipline, he continued to be a believer—even converting his new wife to the faith. But still, the outward appearance of belief didn't assure its power to transform. After he had four more children, his second marriage ended. This time, though, Dad was the "injured party"; his second wife had an affair with the local church schoolteacher.

Dad's second divorce was a bloodbath, with adult children taking sides and testifying for and against each parent, as the younger ones were torn by divided loyalties. The parents often used the children for their own needs, treating them as dispensable pawns. After parental visits, each parent would grill them about the other, acting like children themselves as both vied for position and validation. *Why the appearance without the power?*

I was vaguely aware of the pastor droning on, having long since given up on his make-believe father from some fantasy world. I had escaped to reality, lost in thought as I reflected on the man most never knew—this relative stranger I called "Dad."

The pain beneath the cover-up

Fortunately, my time with Dad was brief; I lived with him less than did any of his other children. However, their experiences with and descriptions of him could have filled volumes.

His volatile anger and his control needs pervaded all his relationships, especially those with his family. There was the explosive temper that burst out in verbal assaults and occasional physical abuse. But this was preferable to the steely, controlled rage—the clenched jaw, cold stare, and the accompanying demeaning voice, dripping with sarcasm, that masterfully decimated the slightest vestige of self-worth. Our home was dominated by abject fear. No one dared question Dad's absolute control. *Why the appearance without the power?*

Dad's dominance spawned constant manipulations, mind games, and intimidations that later became an unending source of family stories. Often, he sought to divide and conquer, pitting one against another. At times, he even named who among us were his favorite children. Frequently, he treated Mom the worst, as his insecurity couldn't allow joint parenting that gave authority to anyone else. His critical, demeaning attitude reduced her to the position of another child who had to compete with the rest of us for his attention.

With the passage of time, the pain diminished. Our stories eventually became a part of casual conversations, even to the point of humor. I often wondered whether all the telling and retelling enabled those involved to become inured and oblivious to the devastating dysfunction of their childhood. But I knew it was no laughing matter for the children when they were living through it. The intensity of overwhelming, inescapable fear was obvious in their stories—particularly one told by my brothers, who, seeing no other option, once plotted to kill our father in his sleep.

Even when we had become adults, his continued manipulations and control were legendary. Much to the dismay of their spouses, my adult siblings would turn into intimidated children, once again paying deference to his dominance and control—even to the detriment of their marriages. How could someone who expressed belief in Christ's redeeming love allow so little of it in his own life? *Why the appearance without the power?*

I found myself focusing on the casket once again. It was difficult to believe that such a powerful presence was actually gone. Suddenly, I felt relief. I realized that we were free. My bride and I would never again be subjected to the control that was an inevitable part of any visit with Dad.

While the sermon droned on, my mind continued to wander as I looked at the youngest among the ten of us. I couldn't imagine what it must have been like. Just a few days ago, John had struggled desperately to save Dad from the stormy seas that had capsized their boat, almost succumbing himself. This was the same father who often responded to his own fear and helplessness by attacking the most vulnerable and helpless—having no tolerance for the normal feelings and neediness of little children. Now, looking over at John, I remembered the hurt once again, recalling Dad's intimidation and control of the younger children. During my brief visits, I had felt the relief of knowing that I would soon leave, while I ached for the pain the younger children were left to endure. *Why the appearance without the power?*

"He was a good man." The very words were becoming painful. Would the preacher never stop?

"He was a good father. Every one of his ten children has honored him with their presence today. He was a good man."

Now that was driving in the knife. I'd certainly had no interest in attending and was present only due to some arm-twisting. In fact, I was feeling used as I realized that Dad's power and control extended beyond the grave.

I glanced over at Clarence once again, wondering what he, as a pastor, was thinking of this sermon. He had spent the most time with Dad and was often his confidant, lending his ear in late-night conversations. I knew I would be asking for his thoughts on this tribute—one that Dad could elicit only in death.

With the pastor's closing prayer, I breathed a sigh of relief, knowing I had finally heard the last "good man." As we gathered outside, the warm Florida sun provided a marked contrast to the somber mood. I joined the others in giving and receiving encouraging hugs—observing my brothers and sisters and wondering what the future held for each of us. How would the wounds and scars we had suffered play out in our lives and those of our families? I watched as several cried, wondering what they were feeling and thinking. But I couldn't share in their tears. No, for me there was no sadness, no sense of loss with my father's passing. I had already done all my crying—years before—for the father I never had.

The reality behind the cover-up

During the twenty-five years since that memorable service, Clarence and I have often reflected on Dad's life and death. Although he had some positive qualities and we had known some pleasant family times, these were overshadowed by the negative. Unfortunately, the latter had far more impact, leaving us reflecting on the dramatic difference between the cover he displayed and the reality we knew. We frequently wondered about the overwhelming pain he must have experienced at some time—pain that he, in turn, inflicted on others; pain that he was never able to trust God to relieve.

You probably are asking the question we asked ourselves: how could someone with such a strong belief and commitment fail to allow Christ's transforming love into his life? As we explored this question, it became clear that our father's experience— in which belief alone hadn't worked—carried wider implications for Christians today.

How often do we honestly consider the difference between our professed belief and the reality of our life? Surprisingly, our father did just that in what Clarence recalled was a telling conversation a few years before his death. As Dad spoke disparagingly of his life in an unusually vulnerable manner, he shared that it would take either years of psychotherapy or a total spiritual conversion to bring about the needed transformation. It is amazing how often we are fully aware of what we need and yet, tragically, lack the will to obtain it. What heartbreak! Knowing the desperate need, realizing the inability to love—even one's self—while struggling to maintain an appearance of godliness that denies its power. Dad seemed helpless to give up on his own futile efforts—refusing to let go, risk all, and let the power of God effect the radical changes necessary for peace and reconciliation. *Why the appearance without the power?*

Some might suggest that our father's life was an aberration, hardly representative of the typical Christian today. Unfortunately, objective evidence suggests otherwise. Polls conducted in recent years by the Barna research group suggest that in several areas of life, believers differ little from nonbelievers. The rates of divorce, gambling (buying lotto tickets), viewing adult-only material on the Internet, and watching videos with explicit sexual content are the same for born-again Christians as for nonbelievers. More than one-third of those who call themselves Christians have cohabited (lived with a lover without marriage)—about the same rate as the general population. Almost 50 percent of born-again Christians believe that cohabitation, sexual fantasies about others, and gambling are morally acceptable behaviors. Believers are even described as rather lukewarm about God. In fact, less than one-fourth of Protestant

Christians have fallen in love with their religion.

churchgoers indicate that faith in God is a top priority for them. Polls suggest that Christians have fallen in love with their religion rather than with the object of their faith.[1]

One researcher observed, "Regardless of its true character and intent, the Christian community is not known for love, nor for a life-transforming faith. . . . America remains one of the largest mission fields in the world, and the American Church remains the most richly endowed body of believers on the planet. There is no lack of potential."[2] Given how this potential is being squandered, it's rather discouraging, isn't it?

Aside from these disturbing polls, we know that the majority of Christians—even those who do not indulge their darker passions—are avid consumers of popular culture. This includes the latest trends, whether in fashions, entertainment, values, or modes of expression. In most Christian homes, children are well versed on the names and lives of TV and movie personalities, as they watch MTV, play video games, and spend entire evenings on various Internet sites. Observations certainly suggest that the majority of professed believers have failed to experience the transformation we believe is possible.

Uncovering the cover-up

Obviously, many Christians are somehow blocked from experiencing the spiritual power they so ardently profess that they want. As our father's story clearly demonstrates, knowledge and belief alone—no matter how profound—are not enough. Absent of Christ's transforming power, Dad's belief was only a cover-up that gave the appearance of godliness, while hiding the desperate need he had, the pain he sought to assuage through his own futile efforts. As we reflect on his life, we realize it was fear that motivated Dad to maintain the form of godliness, just as that emotion motivates all other cover-ups. Despite his aggressive posture, Dad was actually afraid. That's why he avoided risks.

Dad's fear was evident in one of his favorite pursuits—boating. He loved nothing better than to be out on the water. Over the years, he acquired a wealth of nautical information. However, his risk avoidance kept him from completely submerging himself in his favorite pastime. He never fully experienced the love of his life, the water, because he never learned to swim. Ironically, the river he lived on—his greatest source of pleasure—took his life. Paradoxically, the only safe course he could have followed was to give up the fear and become fully immersed as he learned to revel in the joy and power of becoming one with the water.

There was a similar irony in the failure of Dad's spiritual beliefs to transform him. Again, despite great knowledge and intense interest, he played it safe, avoiding the risk of immersing himself in the life of faith he had studied so well. Instead, he clung to self-interest, which he attempted to overlay with spiritual commitment. He pretended faith, engaging in the "appearance of godliness," while refusing to allow its power in his life. It was a cover-up, one with devastating consequences.

Unfortunately, we all share in this same tendency to perpetrate our own cover-up. It is a distressing dichotomy of immense consequence that finds us pursuing spiritual transformation with the very attitude that blocks Christ's life in us. We pretend we can have it both ways, professing Christ as our only need, while attempting to preserve our safety and comfort in the world. This illusion covers up the reality.

We can be rescued from the destructiveness of self-preservation only by letting go of our fear—by understanding that "perfect love casts out fear" (1 John 4:18,

NKJV). We can obtain this promised love only if we are willing to immerse ourselves fully in Jesus, the Living Water, and make our daily life in Him of paramount importance—more important even than knowledge about Him. We must risk uncovering the cover-up.

When it comes to investing money, I've never been much of a risk taker. I prefer to stick with the safety of a sure thing rather than to go for a potentially greater return that carries the risk of leaving me worse off. Of course, when it comes to finances, everything is risky—even stuffing money under the mattress; over the years, the ravages of inflation will diminish the value of money hidden there. However, some ventures are clearly more risky than others, and the natural instinct of self-preservation motivates us to limit the risk. You know the feeling when you perceive some threat and you seek protection.

In the Christian walk, however, responding to our innate desire for safety places us in danger. Our natural inclinations are misguided, since self-preservation is a contradiction in terms. Self is and will always ultimately be a loser, making our choice a no-brainer. So while playing it safe feels less threatening, paradoxically, in the Christian experience, it is the riskiest choice—jeopardizing our very soul!

Christ warned about the human fallacy of playing it safe when He taught the seemingly contradictory way we must strive for survival. Immediately after Peter confessed his belief in Him,

Responding to our innate desire for safety places us in danger.

Christ warned of the radical changes this belief would inevitably demand: " 'If you try to keep your life for yourself, you will lose it. But if you give up your life for me, you will find true life' " (Luke 9:24, NLT).

This essential paradox—one that we tend to fight with every fiber of our natural being—bears repeating with some further reflection. If we try to keep our life for our pleasure, our comfort, our protection, we will lose the Christ-filled life we were created to have. But if, for the sake of being filled with Christ, we die to our self-interest, letting go of any attempt to salvage our fallen humanity, we will discover the real abundant life that we can have only when Christ lives in us.

This, then, is the essence of what our father was missing—what we often miss.

Christ seeks to replace the very core of our fallen humanity—our self. He says that we can become the spiritual entity He intends us to be only by losing the self that every ounce of our natural being seeks to preserve and protect.

Ending the cover-up

The lessons here are inescapable. To whatever extent the natural self is alive and well, we cannot and will not experience Christ in our lives. The evidence is overwhelming. We may be very religious—even living a life of daily study and prayer. But if we're trying to overlay that spirituality on a self that is alive, it won't amount to much. Little of Christ's transforming love will be seen. If we adhere to an intellectual belief that permits us to continue our attempts at self-preservation, bringing a false sense of security, the self grows ever larger and squeezes out the Christ life.

This, then, is the first step in dying: understanding the basis of this cover-up so we can end it. Our pretense is like acting in a play, only instead of doing it just for an evening, we hang on to the role for life—a role that will destroy us. When we have just a religious facade, our condition is far more hopeless than is that of non-believers. This pretense leaves us operating under the delusion that we are saved by belief alone. James 2:19 says, "Do you still think it's enough just to believe that there is one God? Well, even the demons believe this, and they tremble in terror" (NLT). That is hardly a ringing endorsement!

When I first accepted Christ, I thought my belief, along with my reasonably moral life, would save me. With this thought in mind, I attempted to make Jesus a component of my life. After all, He taught some wonderful principles, and, while I was already relatively good, making Him a part of my life could only lead to further self-improvement. But I soon learned that He cannot simply be *part* of my life; He must be my *whole* life. Please understand that this is not essential because He demands it. It is essential because His very nature necessitates it. His heart can live in us only to the extent that we allow our heart, our self, to be removed. Trying to add Him to our natural life is like trying to mix oil and water. It will never work because the natural properties of Christ and self will always be incompatible. He can occupy our life only if we allow Him to take over completely—*daily*.

This endeavor reminds me of a lesson I learned when my computer went on the fritz, something that usually leaves me clueless. We had usually been able to depend on our computer geek son Jeffrey—that is until he left for college. I still recall the first time I had problems after he was gone. I immediately called him, hoping that he could walk me through the necessary steps to restore the machine. But I had barely described the problem when he cut me off, requesting that I hold on just a minute.

While I waited, I idly moved the cursor around, hoping that I might accidentally click on something that would make the computer work. *This is pathetic,* I thought, shaking my head as I waited. Suddenly, the cursor darted across the screen, away from the place to which I was directing it with the mouse. Thinking my computer was going crazy, I attempted to move the cursor back. It responded only briefly before taking off on its own again. I watched that cursor dance all over the screen as I fought for control.

Just then, Jeffrey's voice broke in. "You're an idiot!" he said jokingly. "Leave it alone; I've taken over."

Indeed, he had taken over my computer with something called remote access. But as long as both of us were trying to move that cursor, we just ended up fighting each other. I quickly learned that Jeffrey could help me only if I stopped trying. So I gave up, ending my efforts to fix things. I simply sat back and marveled, watching my screen as Jeffrey clicked here and there, opening and closing various programs to get things back on track.

Clarence often says that rather than trying harder, we need to die more fully. I frequently wonder how often Christ shakes His head at our feeble attempts that get in the way. When it comes to fixing ourselves, we are indeed spiritual idiots! He asks only that we let go of the controls, sit back, and watch Him work. Only then is He able to close down the programs of self while opening programs to His heart.

If you have as many control issues as I do, keeping your hands off the controls and trusting Someone Else to handle things is extremely difficult—anything but a passive process. Yet this is an essential task if Christ is to do His work in us. Our spiritual survival absolutely depends on our *continually* dying to self. To do this, we must understand self's basic operating principle—self-deception.

Chapter 5

Self-deception: The Lies We Believe

(Clarence)

If we claim to be without sin, we deceive ourselves and the truth is not in us.
—1 John 1:8, NIV

I had just finished balancing our checkbook for the month. As I observed the dwindling amount left for savings, I shook my head and reached to turn up our thermostat. The southern Virginia sun had pushed the temperature to well over ninety humid degrees, and, after seeing our utility costs, I thought we could handle eighty degrees in the house rather than our usual seventy-eight. Just then, Dianna walked through the door, packages in hand.

"What did you get?" I asked.

"Just some stuff from Kmart," she replied, laying the bags on our dining room table.

I glanced up to see some cleaning supplies, paper towels, and toilet paper. Having just gone over our finances, I was relieved to see these minor purchases. I should have left it at that, but I couldn't resist looking through the bags.

"Don't worry, honey," Dianna reassured, with a hint of sarcasm, "nothing but the essentials."

"Like bug spray?" I challenged, pulling out a can of Raid.

"You know we need it," Dianna responded defensively.

"I told you I'd find some in the garage."

"Right. That was a month ago. I'm sick of watching you run around the house with that stupid flyswatter. You're getting hyper over two dollars and fifty-nine cents? Unbelievable!"

"Every little bit counts," I insisted.

"I can't believe you're griping over bug spray!" Dianna exclaimed, and she stomped into the bedroom, slamming the door behind her.

I self-righteously reminded myself that I was above this petty fighting, taking comfort in knowing that I rarely lost my temper. In fact, I was usually the peacemaker, apologizing even when an apology wasn't deserved, just to maintain harmony. Indeed, I often reassured myself that I didn't need to come out looking good to know that I was in the right (which shows the typical response of wrongheaded rightness—something we'll learn more about in chapter 15).

Money was our touchiest subject, a source of ongoing conflict in our relationship. It is easy to see why experts find that financial conflicts are the number one cause of divorce. The pattern between us always followed the same path. Dianna would spend more than I thought she should or buy something I deemed nonessential. I was constantly plagued by anxiety about our finances, making any contemplated purchase an opportunity to save. My worry would turn into irritation at various levels, depending on her spending. When I voiced my fears and frustration—I never was able to shut up, even when I should have—she became angry and defensive. This destructive dance was so predictable that it seemed choreographed. But no matter how often we repeated it, we seemed hopelessly caught up in playing out our parts.

It wasn't that I sought conflict over money. I simply felt it incumbent on me to protect our financial position. However, the reality was that Dianna was hardly a spendthrift—anything but. Still, there were always opportunities to save, and I convinced myself throughout most of our marriage that I needed to pinch every penny to improve our financial standing. Of course, I never doubted the implicit assumption that my decisions on money were better than hers—never mind that my own high-risk investment schemes had cost us far more than all the minor purchases we had argued about. Clearly, I had a serious problem with money—a fact I spent most of my life avoiding by making it her problem.

Deceptive conflict

I was raised in a home where financial concerns were a constant source of conflict. The fighting over money was so pervasive that throughout most of my childhood, I thought our family was poor. I was constantly reminded of the need to save. For instance, one time I was lectured for wasting money by using too much polish on my shoes. It wasn't until I was in my early

I had . . . the notion that emotional security and financial security go hand in hand.

teens that I realized what had previously eluded me. We couldn't be poor; doctors are rarely poor, and my father was a doctor. Besides, people in tight financial straits couldn't afford a nine-passenger Imperial limousine or a fifty-foot yacht docked in the most prestigious harbor in Chicago. Obviously, my father had his own rather unique priorities, in which his extravagant purchases took precedence over what most would consider basic necessities. However, by the time I realized limited finances were not the real issue, the emotional damage had already been done, guaranteeing major problems in my relationship with money.

Unknowingly, I had been thoroughly brainwashed with the notion that emotional security and financial security go hand in hand. Of course, no amount of money can bring emotional security, so my unconscious premise was a setup, leaving me hopelessly and helplessly programmed to make the subject of finances a constant bone of contention in our marriage.

Dianna was also set up for this, as she too grew up in a home where her dad was always complaining about money. These dynamics assured that she would be attracted to someone who had the same unhealthy tie to money as her dad. It is scary, the way we are helplessly driven to seek out familiar bents, even if they are very unhealthy.

Self expresses itself in a myriad of ways, which was evident in how I dealt with money. But strangely, while most people would readily see that I had a problem, I was totally blind to it. I spent years deceiving myself and defending my distorted perspective. We have already learned how self deceives with a cover-up to preserve its own agenda. However, there is an even more insidious and far more destructive lie: self-deception—self lying to itself. The Arbinger Institute defines this concept as follows: *Self-deception is the problem of not knowing and of resisting the possibility that I have a problem.*[1]

When self is alive, I can't see that I'm the one responsible for causing the problem. I will also be highly resistant to any suggestion that I'm responsible. Furthermore, I'll fight against anything that might keep me from perpetuating the problem, as this is clearly seen as a threat. This deception is at the foundation of our struggle with self. The Bible describes it in sobering language. "If we claim to be without sin, we deceive ourselves and the truth is not in us. . . . If we claim we have not sinned, we make him out to be a liar and his word has no place in our lives" (1 John 1:8, 10, NIV).

This seemingly simple passage carries profound implications that merit a closer examination. Twice it mentions people's claim to be without sin. For years, as I read these verses, I wondered why this concern was included. After all, who claims to be without sin? But as I gave up on self and began adopting a new life in Christ, I considered this in a whole new light. I began noticing that whenever my self was alive, I was extremely resistant to seeing any of my faults. Our pride gets us totally wrapped up in defending self and tearing down others, guarding our turf with the tenacity of a bulldog. As we attempt to maintain and defend self, we fall into three major traps: we exaggerate the faults of others, we embellish our own virtues, and we blame others. In other words, when we are at fault, the only way self comes out ahead—which is something that human nature insists on—is to distort our view of ourselves and others. And here's the scary part—not only do we claim to be without sin, when self is alive, we actually believe it! We cannot see the truth when self is alive. To preserve its existence, self constantly works at deceiving us.

Self-deception

My personal experience and those verses from Scripture illustrate certain key principles and the ripple effects of self-deception. As I previously indicated, Dianna was a very conservative spender. But did I see her that way? Not at all. A part of my self that was alive involved my attitude toward money. And in order to justify this attitude, I had to defend my criticisms of Dianna's spending, convincing myself that she was careless with money, which was absolutely false. One of the things the verse says is that when we lie to ourselves, the truth is not in us. This is the first principle of self-deception: *When self is alive, it is impossible for us to see the truth of the situation. We cannot see self or others accurately.*

But it goes beyond this. Not only are we blind to the truth, the entire foundation of our self is based on lies. Notice one of the lines in our text. "If we claim we have not sinned, we make him out to be a liar." Christ speaks to this issue in another passage: " 'You belong to your father, the devil, and you want to carry out your father's desire. . . . When he lies, he speaks his native language, for he is a liar and the father of lies. Yet because I tell the truth, you do not believe me!' " (John 8:44, 45, NIV).

Trust is at the heart of our self-deception. We must either trust God or self, the same choice given to Adam and Eve. Believing they could enhance the position of self by disobeying God's instructions, they accepted Satan's lie. First, they distrusted the truth, choosing to believe the lie that self can be trusted, and then they behaved accordingly. Similarly, I chose to believe self's flat-out lie about money. While money cannot bring happiness or even emotional security, for far too many years, I believed that it could—a complete distortion of the truth. Further, once I chose to protect my self by defending my take on money, I had to distrust Dianna, distorting the reality of her spending. She in turn responded with understandable anger. The broken trust led both of us to act destructively, which usually meant saying hurtful words in our quarrels over money. This brings us to the second principle of self-deception: *When self is alive, we will believe lies to protect it, with the ripple effect of damaging trust and destroying relationships.*

Another characteristic of self-deception is that it compels us to cling to distorted beliefs with a defensive stance that blocks any reasonable insight. I was totally irrational in my arguments with Dianna over her spending. Sadly, that only drove me to further self-justification. By nature, self's position is always rather precarious, and the more tenuous it is, the greater the efforts needed to prop it up. I would shamefully cook up any argument, no matter how irrational, to defend my stance on money.

Think of the conflicts you get into or have witnessed in others. When you step back and take even a cursory look at them, you'll likely be shocked at how unreasonable they really are. Our irrationality is based on the fact that the truth so threatens self's existence that we must continue to justify our distorted position at all costs. Paul recognized this when he stated, "The sinful mind is hostile to God. It does not submit to God's law, nor can it do so. Those controlled by the sinful nature cannot please God" (Romans 8:7, NIV).

This fact calls into question our common perception of freedom. Any seasoned believer knows that the idea of freedom is an illusion; we must always submit. So the only question is whether we submit to God or to self. Since self is based on lies, it is hostile to God because His truth is a constant threat to its existence. While we claim to want harmony, self will trump harmony in order to be right. It will say, do, and believe anything, no matter how irrational, to justify its position. This brings us to the third principle of self-deception: *When self is alive, it thrives on lies that support a fundamental character flaw—self-justification.*

Self-justification's destructive effects

Thus far, our principles have focused primarily on what self-deception does to us. Equally important is the consideration of how self-deceit affects others. It was only after years of marriage that I learned of the destructive influence my self-justification had on Dianna. In terms of finances, I was able to deceive myself about the rightness of my position and the wrongness of hers. This allowed me to feel fully justified in my treatment of her. I was absolutely sure that my approach to money was right, so when Dianna didn't concur, I believed it was appropriate for me to do whatever was necessary to ensure adherence to my "correct" financial decisions. This thinking led me to treat Dianna in very hurtful ways. And no matter how despicable my conduct was, I believed it was really Dianna's fault, since it was the consequence of her refusal to see the "truth" of my position and to behave accordingly. This illustrates the fourth principle of self-deception: *When self is alive, it convinces us that other people are wrong, allowing us to treat them any way we want, while blaming them for making the treatment necessary.*

This kind of thinking inevitably affects the attitudes of those with whom we interact. It has been said that we teach others how to relate to us. When Dianna and I dealt with the subject of money, I was a very effective teacher. Through my constant badgering and judgmental approach, I taught her to become defensive and resistant. This distanced us from each other. Furthermore, it prevented her from hearing even reasonable comments about our finances—though, tragically, my comments were seldom reasonable because my self was vigorously alive. *People hear us only when they are moving toward us emotionally.* By our "discussions" regarding money, I had so conditioned Dianna to move away from me that she became deaf to me, demonstrating our fifth principle of self-deception: *When self is alive in relationships, we provoke self to rise in others, blocking trust and causing them to distance themselves from us.*

The expression says it takes two to tango, which is certainly evident when it comes to self. Dianna and I each contributed to the conflicts in our marriage, and she will now readily admit her own issues of self. Remember, through our behavior we teach

Through my . . . judgmental approach, I taught her to become defensive.

others how to relate to us. Dianna's dad taught her to distrust all his assurances. Over and over, he would agree to things and then renege on the promises. This provoked self to rise in her, causing hurt and then anger. And it was reinforced frequently enough to program Dianna for self to rise and for her to become highly reactive whenever there was even a threat that someone might break a promise.

While I am not one to break promises, I have occasionally agreed to do something and later forgotten the promise. Dianna's reaction to this always took me off guard because it was far more extreme than the situation merited. On one such occasion, for instance, we were driving home when Dianna suggested that we drop by an ice-cream shop. I readily agreed. However, we became caught up in conversation, and I totally forgot about the plan. When Dianna realized we had missed the turnoff, she immediately responded with hostility. And the rising of self in her provoked the same in me. I became defensive, telling her this was a small enough mistake; it certainly didn't justify her reaction. We've all participated in this kind of blame game, which usually goes nowhere good.

However, this time the conclusion differed. We had both committed ourselves to a life of attempting to recognize the workings of self and of inviting Christ to keep it in check, altering our responses. After driving in silence for a time, I reflected on what had happened, keeping in mind my new paradigm as I considered a different approach. At my suggestion, Dianna agreed to step back and look at what had just happened between us.

I began by asking if she considered me to be a habitual promise breaker. She readily agreed that I was not. I then reminded her of her dad's broken promises, suggesting that my breaking a promise might trigger feelings occasioned by all the broken promises she had experienced in childhood. Fortunately, she had successfully quieted self and was able to hear me instead of the lies that had served to protect her self all these years. When I suggested that in her reaction to my broken promise she was

> *We* learned the truth about the lies we had brought into our marriage.

sending me "mail" that really belonged to her dad, she immediately agreed. With her new openness, she was able to distrust self and all its protective lies, ending this type of response. Her reactivity to broken promises has not been a problem since.

Once Dianna was vigilant to the rising of self—refusing its lies in favor of the truth about her life—the change in her responses to my occasional lapses of memory was amazing. The same thing happened regarding my sick relationship to money. Ten years into our marriage, I rather suddenly saw the lie I was caught up in about our finances, and I allowed God to totally change my attitude toward money. For both of us, this truth hit well beyond an intellectual level; we were convicted at a deep, emotional level. As a result, our understanding was much more than a head trip. In a way that was transforming, we learned the truth about the lies we had brought into our marriage.

This illustrates another important concept about self-deception. Our experience taught us that clearly, for new insights to effectively overcome the determination of self to rise at every opportunity, we must be convicted of truth at an emotional level. As outlined in the previous principles, self distorts truth, leading us to believe lies to protect self. It also insists on self-justification that blames, which provokes the rising of self in others—which, in turn, further aggravates self in us. This vicious and damaging cycle of self-preservation can end only when the truth about self breaks through at a deep, emotional level. This leads to the final principle of self-deception: *Until truth convicts us at the level of our emotions, fixed patterns involving the rising of self will rule, driving us to revert to our self-protective mode at the slightest provocation.*

Six valuable truths

These six principles present valuable truths regarding our self—truths essential for our breaking through the deceit it perpetuates and successfully guarding against its rising to damage our relationships.

1. When self is alive, it is impossible for us to see the truth of the situation. We cannot see our self or others accurately.
2. When self is alive, we will believe lies to protect it, with the ripple effect of damaging trust and destroying relationships.
3. When self is alive, it thrives on lies that support a fundamental character flaw: self-justification.
4. When self is alive, it convinces us that other people are wrong, allowing us to treat them any way we want, while blaming them for making the treatment necessary.
5. When self is alive, we provoke self to rise in others, blocking trust and causing them to distance themselves from us.
6. Until truth convicts us at the level of our emotions, fixed patterns involving the rising of self will rule, driving us to revert to our self-protective mode at the slightest provocation.

The characteristics intrinsic to self's survival paint a rather bleak picture of our position, inviting us to ask whether there's any hope. Left to our own illusions about the viability of self, the answer is a resounding No! But providentially, when we face this reality and relinquish its deception on a daily basis, Christ can live in us. This is what it's all about—not simply a trip of self-denial but the death of self that allows Christ's complete takeover in our lives. This is far more than some lofty ideal or demand for perfection with little practical application. Rather, it is a very realistic way of living, for which there are clear guidelines that will be explained in the third section of this book.

But first, if we are to remain open to Christ's radical and immensely rewarding call, it is essential that we explore further the basis of our resistance and how we arrive at our distorted understanding. These lie at the heart of our desperate attempt to deny Christ's reality—our protest: illusions of self.

Chapter 6

Protest: Illusions of Self

(Clarence)

Trust in the LORD with all your heart. Never rely on what you think you know. Remember the LORD in everything you do, and he will show you the right way.
—*Proverbs 3:5, 6, TEV*

It was a surreal moment—emotionally charged and life altering. Even fifty years later, the scene remains vivid—the day I lost my family. It was a moment that called for intense emotion. But at fourteen years old, I had already learned that my emotional survival depended on hiding my feelings. As the oldest brother, I couldn't show my inner turmoil even when my family was splitting.

The warm, moist air hung heavy, as it did on most other Illinois summer days. It was the kind of day that often found our family out boating, enjoying the cooling breeze off Lake Michigan. But this was no family outing. My mother and my four younger siblings were leaving—for good! I had known it was coming. The marriage had been tense and strained for as long as I could remember. But at my age, I was far less concerned with my parents' relationship than with my own emotional survival. It wasn't just that the family was breaking up, with Mom and my younger siblings moving to Denver. The life I'd had in Illinois was also ending. Those of us left behind would soon be moving to Maryland to begin a new life. I couldn't imagine what it would be like—a new home, new church, new school, and on top of all that, my older sister and I would have to adjust to a new stepmother, just ten years my senior. But one thing I knew wouldn't change—my father. Wherever I went there would be no escaping the constant sense of appre-hension and fear that ruled my life.

Divorce—the word carried with it a sense of complete destruction and finality. Now the moment of separation had arrived. At five years old, Steve was bliss-fully oblivious to the impact of what was happening. But the rest of us stood by awkwardly—as emotionally paralyzed in our parting as we were in our previous relating. We shed few if any tears. Over the years, our family knew that expressing feelings of hurt would only result in further pain. While living together, we had learned suppression well, making the stoicism in our parting no sur-prise.

> I was stuck—trapped in the life of fear my siblings had escaped.

I continued smiling and waving as my mother and brothers and sis-ters got into the blue Plymouth station wagon. I watched Steve and the others return my wave as they drove away. I never dreamed that it would be eight long years before Steve and I would meet again.

My smile hid overwhelming feelings I dared not express—feelings that were surprisingly unrelated to my loss. Rather, as I watched the car disappear, I experi-enced intense feelings of jealousy, envy, and dread. They were the lucky ones, es-caping into a whole new life. And while I didn't know much about what that new life would be, I knew the most important thing: they wouldn't be under Dad's rule. They were free of the constant fear that consumed me—fear that I spent my life trying to escape. As I returned to our suddenly empty house, I felt resentment, knowing I was stuck—trapped in the life of fear my siblings had escaped—with no choice and no way out.

During my teens, I often wondered what it was like for my younger siblings. I ached, longing for a different life—imagining how it might feel to be free from Dad. Often, I dreamed of leaving it all, hitchhiking the seventeen hundred miles to Denver, and joining the rest of my family in their freedom. But in the early years, I knew this wasn't an option, and later, I was simply too afraid. The divorce had forever altered my life. Clearly, I was trapped with no options. Or was I?

False assumptions

Years later, I learned that I, too, could have joined the others in their new life. My parents had agreed to let the older children choose where they lived. But our poor-to-nonexistent family communication played out in the decisions regarding child custody. Dad informed Mom that I was staying with him, and over the years she, like me, had learned not to question things. She assumed that this was my choice, and, with her desire to placate Dad and avoid confrontation, she chose not to ask me about it. Unfortunately, I never asked either one—unaware that I had a choice.

I was so certain about what I knew. But what I thought I knew wasn't true; it was based on a misperception—an illusion. The assumption that I refused to question kept me locked in a prison of my own making. The illusion that I believed robbed me of opportunity. This tendency to jump to conclusions is all too common. What is the basis of our misperceptions, and why do we so readily rely on and act on beliefs that are often inaccurate? What caused me—what causes us—to miss the opportunity to see reality?

The culprit is self. Our paramount need to preserve and protect self frequently causes us to distort reality, with devastating consequences. This propensity often results in us serving a God of our own making—something noted theologian David Wells warned of more than a decade ago. "They [Christians] labor under the illusion that the God they make in the image of the self becomes more real as he more nearly comes to resemble the self, to accommodate its needs and desires. The truth is quite the opposite. It is ridiculous to assert that God could become more real by abandoning his own character in an effort to identify more completely with ours. And yet the illusion has proved compelling to a whole generation."[1] Author Anne Lamott adds some wit in this more succinct description of our self-made god. "You can safely assume that you've created god in your own image when it turns out that God hates all the same people you do."[2]

Obviously, there is a very real danger that we might develop an allegiance to a god of our own making—an illusion based on our human self-interests. Such an understanding has little to do with the reality of God. It raises self to a whole new level and gives us a watered-down message that's far more palatable than His radical call.

Unfortunately, misperceptions and illusions have been the story of professed believers throughout history. As my father's story shows, information, intellectual belief, and even extensive time spent in worship, Bible study, and prayer often have little to do with either transformation of character or true understanding. Arguably, no group was more disciplined, more faithful, and more biblically informed than the religious leaders of Jesus' time. Yet when the Messiah appeared, they failed to recognize Him.

Deaf believers

Christians usually view the blindness of the Jewish leaders with smug dismay. Instead, their failure should be cause for sober reflection. Jesus was literally in their faces for three and a half years—tangibly present, where they physically heard with their ears, saw with their eyes, and could touch with their hands. But they didn't recognize Him!

Peter's words must have brought Jesus tremendous joy.

More disturbing yet is the blindness of His disciples—His closest companions. While they accepted His divinity, they were unable or unwilling to understand His mission. Think about it: during the latter part of His ministry, Christ gave them every opportunity to grasp and accept the true nature of His kingdom of love. They had spent more than two years listening to His revolutionary message and watching the unending string of miracles. Just after He had fed the four thousand and healed the blind man at Bethsaida, He confronted His disciples with the crucial question that others were increasingly asking. Was Jesus simply a loving individual or was He the Creator and the embodiment of love? Repeatedly through the ages, people have been asked this question that we all must answer, the question that Jesus put to His disciples. " 'What about you?' he asked them. 'Who do you say I am?' Peter answered, 'You are the Messiah' " (Mark 8:29, TEV).

What a breakthrough! Peter's words must have brought Jesus tremendous joy and validation. These simple men He had recruited to join His mission were finally getting it. He was seeing the formation of a nucleus of the believers who would spread His message of love throughout the world. But Jesus knew that before this could happen, His disciples would have to endure terrible trials. So, His love for His earthly companions moved Him to focus on the pain they would experience rather than on His own anticipated suffering. Surely now that they understood His true identity, they could hear the rest of the story. Hoping to strengthen their faith and cushion the disappointment that lay ahead, Jesus decided it was time to reveal how His earthly mission would end. He said, " 'The Son of Man must suffer much and be rejected by the elders, the chief priests, and the teachers of the Law. He will be put to death, but three days later he will rise to life.' He made this very clear to them" (Mark 8:31, 32, TEV).

This was a message of love and care that Christ hoped the disciples could hear for their own sakes. But belief in His divinity didn't translate into acceptance of what He plainly told them. Taking Him aside, Peter, who had just acknowledged His divinity, basically told the Son of God that He didn't know what He was talking about!

However, Jesus didn't give up. Six days after that exchange, the Transfiguration provided further confirmation of His divinity. A few days later, Jesus tried to inform them once again. Surely the overwhelming evidence of who He was and their love for Him would now find them ready to hear and believe predictions concerning His coming sacrifice. He said, " 'The Son of Man will be handed over to those who will kill him. Three days later, however, he will rise to life.' But they did not understand what this teaching meant, and they were afraid to ask him" (Mark 9:31, 32, TEV).

Obviously, they didn't have the perfect love that casts out fear. They were afraid—afraid to ask, afraid to admit ignorance, afraid to learn things that might shake their complacency and threaten what they believed. Something took precedence over the disciples' love for Christ and interfered with their ability to understand what He was telling them. Instead of asking about what He was saying and trying to understand it, the disciples focused on their own self-interests and began to argue about who would be greatest in the kingdom.

One more attempt

A few months later, on their final trip to Jerusalem, Christ tried once more to let the disciples know what was coming. By now, He had lived with them for three years and knew from all their discussions and bickering how off base they were about His mission. But He didn't attack their misperceptions. Instead, His love prompted Him to be concerned once again for the suffering their misunderstandings would cause. His concern for them must have been overwhelming—knowing that they were deaf to words that could assuage their suffering. If only they were open to His love and could hear! Knowing how little time remained before the devastating events surrounding His crucifixion would begin, He tried for the third time to warn them, with even more detail. " 'Listen,' he told them, 'we are going up to Jerusalem where the Son of Man will be handed over to the chief priests and the teachers of the Law. They will condemn him to death and then hand him over to the Gentiles, who will make fun of him, spit on him, whip him, and kill him; but three days later he will rise to life' " (Mark 10:33, 34, TEV).

They couldn't hear or accept His repeated explicit message.

Once again, the love in this message couldn't overcome the deafness of the disciples, which was caused by their own self-interest. This time James and John, instead of understanding or discussing the gravity of the situation, vied for status, requesting to be seated at the right and left hand of Christ in His kingdom.

On at least three separate occasions, Jesus communicated information to the disciples in the clearest possible manner. Because He spoke to them privately, He didn't need to hide His message in parables or metaphors. Besides, this information was far too important for anything but the plainest talk. Still, despite their obvious belief in His divinity, they couldn't hear or accept His repeated explicit message. How was this possible?

Clearly, this conversation that the disciples overlooked was no casual one. Given the nature of the message, Jesus must have had an extremely serious demeanor. How many of us would miss or ignore such a compelling discussion—a companion telling us that he was facing imminent death? I am reminded of what Steve experienced when his wife shared her thoughts on terminating dialysis. The whole family discussed it in tears, knowing death would soon follow if she made this choice. Obviously, it was a conversation that had commanded their full attention.

It seems inconceivable that Jesus' disciples could have missed, ignored, or denied such an important revelation—and to do so on no less than three occasions. In fact, the Gospel reports that they did talk about it: "They kept it to themselves, but they often asked each other what he meant by 'rising from the dead' " (Mark 9:10, NLT). Most people would say the meaning of "rising from the dead" is more than obvious. But it was so inconceivable and so incongruent with what the disciples were anticipating for Christ's mission that they couldn't accept it at face value. Instead, they looked for some hidden meaning that would fit their agenda better.

This blindness of the disciples should teach a rather sobering lesson to believers today. If those who lived in Christ's physical presence and audibly heard His words couldn't get what He was saying, how can Christians today expect to perceive His calling accurately? If we hope to hear any better than the disciples, we must understand what kept His message from getting through to them.

Christ often spoke of the difference between physically hearing and seeing, on the one hand, and genuine understanding on the other.

" 'They see what I do,
    but they don't perceive its meaning.
They hear my words,
    but they don't understand' " (Mark 4:12, NLT).

He often commented about the fact that the Jewish leaders couldn't see the Messiah among them. But this also applied to the disciples. While they accepted His divinity, they were equally blind when it came to accepting His mission of love. " 'He who has ears, let him hear' " (Matthew 11:15, NIV).

What kept them from hearing? And what keeps us from hearing today? Unfortunately, both the disciples and the religious leaders who killed Jesus shared a common flaw: they were human and had self-centered desires that motivated them to attempt to preserve their concepts of how the Messiah would come and what His mission would be. Their selfish motivations prevented them from hearing and accepting Christ's message of love.

What about our motivations? How much do they interfere with our hearing His message for us?

The beginning of wisdom

What underlies people's lack of understanding and acceptance today is the same as what did two thousand years ago—the all-too-human basis for all moral weakness: self. The disciples were alive to self, seeing only self-generated ideas about Christ's mission. This understanding led them to focus on gaining and keeping a hoped-for status, and left them deaf to the explicit statement that contradicted their desires. The difference between having closed or open ears is whether self is dead or alive. Clearly, spiritual commitment and religious beliefs—even belief in the Son of God—cannot penetrate our own distorted understanding. It won't allow us to include Christ in our lives the way He intends to be there—not as long as self is alive. This is why we are told, "Never rely on what you think you know" (Proverbs 3:5, TEV).

While the disciples filtered Christ's message through selves that were fully alive, they could hear little of His love, His true mission, or how His earthly ministry would end. With the advantage of hindsight, we find the disciples' blindness un-believable. What an incredible opportunity—to spend three years in constant companionship with the Son of God! We think it certainly must have been much easier to be a believer two thousand years ago than it is now. But was it?

Just as was the case with the Jewish leaders and the disciples, many today are not hearing—for the same reasons. Modern hearers share the same vulnerabilities to self that made the disciples miss His message and the religious leaders call for His death.

We cannot answer the call to trust in the Lord without distrusting and renounc-ing our own understanding. Anything less will end—as it did for the disciples and the religious leaders—in us worshiping an illusory messiah of our own making. Self constantly calls for us to meet its needs, leaving us spiritually bankrupt. This dying to self-generated illusions is essential if we are to have any hope of trusting in the Lord and His design for our life. Until we despair of self, seeing it in all its helplessness, we will be resistant to adopting this challenging new life.

"Sounds pretty grim," observed my brother Nathan, after reading an early draft of this book. "I guess we may as well get on board for the Bataan death march!"

While I couldn't help laughing at his observation, I also realized that he had identified an issue that likely resonates with others. I certainly don't want to leave the impression that Christ's call is virtually impossible to fulfill. If you feel like Nathan did, it is likely due to the emphasis on the hopelessness of self. This can leave a dangerous misimpression concerning what *we* must accomplish. Christ wasn't—and isn't—making a self-based call. We need only to surrender our will—to give up on keeping self alive—so that Christ can effect our daily dying to self. We emphasize the hopelessness of preserving the self because it is an understanding essential to our surrendering self fully and accessing the boundless hope Christ offers through His making us new creations.

When we accept the need to die and then consider the task of dying to be our job, it is more than discouraging. It leaves us with the expectation that we must attain a self-flagellating perfection. If this were true, we might as well take a hike to the nearest monastery to try to limit the opportunity for the dead self to rise by cutting ourselves off from the normal temptations of the world. But the work we find so overwhelming when we consider it our work becomes easy when we give up and let Christ do it. He said, " 'My yoke is easy and my burden is light' " (Matthew 11:30, NIV).

Steve illustrated Christ's work in us with the story about Jeffrey's computer repair through remote access. As long as we're at the controls, working on fixing things ourselves, Christ can't work in and through us. Admittedly, turning control completely over to Him involves enormous trust in Him, and doing so—giving up on self's will to survive—poses life's greatest challenge. But when we surrender control and Christ becomes fully alive in us, He brings peace and security beyond belief!

Before we look at Christ's takeover, though, we must understand our part in this process. Giving up on self is an unending battle, requiring constant vigilance. We must experience the despair of knowing our solutions will inevitably fail.

Chapter 7

Despair: Solutions That Fail

(Steve)

Oh, what a miserable person I am! Who will free me from this life that is dominated by sin?

—*Romans 7:24, NLT*

The sunlight, just beginning to stream through my office window, illuminated a scene I could only wish had never seen the light of day. I had totally lost control of my psychiatric evaluation. Jimmy, the eight-year-old focus of concern, was dancing around my office naked! My nurse and I, along with his mother and grandmother, watched in shock as the scene unfolded.

The initial presentation certainly had given no hint that this appointment would turn into a complete fiasco. Jimmy's problems were rather typical of those displayed by many of the children I saw at the mental health clinic. His problems included impulsivity, defiance, and a low-frustration tolerance that resulted in frequent, extreme tantrums involving physical attacks and property destruction. In such cases, parents often feel unable to gain control and seek a psychiatric referral to determine whether medication might help.

Jimmy's guardians were at their wits' end over his moodiness, aggression, and constant defiance and were questioning whether they could even continue parenting him. "We just want to find the right diagnosis," they observed, reminding me of today's informed consumer. With the Internet and media hype over supposed psychiatric breakthroughs, everyone has become an amateur psychiatrist. The result is information overload for people whose ability to filter and critically evaluate the data provided is limited. *Here we go again,* I thought as I continued listening to their concerns.

"Someone diagnosed him with oppositional defiance," they said. "But do you think he might have attention deficit disorder? What about bipolar? We read about that online, and it certainly seems to fit."

I found myself repeating the same timeworn responses I had been providing through the years. Again I attempted to offer some sanity in the face of psychiatry's headlong embrace of diagnoses and of medication as the cornerstone of treatment. Explaining this to clients was a tall order, given the popularity of that approach. As I tried to point out the realities of psychiatric diagnosis and treatment, Jimmy's antics in the office only added to the challenges at hand.

I began to explain. "Psychiatric diagnoses are simply labels for groupings of symptoms. They say almost nothing about what is going on inside the brain." I tried to ignore Jimmy as he darted around the office and interrupted my explanation. "Compared to diagnosing strep throat, a psychiatric diagnosis is more like blind men describing an elephant, with each having a different opinion. Often our diagnoses don't translate into specific treatments. When we add the normal differences in how children mature and develop, trying to make a mental health label fit a child is even more impossible."

"Well, his moods go way beyond normal development," his grandmother observed, still trying to pin down the diagnosis, despite the reservations I expressed. "When he explodes, it's like he's a different person. He gets this glazed look, as though he's in another world, and then he goes ballistic."

"Do you notice any pattern or cycle? Is there any predictability to his moods?" I asked. Increasingly, any moodiness tends to be diagnosed as bipolar disorder, though most children who get this label don't have distinct cycles and don't turn out to be bipolar as adults.

"Oh no. He just blows up whenever he doesn't get his way," she responded, shaking her head in dismay.

"After he hits you or breaks things, is he upset with himself? Does he apologize or show any remorse?"

"Oh no, he never apologizes," Mom chimed in. "He just goes on like nothing happened."

Happy or sad?

"Jimmy. Jimmy!" I said, getting his attention just as he crawled out from under the table. "Do you feel happy or sad most of the time?"

"Happy," he responded.

"And do you think your anger is a problem?" I asked.

He grinned somewhat sheepishly and shrugged, obviously wanting to avoid the question.

"Do you think you could control your temper if you really wanted to?" I asked, pushing for his thoughts. Again he shrugged.

"How about if someone were to promise you a new video game system if you stopped having tantrums for one week—could you do that?"

"Sure!" he responded. "Will you buy me one?"

I laughed, and continued with my point. "I'm glad you can control your anger if you want to badly enough. Of course, since you are in control, that means that you are choosing to blow up when you get angry. It's great that you can make that choice, but it also means that you will get punished when you choose to have a tantrum."

A puzzle piece narrowly missed my head.

He didn't seem very thrilled with this observation and frowned as he threw one of the wooden blocks. His mother admonished him to stop throwing things, but he picked up a puzzle piece and threw it. She tried to grab him, but he scampered across the room.

"See, he just won't listen to anything," she said in exasperation. "I don't think he could control himself, even if he wanted to."

"You might be right," I conceded. "He has certainly developed bad habits of losing his temper and doing whatever he wants. Habits are extremely difficult to break, and it doesn't appear that he even wants to try."

"This is more than a bad habit," she observed with growing irritation as he bumped into her legs and then crawled around the sofa again. "Jimmy! Will you please sit down?" she pleaded. Then turning to me, she asked, "Why wouldn't he want to try to control his anger?"

"Because it works for him," I responded. "Like other animals, we tend to do what feels good and works for us. As we mature, we learn to resist this at times, but in children, the urges to satisfy self are often controlled only by the environment. When we become angry and the tension builds, we want relief. Exploding gives a wonderful feeling of release, and most children don't want to give that up. In fact, most people who have trouble with anger don't think they have a problem. They think it's the people around them who have the problem."

"We have a problem, all right," the grandmother agreed. "That's why we're here. Nothing we do has any effect, which is why we're wondering if he really *can* control himself."

"In my experience, very few children are unable to control their anger. Only God really knows, but when we assume that children can't control it, we're in danger of enabling their actions. The jails are full of people who struggle more with control than do most of the population. But society still expects all people to control their anger. For some, the impulse is stronger than for others, but it is rarely irresistible."

A puzzle piece narrowly missed my head, and once again, Jimmy's mother grabbed at him, this time catching his arm. But he soon squirmed away from her and darted across the room.

"But he's just so out of control!" his grandmother exclaimed as he began throwing more puzzle pieces around the room. Jimmy's mother kept telling him to stop, but he simply ignored her. "We can't take much more of this," the grandmother continued. "Isn't there something you can give him?"

"Some medicines tone down aggression," I replied, "but behavioral approaches are most effective. Since he doesn't think he has a problem, it is up to the adults to change the environment, making sure his tantrums don't work. Then he'll discover that he does have a problem."

Out of control

As I began to review basic behavioral interventions, they said they had tried everything, and nothing, including punishment, affected Jimmy's behavior. Jimmy obviously didn't appreciate my attempts to institute consequences. He began more frequent interruptions, dancing around in front of me and tossing toys around the room. I could see that the session was getting out of control. But when he ran to the other side of the nurse's desk, his ability to control himself became obvious. When she gave him one stiff shake of her head and stared at him with dagger eyes, he quickly halted and backed away. Unfortunately, neither of his caregivers had that kind of control, and he knew it.

My input was threatening Jimmy's control over things, and he wasn't about to relinquish any power—not without a fight. As he danced around throwing things, his mother and grandmother began taking the toys away. Soon there was nothing left to throw—or so I thought. But then he pulled off his shoes and threw them at his mother. As she tried to grab his arms, he pulled off his socks, laughing gleefully as he tossed them in her direction. She persisted with her verbal reprimands, which he continued to ignore. His intention to provoke was so blatant, and she was so obviously hooked—her objections only fueling the fire—that I advised her to ignore him. So she sat still.

His mother couldn't tolerate allowing him to experience ... disappointment.

I was sure that without any attention, Jimmy would de-escalate. Unfortunately, I hadn't counted on the years of programming he had received. His mother's attention had reinforced his demands for self-satisfaction throughout his life. Now he had every expectation that if he persisted in acting out, he would be rewarded once again. When it comes to satisfying self, our demands know no bounds, and there is often no shame—no lengths to which we will not go to gain the fix we want. Jimmy proved that. He began stripping off his clothes and throwing them at his mother until he tossed the last item—his undershorts!

I still wasn't willing to get hooked by this ridiculous display, so I pretended indifference, though I certainly felt the same shock that the others were showing. Then Jimmy began peeing on the sofa!

His grandmother, who could only see his back, was oblivious to this latest development. She warned, "I think he might need to go to the bathroom."

"No. I think he's already taken care of that," I deadpanned.

Still, Jimmy wasn't about to be ignored. He insisted on further attention by dashing out of the office and down the hall. *Great,* I thought, *now the entire clinic will know about this fiasco!*

While his mother chased him down the hall, his grandmother shared tidbits she hadn't felt comfortable telling me in her daughter's presence. She reported that her daughter had very volatile moods and had been diagnosed—you guessed it—with bipolar disorder. In the early years, she gave Jimmy whatever he wanted. She was reactive and often had little control, either giving in to keep the peace or exploding in anger. The grandmother was able to see Jimmy's manipulation and finally agreed that this was a behavioral problem that needed to be addressed primarily with appropriate parenting. But she was doubtful that her daughter could be convinced or was even capable of disciplined parenting.

Contrary to what some professionals might posit, Jimmy's severe behavioral impairment didn't stem from an inherent brain dysfunction. Rather, it was the result of behavioral reinforcement from years of exposure to an inconsistent and permissive environment. Like many parents, his mother couldn't tolerate allowing him to experience the disappointment and frustration that is an inevitable part of refusing to gratify self. Over the years, this kind of parenting—increasingly evident in society—programs children to expect their wishes to be met at every turn. As they become increasingly addicted to self-gratification, they also become unable to accept refusal or delay of their desires.

Our culture's progressive obsession with self is driven by multiple forces, not the least of which is the mental health movement, of which I am a part. It is rather ironic that my chosen profession, which primarily treats problems related to the narcissistic self, is steeped in theories that have raised the self to a whole new level. This perspective wasn't taught in my psychiatric residency; it is one that I have come to understand only after years of practice. Initially, I enthusiastically embraced my education on the latest psychiatric cures. I fully believed in humankind's ability to solve our problems and looked forward to having a role in learning and providing my own solutions. I hadn't yet learned the ultimate futility of human solutions.

I was taught that mental disorders almost always involved dissatisfaction with the self and that they indicate an underlying abnormality that requires outside treatment to reestablish normal functioning. Of course, this paradigm supports the view that the self is a victim that needs to be rescued and enhanced. With the recent change in my perspective, I have come to understand that psychiatry's underlying philosophy often translates into more human-made constructs that champion the self. Our temporary solutions, which ultimately fail, have been progressively incorporated into mainstream thought, providing a rationale for satisfying self that we are more than happy to embrace.

Self-promotion therapy

Amy, the nurse in my office that day, had only recently begun working with me when I first saw Jimmy. "That kid was a brat!" she observed after he left.

I laughed and said, "We don't like to call them brats," but I couldn't really disagree with her assessment.

This was Amy's first experience in a child psychiatry clinic, and she had many questions. "How does a kid get like that anyway?" she asked.

"By getting his desires met whenever he wants," I responded. "It's all about self. The more self is gratified, the more dissatisfied and demanding it becomes. In fairness to Jimmy, he has spent years living in an environment that taught him he could best meet his needs by being a brat."

"But how can you say the problem is self? I thought that's what psychiatric treatment was all about—improving self and building self-esteem."

"True, which is why I often part company with the tenets of my profession."

"I don't understand. Why did you even go into psychiatry if you don't agree with it?"

"Sometimes I ask myself the same question," I said, laughing. "But initially, I fully bought what I was taught."

"So what changed?"

"Over time, I learned that psychiatric solutions, like most others, are temporary at best and often, by enhancing self, actually make problems worse."

"How? I thought that's why people get treatment. Therapy is supposed to make them feel better about themselves."

"That's certainly the idea," I agreed. "And it clearly explains the popularity of psychotherapy. We love any notion that suggests self needs to be our primary focus."

"So what's wrong with that?"

"Nothing, if you think that feeling good about ourselves is the ultimate goal in life. But this tends to become a narcissistic trip that often dooms us to helplessly follow the dictates of self."

"So you're saying therapy makes people more self-centered?"

"It certainly has that danger. Psychiatry tends to trash our tendency to repress drives and emotions as irrational and unnecessary. Freud taught that proscriptions against self-gratification are often based on irrelevant parental constructs—relics of the past that were at the root of frustrating the desires of the self. It's really a wonderful rationale for meeting the 'needs' of the self!"

"But isn't that why people come to see you—to feel better about themselves so they can function better?"

"Yes. And how do you think it's working?" I countered.

"What do you mean?"

"Well, just look at how we're behaving. Is all the push to make ourselves feel better and increase our sense of self-satisfaction really working? Over the past couple decades, we've been able to take care of self far better than at any time in history. Yet most would say we are increasingly dissatisfied and demanding. And few would argue that overall there has been a rather marked moral deterioration as the needs of the self are better met."

"I guess that's true," Amy agreed. "And you think psychotherapy adds to the problem?"

"At times. I have to admit that other therapists and I collude—albeit often unwittingly—in a process that champions and boosts self's position. We are supposed to give unconditional acceptance to the client, which often leads to the unspoken assumption that no one is really responsible or at fault for anything. I was trained to listen to patients in a warm, empathic, nonjudgmental manner no matter what they might share. This often results, although unintentionally, in the perception that I'm giving tacit approval for what the patient is sharing, regardless of how reprehensible the behavior might be."

Avoiding balance

"So we're all supposed to feel bad about ourselves?"

"Certainly we should when it's deserved. But that seldom happens in therapy.

Did you notice how quick Jimmy's family was to suggest that he might have bipolar disorder?"

"Yeah. I wondered about that since I thought it was a somewhat rare diagnosis."

"It used to be, but that's changing. Now people want a psychiatric diagnosis, as it tends to reduce the sense of individual responsibility. The anti-blame game is supported by neuroscience research as biological approaches lend further impetus to the notion that those in treatment aren't really responsible—that we simply need to come up with the right medication.

Psychotherapy has…increased its popularity through promotion of the self.

Psychotherapy has also increased its popularity through promotion of the self by offering to explore the causes of pain: family of origin, traumas, unfulfilling marriages, financial setbacks, et cetera, everything but the client's own doing."

"So why does therapy have to avoid any blaming of the client?" Amy asked.

"It doesn't have to, but it usually ends up doing that. We have to avoid blaming the client if we want to preserve the all-important self-esteem, which could be jeopardized by negative feelings of guilt and shame. Have you noticed how today's culture is increasingly rejecting such depressing feelings?"

"Yeah. No one likes to feel bad about themselves."

"No kidding. We naturally want to be as pain-free as possible. My training involved techniques that would tend to mitigate what was considered self-defeating guilt and shame. After all, such feelings don't do much to meet the goal of making the client feel better. Besides, we therapists also have our own needs—earning money! While most don't like to talk about this motivation, if we don't have a happy, self-satisfied clientele, our incomes will drop, which won't do much for our own desires to satisfy self!"

"That sounds rather self-serving," Amy observed.

"At times, it is. In my practice, I have been guilty of attempting to assuage the clients' pain, building them up when it wasn't warranted. Such treatment promotes an undeserved sense of self-esteem and raises the expectation of even greater self-esteem. Regardless of how much this may distort reality, feeling esteemed increases the sense of self worth. And no matter how unwarranted, this feels great—not only for the client but also for the therapist, who gets both positive feedback and a growing bank account."

"Isn't that rather cynical?"

"Maybe. But we need to be honest about the downside of the treatment process. The self-satisfied clientele turn into self-esteem junkies who keep coming back for more, with the therapist only too willing to act as their well-paid pusher. While this results in clients feeling good about themselves and the therapeutic experience, it often does so at the expense of long-term growth. Such therapy seldom produces development of character that incorporates discipline and willingness to deny the wants of the self. That would be a rather painful process that few would seek out, let alone pay for."

"So as usual, it all boils down to money."

"Unfortunately, it often does. And the financial motivation of therapists is not the only economic driving force. Managed-care organizations save themselves money by limiting health care. They're only too happy to find quick fixes for the short term, in order to make the bottom line look good. Financial incentives also motivate the pharmaceutical industry, which welcomes the opportunity to increase its sales by promoting chemical solutions for any and all emotional and behavioral problems. And most patients would rather pop a pill than engage in the hard work of character change."

Passing it on to the kids

In addition to the premise that children are victims of their environment and of their parenting, my profession now increasingly includes the idea that because they have defective brains from bad genes, they have little control over feelings, thoughts, and actions without the medications they need to bring about change. Of course, we are all born with defective brains—they're pathologically programmed to worship self. But that hardly makes us victims. Many of the so-called psychiatric disorders we see are the outcome of making self-addicted choices over years, which leads to self-driven bad behavior. When treatment focuses primarily on unconditional support that gratifies the self, it simply encourages greater demands by the insatiable self.

Unfortunately, the self-help culture has also adversely influenced our parenting, which has had a devastating impact on today's youth. When I began child psychiatry training twenty-nine years ago, children were viewed as unsocialized, potential monsters who needed to be shaped within an environment of firm limits and consequences. People's perspectives have shifted dramatically since then. As "modern" parents, we're far more permissive because we want to avoid raising repressed, neurotic children who might grow up to resent us the way we do our parents.

In our zeal to avoid disappointing our children, we often give in to their desires rather than allow them to experience frustration. We fool ourselves into thinking that this is a loving, caring approach. In reality, we're caring for our own desires to have happy, self-satisfied children who make us feel good, and we're denying our children the opportunity to build their frustration tolerance through disappointment. The growth in this style of parenting over the years has produced children who are programmed to expect that their desires will be met at every turn. They can't delay pleasure, and they become ever more addicted to self-gratification.

"We usually provided far more than you kids really needed."

Recently, I had a conversation about this with my oldest son, Justin. "You know, Dad, we were rather conservatively raised," he observed. "I mean, you didn't give us whatever we wanted, like a lot of parents do."

"That's in the eye of the beholder," I responded. "Your grandmother would say you were given far more than I was. Today, parents seem to give more to their kids, and the kids expect more. You may not have gotten as much as most kids raised in a doctor's family, but we still probably gave you too much."

"Like what?" Justin challenged.

"Well, take Christmas for instance. We loved the excitement and magic of the season and did all we could to pass this on to you kids. In the early years, it was easy. With five of you under the age of ten, spending one hundred or one hundred fifty dollars on each of you at Toys "R" Us filled our van with gifts. With one evening of shopping, we could amass a pile of presents under the tree guaranteed to elicit squeals of joy from all of you on Christmas morning."

"You definitely gave us the *wow* factor back then," he said, laughing.

"Unfortunately, as you grew up, it became increasingly expensive and difficult to get the same response. Still, we spent unnecessary money trying not to disappoint the expectations previous Christmases had raised in you."

"Yeah, I remember when that excitement began to end in my teens. As reality set in, we had to learn that we couldn't be overwhelmed that way."

"But it goes far beyond Christmas," I continued. "Most of us are so blessed that we are able to give our children far more than is good for them throughout the year. Middle class was way different twenty years ago. With all our conveniences, increased time, fast food, recreation, TV, video games, et cetera, raising happy, frustration-free children who receive all they desire is easy in the early years, easier than it has ever been in history."

"True," Justin agreed. "Even the poor kids I knew had plenty of TV and video games."

"That's what I mean. You think you had more limits than usual, but that's only when compared to others in your generation. Previous generations would say you were rather spoiled."

"Thanks, Dad," he responded sarcastically.

"Seriously, if you think about it, we usually provided far more than you kids really needed, far more than was best for you, though often still less than we could afford. We continually attempted to restrict ourselves from indulging you with as much as we were tempted to provide. Today, almost all parents must deal with this struggle at some level; a struggle that many have already given up. Unfortunately, as you kids grow older, your demands and sense of entitlement often become greater, and your wants become 'needs' that are increasingly difficult to satisfy."

Treating the children

Parents realize, often too late, that they have raised spoiled brats who expect immediate gratification. Often, that's when they seek my professional help, which, given that we are a society of victims, is not always well received. Clients are often looking for validation rather than confrontation on their parenting.

Many psychiatrists avoid directly focusing on individual or parental responsibilities. They ignore family concerns and simply diagnose the child as having a disorder. And now the children of these parents have become parents themselves—parents who have even less tolerance for blame or guilt, even when it is called for.

I have observed over the years the dramatic influence the mental health movement has had on the way parenting has evolved in recent decades. When parenting was seen as a culprit that produced unhappy, repressed adults, professionals began advocating increasingly permissive parenting. Remember the famous parenting guru Benjamin Spock? He used Freud's principles in his advocacy for more permissive parenting. We moved from the authoritarian oppression of the early 1900s to the permissiveness, rebellion, and sexual freedom of the sixties, and the baby boomers who questioned authority began to question even their own authority, preferring to let their children decide for themselves rather than force any choices upon them. This resulted in the narcissistic Generation Xers, who, in turn, have given us Generation Y, which has an even greater sense of entitlement—illustrating the biblical warning that " 'the iniquity of the fathers' " would be visited " 'on the children to the third and the fourth generation of those who hate me' " (Exodus 20:5, ESV).

Can you see the gradual shift in society with each generation? We have become increasingly invested in our own feelings that, unfortunately, dominate our choices in parenting. Spock, who was the recognized child-rearing authority for decades, appeared to advocate this when he suggested that "what good mothers and fathers instinctively feel like doing for their babies is usually best after all."[1] Of course, as we observe the increasing deterioration in the character of individuals and society, it is difficult to make the case that simply doing what we feel like doing has been successful.

Even Spock recognized the terrible fallout from what he had been advocating for years. He wrote, "We have reared a generation of brats. Parents aren't firm enough with their children for fear of losing their love or incurring their resentment. This is a cruel deprivation that we professionals have imposed on mothers and fathers. Of course, we did it with the best of intentions. We didn't realize until it was too late how our know-it-all attitude was undermining the self assurance of parents."[2] If we had a generation of brats in 1974, what would he say about the generation now being raised by that generation?

Jimmy's case exemplifies what happens when parents don't meet children's needs to experience the frustration of unmet desires. Many in my profession, seeing these types of serious behaviors, conclude that they are so extreme there must be an underlying brain disorder. At some level, they are correct, though the brain disturbance is often one of nurture rather than nature. Jimmy indeed had a "brain disorder"—as do all of us. Each brain is in some way impaired and hopelessly driven by the desires of the self.

This surrender to the desires of the self is progressively more evident in each generation, making our plight seem ever more hopeless. Actually, it is hopeless! No matter how well meant the attempt to rehabilitate the self, no matter how convincing the latest theory that claims to solve its existential crisis, it is doomed to fail. We are already slaves to self, and any purported solution will simply provide false hope, further enhancing self in a way that ultimately leads to greater enslavement. And awareness of our desperate condition inevitably produces an overwhelming despair.

However, admitting our desperate condition is actually a major breakthrough. It represents one more step in our acceptance of the fact that self is terminal, with no hope of recovery. Given our enslaved condition, there is only one avenue through which we can gain emancipation: the Christ-filled life. In order to avail ourselves of freedom in Him, we need to understand the basis of our hopeless condition, our addiction to self. This will lead to an essential prerequisite for change: admitting our true nature—that we are wired to exalt self.

Chapter 8

Acceptance: Wired for Self

(Steve)

I know I am rotten through and through so far as my old sinful nature is concerned.
No matter which way I turn, I can't make myself do right. I want to, but I can't.
—Romans 7:18, NLT

I felt my irritation growing as I attempted to convey the concept of self to my eighteen-year-old daughter, Jaclyn. "When it's all about us, Christ can't live in us," I said, trying to explain.

"You still don't understand, do you, honey?" Dee Dee said, verbalizing what our daughter was hesitant to share. Jaclyn had frequently been on the receiving end of our frustration over the years. Our lack of patience with her "not getting it," especially when homework was involved, only added to her anxiety, further interfering with the learning process. By the time we discovered that there was a reason for her problems, our critical responses had already caused her to develop a pattern of avoidance when it came to learning. So, engaging her in discussion took a great deal of time and patience—qualities that unfortunately were not my strong suit.

I sighed, feeling my irritation moving toward complete exasperation. Given Jaclyn's avoidance, my lack of success in communicating with her often left me feeling like a failure. If that wasn't enough to push my frustration, the timing of this whole discussion was terrible. After a long day of work, I had just settled down to watch the evening news, a favorite pastime. I enjoyed debating about and sharing solutions to world problems—especially when I couldn't solve my own!

Dee Dee asked that I help explain this whole self thing to Jaclyn. I had questioned the urgency, suggesting it could wait, but she had insisted, saying they were already in the middle of talking. It was hard to argue this. Because Jaclyn was somewhat reclusive by nature, engaging her in any dialogue was a major accomplishment. So, Dee Dee didn't want to lose the moment, though I still wished it didn't have to include me. However, I realized getting tapped for input came with the territory of my know-it-all attitude. Besides, this was about some exciting recent discoveries—that week we had just finished watching Clarence's DVD.

While I climbed the stairs to join them, I reasoned that Jaclyn could certainly benefit from understanding and overcoming the self-driven life. (Somehow, it's always easier to see other people's need to die to self than one's own need.) So, although I was still feeling irritated at the interruption, I could hardly object. And how could I claim commitment to ending the dominance of self if I was selfishly refusing a discussion on overcoming it? I didn't want to look like a hypocrite. (Ironically, I was motivated to explain the battle of self by my desire to preserve the status of self!) I had a good grasp of the concept and, figuring this wouldn't take much time, already anticipated getting back to the news.

Unfortunately, I seemed to have conveniently blocked out the fact that I was much better at grasping concepts than I was at explaining them. That had become obvious when I had tutored Jaclyn in algebra, often sinking from explaining to yelling and pounding the table because of her failure to understand what was obvious to me. Regrettably, no matter how many lessons life provides us about self, self-deception always seems to rule. In this case, my self was still well defended, as my obvious limitation never even crossed my mind.

"Self is that part of you that wants to protect and defend," I said. Jaclyn's only response was to look down, and I knew I was losing her. I heard Dee Dee clear her throat, an action that was plainly directed at gaining my attention. I glanced up to see her shaking her head, signaling her disapproval of my attempts, which were falling on deaf ears. A sense of rage welled up in me. "What?" I asked accusatorily. Dee Dee signaled that I was over Jaclyn's head. That was the last straw—I lost it. "Why in the world did you call me up here?" I snarled. "You can talk to her yourself." And I stomped down the stairs with a sense of righteous indignation.

I felt my anger was well justified. Here I was interrupting my news, sacrificing my free time to help out, and after asking for my help, Dee Dee had the nerve to criticize my explanation! That's what I got for trying to be a responsive, understanding father. Unbelievable!

But as I cooled and came to my senses, I was horrified about what had happened. I suddenly remembered Clarence's insight that self is the most dangerous when we feel the most justified. I became painfully aware of how well my behavior proved his point and was soon apologizing to both my wife and daughter.

As I reflected on my response, I was dismayed. I had learned all about the foibles of self, was committed to daily ending its rule, and had invited Christ into my life. Yet here I was, blatantly advertising how very alive my self was, right in the midst of attempting to

"*I* do the very thing I hate."

explain what it meant to die to self! It was more than ironic and disconcerting, and reminded me of the dilemma Paul experienced. He wrote, "I do not understand my own actions. For I do not do what I want, but I do the very thing I hate" (Romans 7:15, ESV).

What causes this dilemma that mystified even a spiritual giant like Paul? What made me so vulnerable to the power of self, when I was so obviously committed to overcoming it?

The answer is found in our nature. All of us are wired for self.

The self-driven brain

We are indeed fearfully and wonderfully made, and among all the phenomenal structures of the body, none makes a better case for this than the brain. Looking at this organ gives a glimpse into its astonishing complexity and how we can influence it.

Our brains have a hundred billion neurons. Both before and after birth, these neurons begin forming connections with each other. Half these synaptic connections are lost through childhood, leaving us still with a mind-boggling hundred trillion of them, as each neuron connects with up to ten thousand other neurons. These neurons are genetically programmed to give chemical messages to the others, which in turn relay their own messages.

The neuronal connections are anything but static, as throughout life we are constantly forming new ones while others die out. Various influences can make connections that are barely a path at first grow into a major freeway of communication, while other circumstances shrink pathways. The expression "use it or lose it" applies here.

So, thousands of messages relayed from the brain and various parts of the body arrive at a given neuron, and the combined influences determine the actions within the cell and what messages that cell sends to other cells. This process is taking place among billions of cells on a constant basis, with hundreds of billions of messages that must be translated and passed on within milliseconds. The sum total of these messages from all the millions of neuronal networks is what determines every thought, feeling, and action we have. So when someone says, "It's all in your head," it really is!

"What does this have to do with the discussion of self?" Dee Dee asked, after I read about the brain wiring.

"Everything!" I exclaimed. "All those connections are created for various physical functions, along with complex thoughts, emotions, and actions, and our wiring predisposes us to a life driven by self."

"Sounds discouraging," she lamented.

"It should be discouraging, considering how much we trust ourselves. We aren't in nearly as much control as we like to think. Research and our experience in life tell us that those trillions of connections and messages are, at a basic instinctual level, driving us toward a singular purpose: taking care of number one."

"So we're just like other animals, trying to feel good and do whatever comes naturally?" Dee Dee queried.

"Left to our own natural state, yes. We are programmed to follow instincts of self-survival, attempting to relieve pain and gain gratification for ourselves as much and as frequently as possible. But there is one difference between our natural drive and that of other animals."

"What's that?" Dee Dee asked hopefully.

"When our natural self dominates, we often behave even worse! Many animals take care of their own far better than do many humans. Where in nature do you see animals committing the senseless crimes we see in the daily headlines?"

"But it doesn't seem fair. Since we're programmed that way from day one, we're bound to be self-centered."

"True, we start out this way—babies who want it and want it now! But we can't allow this to go on. Blindly following our natural inclinations has disastrous consequences."

"No kidding. We constantly punished our kids' selfishness and tried to teach them the golden rule."

"Yeah, we spend years attempting to eliminate the self-driven nature in our children, though we do far less about it than our parents did when we were kids. But then as adults, we often pursue the self-indulgent life with a vengeance."

"That's sad. It's the old 'do as I say, not as I do.' "

"You're right. But knowing the futility of self-gratification usually isn't enough to overcome our predisposition to pursue it. The self-wiring I've described is another evidence of the nature of fallen human beings."

The entrenched sinful nature

"But I thought that accepting Christ kind of takes care of our sinful nature."

"Well, it does provide our salvation. But accepting Christ doesn't wipe out our inclination to be controlled by self. This has to be an ongoing concern if we hope to counter it."

"Why? This whole thing sounds like a real downer. I'd rather not think about it."

"To the extent that self is viable, Christ cannot occupy our lives."

"Unfortunately, we don't really have a choice if we want to have a life in Christ. Being blindsided by self because we're ignorant as to what we're up against is even more discouraging."

"Then how come we don't hear much on this from mainstream Christianity?"

"For the same reason you don't like it. Let's face it: a message that says we're hopeless isn't exactly popular, given our culture that believes primarily in man-made solutions. This perspective is the opposite of the messages preferred by the current culture. The latter suggests that self should be championed and disparages the notion that we have any need for self-defeating feelings of shame or guilt."

"Yeah. Sounds like the victim society we hear about. We're all victims: of the brains we inherit, our parenting, or our environment."

"Exactly. Culture says there's really no need to feel bad about anything. But the Christian walk has no place for this rationalization. The fact that this notion survives indicates the deceptiveness of self. Sadly, in the interest of self, Christians have increasingly joined the modern-day movement of humanism that suggests that we are intrinsically good and that self isn't really bad; it needs only some tweaking here and there to maximize the good and eliminate the bad."

"So you're saying we're beyond fixing?"

"No. I'm just saying what God tells us—that we'll fail to gain the life Christ offers as long as we refuse to see that we are truly hopeless and in desperate need of His saving grace."

"That makes sense. Why would we want to die to self if we don't consider it to be all that bad?"

"Now you understand why this seemingly discouraging message is so essential. To the degree that we think we're not all that bad, self will remain fully alive. And to the extent that self is viable, Christ cannot occupy our lives."

"So you're saying that before we can access the good of Christ, we have to accept the fact that evil lives in us."

"That's a good way of putting it. After all, how can we possibly hope to win the battle of self, if we start with the notion that it is something to be protected, preserved, and enhanced? If we can't recognize that there is something to combat, we'll have lost the war before the first battle—a war that is essential if we are to have Christ in us."

Self found wanting

Christ addressed the seductive illusion of self when He told the rich young ruler to " 'go and sell all you have and give the money to the poor, and you will have riches in heaven; then come and follow me' " (Matthew 19:21, TEV). Scripture says, "When the young man heard this, he went away sad, because he was very rich" (verse 22, TEV).

Why the sadness? Jesus cut to the chase, providing him the key to his salvation: giving up on trusting in self's possessions and security. (It makes one wonder what Jesus would have to say about our 401[k]s.) The illusionary security of money is a serious threat to our spiritual existence, as Christ indicated when He said, " 'You cannot be a slave of two masters; you will hate one and love the other; you will be loyal to one and despise the other. You cannot serve both God and money' " (Matthew 6:24, TEV). In the ultimate sense, our only freedom is in choosing which master to serve.

The wealthy young man longed to follow Christ. The problem was that Jesus could not be just a part of his life. Jesus would have to be his whole life, completely replacing all the comfort, security, and pleasure of self. By asking him to sell all and give to the poor, Jesus was asking for more than a behavioral ticket to salvation. He was challenging him with the need to fully relinquish every last vestige of self, which for the ruler, and for many of us, is all about money. Sadly, his addiction to his riches prevented him from losing the life of self in order to experience abundant living in Christ. He couldn't see past his financial well-being in this transient world to the bigger picture. He was unwilling to divest himself of investments that ultimately were losers and shift his portfolio to treasures that would have provided astronomical returns then and throughout eternity!

This story also points to another crucial aspect of our wiring. This is a key human attribute that keeps us from being helplessly dominated, as other animals are, by drives of mere survival and pleasure. When Christ advised the ruler to obey the commandments, he confidently said he was doing that. Why then did he continue questioning Jesus? He could have assured himself that he was meeting the expectation and moved on. However, he persisted, asking what more was needed—clearly indicating his awareness that something was still missing.

This story speaks to the other, more hopeful aspect of how we are wired. We're created with a brain structure that tells us what is right—our conscience. Like the young ruler, most of us know what is right and wrong. Yes, there are a few extreme cases in which people have violated and ignored this moral guide so often that it has been numbed out, but this is rare. We find this guide illustrated in Paul's dilemma: "I do the very thing I hate." He knew what was right, and his life in Christ made him hate behaving in a contrary manner.

Like Paul, most of us are generally well aware of what is right, even when we often fail to do it. The problem with our behavior is not so much a lack of moral knowledge; we simply lack the ability or will to put it into practice.

Unhappy Christians

Christians must struggle with the same temptations regarding self as did the rich young ruler. We are continuously faced with this conflict between what we feel like doing and what we know in our hearts we ought to do, leading to an unhappy state no matter what we choose. It seems that in spite of our beliefs and good intentions, we are doomed to a life of unhappiness.

Clarence often has told me that from all his observations, many Christians aren't living the satisfying life they say Christ offers. They're frustrated and unhappy because they know too much about sin's transient and destructive nature to enjoy its pleasures, but they don't have a level of commitment that lets them enjoy abundant living in Christ. This leaves them even less happy than many unbelievers, who feel far less guilt about enjoying the pleasures of sin.

I am reminded of my own experience in college, during a time when I was an unbeliever. For an English assignment, I wrote a paper titled "Why I Am Not a Christian." Simply stated, I wrote that I would rather pursue a sure thing, spending my life enjoying the pleasures of sin for a season, than to spend a lifetime devoted to self-denial for the somewhat iffy and remote possibility of heaven—for some pie in the sky that, for all my efforts, I still might not be good enough to attain.

On the surface, it still makes sense, especially in view of the many Christians who are laboring under the delusion that improving self will gain salvation—if they make enough improvement. Now, however, with maturity and deeper insights, I see the errors in my reasoning. First, my youth and inexperience led me to exaggerate greatly the pleasures sin offers. The suggestion that self can be satisfied with such pleasures is false. The temporary satisfaction simply leads to greater enslavement to self, which results in increasingly frenzied attempts to meet ever higher expectations, and self's unmet desires leave us more frustrated, miserable, and enslaved.

Second, truly committed followers of Christ aren't simply pining away on earth as they await their pie in the sky. They experience immediate rewards—abundant living—when they choose to become slaves to Christ rather than slaves to self. "Now you are free from sin [self] and have become slaves of God. This brings you a life that is only for God, and this gives you life forever" (Romans 6:22, NCV). Our freedom in Christ is truly a cause for celebration.

As I write this chapter, the news is heralding the liberation of fifteen hostages, three of whom were United States citizens, from being held captive by a rebel group in Colombia. It's impossible to imagine, let alone describe, the sense of elation they must have felt when they first realized that they were free. They joked that the helicopter almost fell out of the sky as they jumped and screamed for joy. After six long years of captivity, they had virtually given up, resigned to lifelong imprisonment or death—until they were suddenly freed! The feeling must have been overwhelming. I'm sure they are living in a kind of reverie, permanently wonderstruck. Wouldn't you love to feel that boundless euphoria—having something that phenomenal to celebrate?

We do! We've been prisoners, doomed to a hopeless, helpless life, tortured by enslavement to self until Christ freed us. The freedom He offers is almost incomprehensible. It reaches far beyond the mere physical freedom experienced by the hostages. Christ frees us not only in this life but throughout eternity! However, if we are to experience this freedom, we must fully accept the reality of our condition.

Acceptance

In our natural state, we are wired and predisposed to let self be our master. However, by our choices, both in our parenting and in our personal daily life, we can lay down new brain connections and thus help shape the kind of mind we and our children will have in future years. Recent research shows that despite our original hardwiring, the brain has tremendous plasticity. We modify its connections and form new ones as we develop different habit patterns.

Norman Doidge, a leading authority in the field of neuroplasticity, addresses both the pitfall and promise in the following statement:

> While the human brain has apparently underestimated itself, neuroplasticity isn't all good news; it renders our brains not only more resourceful but also more vulnerable to outside influences. Neuroplasticity has the power to produce more flexible but also more rigid behaviors—a phenomenon I call "the plastic paradox." Ironically, some of our most stubborn habits and disorders are products of our plasticity. Once a particular plastic change occurs in the brain and becomes well established, it can prevent other

changes from occurring. It is by understanding both the positive and negative effects of plasticity that we can truly understand the extent of human possibilities.[1]

God has created these possibilities within us. While people are born with defective brains—pathologically wired for self—many of the psychiatric problems we see are the product of self-addicted, individual choices made through the years, which have laid down stubborn habit patterns. The resulting adverse changes in the brain wiring have led to increasing maladaptive, self-driven behavior.

However, we can create new wiring that is freed from self. The choices we make on a daily basis in thought, word, and deed help determine our brain connections of tomorrow. God is waiting to do the rewiring, but we must allow Him to do it by daily refusing to trust the demands of our self-wired brain and choosing to rely on Him instead. Just as Jeffrey needed me to let go of the computer controls so he could take over and do the needed reprogramming, so Christ is constantly asking us to let Him take over the controls and allow Him to reprogram our self-driven brains in His marvelous ways. This process will influence the brain to develop an attitude that is increasingly open to Christ's presence, enabling us to live His purpose in our lives.

Despite our original hardwiring, the brain has tremendous plasticity.

The view of our terminal condition presented in this section of the book is the antithesis of the usual perspective on self. One needs only to look at the present-day bestsellers on self-improvement to realize this. We hear about how to validate your authentic self, how to trust yourself, how to tap into the power of self, etc. I don't know about you, but after what we have reviewed, I have no interest in learning how to validate or trust my self. And regarding suggestions of tapping into the power of self—obviously, self is already an extremely dominant and destructive force that has little need of further empowerment. The continuous attempts to reinvent self with the newest take on self-fulfillment are futile. No matter what the spin, self is *not* salvageable.

Once we fully comprehend our universal addiction to self, we are in a position to participate in the crucial acceptance of the truth that self is terminal, with no chance for rehabilitation. This understanding of our desperate condition—finally renouncing the dominance of self and the will for it to survive—shifts our full allegiance to Christ. With the complete abdication of self, we are crucified with Christ. As we die with Him, we are finally freed from the tyranny of self, ready for His resurrection power to bring us to a new life in Him. This is truly a life to die for—daily dying to live.

Section III

Dying to Live

The painful grieving we do over our terminal condition leads to surprising freedom. At last, we can give up the battle to protect and preserve self. Our surrender opens us to embrace the life Christ has promised. It is indeed a new and exciting experience as He fully occupies the life emptied of self and uses His power to transform us.

Dying to live is not just an event but an ongoing process. To ensure our success in this new life—to continue dying to live—it is essential that we immerse ourselves in specific methods and approaches.

Chapter 9

The Exchanged Life

(Clarence)

"I will give you a new heart with new and right desires, and I will put a new spirit in you. I will take out your stony heart of sin and give you a new, obedient heart."
—Ezekiel 36:26, NLT

Patience is not one of my virtues. That was obvious as I paced around the waiting room, scanning the magazines while I counted the minutes until Dianna was due out of surgery. No, I wasn't really worried; I was simply impatient. Still, I realized I had little room to complain. It was a routine elective surgery, certainly nothing like the waits Steve had endured with Dee Dee's multiple health crises. Besides, during his waiting room vigils, the outcome was often far from certain. Dianna's surgery would be painful, but we were confident the result would be positive. I felt a sense of reassurance as I reflected back on our conversations with the doctor and the events that led to her surgery.

A few months earlier, Dianna's left shoulder had become painful. For a while, she ignored it, hoping the problem would resolve on its own. However, it progressed, causing increasing discomfort and disability to the point where she could no longer tolerate it. A series of medical appointments along with X-rays led to the conclusion that she had spurs in her shoulder. The only solution to her pain was surgery to remove these bony protrusions. While the prognosis was good, we were told that, like most worthwhile things in life, there would be a significant amount of short-term pain. We were also advised that following the surgery, she would be rather incapacitated for two weeks, with continuing physical limitations for up to two months.

I walked across the waiting room to get a drink of water and glanced up at the clock—which seemed immobile—as I considered what Dianna's recovery at home would entail. After learning that she would be temporarily disabled, I knew this was no longer just about her. Incapacity meant just one thing: my assistance. While for most, this might not pose much of a problem, if history was any judge, this would be a major challenge for me. With some shame, I had to admit to a serious character flaw when it came to helping when Dianna was ill. If she had anything beyond the common cold, she could count on me for one thing—a quiet, resistant attitude in response to her need for extra care and compassion.

It was an attitude I came by honestly. While illness or physical complaints often garner sympathy and attention, I had grown up in a medical family in which most physical concerns were given cursory attention or were dismissed. My father responded to dependency needs with hostility and tended to punish in one way or another any sign of weakness. I learned my lessons well, becoming increasingly stoical in response to physical discomfort.

Unfortunately, I tended to expect the same attitude from Dianna. After all, I was a busy pastor with an entire flock of spiritually needy church members who depended on me. She certainly knew what she was getting into when she married a pastor. Besides, there really wasn't much I could do if she was ill; she just needed to do as I did—suck it up! (I know what you are thinking, and I totally agree with you!)

Mind you, it was not like I was openly resistant. That wouldn't have done much for my image as a loving husband, let alone as a pastor. (When self is alive, image is all important). Instead, when Dianna was ill, I would go through the motions of doing the right thing. But doing so was a chore, and we both knew my heart wasn't really in it. Fortunately, Dianna was rarely ill, or my attitude would have been far more visible and problematic to our marriage.

As I sat in the waiting room, anticipating Dianna's recovery, I knew I would have to step up and serve her at levels we had never before faced. But I believed this time would be different. In fact, during the previous month as I anticipated her surgery and my role in her recovery, I had been surprised at how much I was looking forward to helping her. The change in my attitude was so dramatic that I wondered if I was simply psyching myself up for the inevitable challenge. However, as I felt myself smile in anticipation of waiting on her hand and foot, I realized the feelings were indeed genuine.

I glanced at the clock once again, thinking that she should be in recovery by now, and then began to reflect on our discussions prior to her surgery. I had shared with her how much I was looking forward to assisting during her recuperation, though I wasn't sure she really believed me. (Later, she said she thought it sounded a little weird, given my past attitude!) After learning of the needed surgery, like any other woman, her first thought was about

> *I even convinced her to let me do her hair.*

just one thing—her hair. How could she possibly fix her hair with one arm immobilized? The image of her trying to do so was comical—and surpassed only by the notion of me helping her. These images gave both of us a good laugh, but I still planned on trying.

The seemingly interminable wait finally ended, and I had Dianna settled back at home in no time. I was soon fully engaged, getting her a drink, cooking food, reading with her, and generally catering to her in every way possible. In a few days, I even convinced her to let me do her hair. She wouldn't trust me with her curling iron, not wanting to risk additional pain—a burned scalp! But while voicing reservations, she did allow me to take a stab at using the curling brush. This was certainly a first for me, but with some input from her—I later learned she had winced, watching my awkward efforts—I thought the result was quite good. Dianna was a little less enthusiastic. She said, "Well, I'd go shopping, but I wouldn't go to church!"

I continued to minister to her in various ways over the next several weeks while she healed. It was a very rich and rewarding time for both of us—something we could never have envisioned in previous years. By the time it was over, Dianna was fully convinced my enthusiasm over helping her was genuine. It wasn't just what I did for her—which was plenty. What she found surprising was the attitude I had while helping her. It was the complete opposite of what I'd had in previous times. Now, when we recount precious times in our marriage, the weeks following her shoulder surgery stand out as one of our high points. I really loved caring for her, and it brought a special closeness during her recuperation.

The transformation

The reversal in my attitude was such a radical about-face that it seemed almost inconceivable. It was so atypical that it felt like some kind of force had taken over, exchanging my heart for a whole new heart that was suddenly able to give in ways I never thought possible. Only in retrospect did I realize that indeed there actually had been an exchange. Let me explain.

A year and a half before the surgery, we learned about the crucial step of dying to self in order to gain abundant living in Christ. With awkward and tentative beginnings, we had been engaging in this new life: learning to end the dominance of self and giving up on our own efforts to change behavior as we let Christ freely live in and through us. Often, we see progress in our lives only with hindsight. Such was certainly the case in this new walk. At the time God was transforming us, we didn't realize how radically He had worked in me, replacing my heart of resentment with His new heart—one that allowed Christ in me to minister enthusiastically to Dianna after her surgery.

C. S. Lewis described this phenomenon eloquently:

> It is not a question of a good man who died two thousand years ago. It is a living Man, still as much a man as you, and still as much God as He was when He created the world, really coming and interfering with your very self; killing the old natural self in you and replacing it with the kind of self He has. At first for only moments. Then for longer periods. Finally, if all goes well, turning you permanently into a different sort of thing; into a new little Christ, a being which, in its own small way, has the same kind of life as God; which shares in His power, joy, knowledge and eternity.[1]

What a concept! It is truly awesome and overwhelming! But doesn't it seem rather brazen and grandiose? The notion of turning oneself into Christ's image seems absurd, blasphemous, and yes, even impossible!

It is. That's why it's so essential that we concede we can't even come close through our own efforts. We must give up running things, getting self out of the way so Christ can morph us into His likeness. In my care for Dianna, this didn't mean a minor shift in my attitude—no little bit of self-improvement. It meant a 180-degree turnaround, an exchange of totally contradictory attitudes in the same person.

How? What happened?

These questions have been asked and answered throughout the ages, being first addressed in the Scriptures. There we find numerous references that describe lives that are diametrically opposed. God has promised a heart transplant, exchanging our heart of stone with a new heart (Ezekiel 36:26). Paul described the opposing forces operating within us in the following text: "Those who live following their sinful selves think only about things that their sinful selves want. But those who live following the Spirit are thinking about the things the Spirit wants them to do. If people's thinking is controlled by the sinful self, there is death. But if their thinking is controlled by the Spirit, there is life and peace" (Romans 8:5, 6, NCV).

He further clarifies this process of gaining the life of the Spirit in Galatians 2:19, 20, "I have been put to death with Christ on his cross, so that it is no longer I who live, but it is Christ who lives in me" (TEV). This clearly makes the case for the exchanged life. I like the following paraphrase of this text: "My self has been put to death with Jesus' death on the cross that allows for the exchanged life, meaning that self no longer lives in me, and with self dead, Christ now lives in me."

Further on in Galatians, Paul discusses the contrast of this exchanged life. "Our sinful selves want what is against the Spirit, and the Spirit wants what is against our sinful selves. The two are against each other, so you cannot do just what you please" (Galatians 5:17, NCV). He continues in the following verses to portray the contrasting characteristics of the sinful self versus those of the Spirit in us, concluding, "Those who belong to Christ Jesus have crucified their own sinful selves. They have given up their old selfish feelings and the evil things they wanted to do" (Galatians 5:24, NCV). The dramatic contrast is reminiscent of a passage in the Old Testament:

"My thoughts are
    not like your thoughts.

Your ways are not like my ways" (Isaiah 55:8, NCV).

It is this exchanged life that explains the entirely new attitude I had in response to Dianna's physical needs. I had been dying to the old life, and a different life—Christ's—was living in me and directing my responses. The exchange affected every aspect of our lives, with my attitude toward her illness being just one example.

Out with the old, in with the new

Letting Christ replace self has enhanced Dianna's and my life together immeasurably. We were simply unprepared for just how great the changes would be—primarily because our previous Christian experience left us clueless as to what is possible with abundant living. Before this exchanged life, I had been living mostly by my own efforts. With each failure I asked God to help me—my hopeless self—to do better as I redoubled my efforts to live the kind of life I knew was right. My constant failure left me discouraged and overwhelmed. No amount of effort seemed sufficient.

"The yoke I will give you is easy."

What is amazing about this new life is not just the changes, but also how effortlessly they were accomplished. While the task of ending self's dominance is an overwhelming challenge, once it is understood, Christ's takeover makes the goodness He works through us relatively easy. I had been schooled in my Christian walk to assume that I couldn't accomplish anything without intensive and exhaustive efforts. Only with exchanged living did I begin to understand the true meaning of Jesus' promise, " 'The yoke I will give you is easy, and the load I will put on you is light' " (Matthew 11:30, TEV).

I am convinced that Jesus' words reveal a crucial sign of whether or not we are successfully engaged in abundant living. If we find our Christian experience demanding and exhausting, leaving us with constant feelings of inadequacy and futility, then we are living primarily by our own efforts, trying to force self into imitating Christ. Unfortunately, far too many Christians have this experience. We are constantly inviting Christ into our lives only to have Him quickly squeezed out by self, which is fully alive and insisting on salvation through our own efforts to be good.

Without intending to, we have tried to remodel our sinful nature (self), not realizing this is absolutely impossible. Our own experience and God's Word clearly indicate that we can't fix our sinful nature. "The heart is deceitful above all things / and beyond cure" (Jeremiah 17:9, NIV). Paul also observes, "When people's thinking is controlled by the sinful self, they are against God, because they refuse to obey God's law and really are not even able to obey God's law" (Romans 8:7, NCV).

It is amazing how often we talk in terms of making Christ a part of our lives and having Him help us to become better—seeming to suggest a dedication to making self becoming more Christlike. This has about as much chance for success as a gardener would have in attempting to force a crab apple tree to produce Red Delicious apples. No amount of tending and nurturing will change that crab apple tree. The only way to produce Red Delicious apples there would be to root out the crab apple tree and plant in its place a Red Delicious apple tree. (Let's not confuse the issue with the possibility of grafting!) Likewise, no amount of effort can ever make self produce Christlike virtues. This is why it is so tiring and defeating to attempt to achieve Christlikeness with the self. Our sinful nature can never be Christlike; it is simply *not* fixable!

I was . . . amazed at my energy levels.

Once we have given up on our efforts at self-rehab, there is another added benefit—one that I hadn't anticipated when I cared for Dianna. Not only was I surprised about how much fun it was, but I was also amazed at my energy levels. Though I was doing more than usual, my eagerness to help had me feeling like the Energizer Bunny! In the past, when I had to do extra service for her, seeing it as a chore and an imposition, I would often put forth great effort to do the "right" thing. But my heart wasn't in it, and even when the behavior looked good, it was exhausting because I was in a constant battle with self that was fully alive.

This battle had two fronts. As I worked to do good through the efforts of my natural self, I was fighting any possibility of Christ replacing me. I was trying to be loving and Christlike with a nature (self) that is an enemy to Christ. Also, my attempts to do good threatened to thwart my natural need, placing me in direct conflict with a self that was fully alive. This two-front war of fighting Christ and self demanded far more energy than any physical task did. It left me emotionally exhausted. The Christlikeness that we all strive to achieve is often a false goal; because for many people, it means engaging in a struggle to have self imitate Christ—something that is impossible.

C. S. Lewis described the necessity of Christ's complete takeover in the following analogy:

> Imagine yourself as a living house. God comes in to rebuild that house. At first, perhaps, you can understand what He is doing. He is getting the drains right and stopping the leaks in the roof and so on. . . . But presently [H]e starts knocking the house about in a way that hurts abominably and does not seem to make sense. What on earth is He up to? The explanation is that He is building quite a different house from the one you thought of—throwing out a new wing here, putting on an extra floor there, running up towers, making courtyards. You thought you were going to be made into a decent little cottage: but He is building a palace. He intends to come and live in it Himself.[2]

When self is dead, Christ is able to move in, and His life flows freely through us. This is what happened while I cared for Dianna: Christ living in me made loving service to Dianna the only choice. This wasn't natural to my self, but it was a totally natural choice for Christ, as "it is no longer I who live, but it is Christ who lives in me" (Galatians 2:20, TEV). It is truly amazing what He can and will accomplish when we give up and step aside. "God is able to make all grace abound to you, so that in all things at all times, having all that you need, you will abound in every good work" (2 Corinthians 9:8, NIV). He was working in and through me to accomplish every good work during Dianna's convalescence.

Born with the mind of Christ

Jesus spoke directly about our need for an exchanged life in His late-night conversation with Nicodemus. When He told Nicodemus that he had to be born again, Nicodemus was obviously amazed and perplexed, asking how this could be.

When one considers the implications of what Christ was suggesting, it is certainly a reasonable question. If we were born again physically, we would have a different set of parents, which would mean we had a totally different genetic code that would make us completely different in every aspect of our being. The contrast would be huge—one both we ourselves and other people could see.

By using the analogy of rebirth, Jesus was describing the radically transforming nature of His call. Nicodemus was born with sinful genetic hardwiring that was intrinsically at enmity with God. No amount of reading, knowledge, or pious behavior—which the Pharisees did so well—would change the core self. There is no way to rehabilitate it. The only way Nicodemus could experience the kingdom of heaven, both now and at the Second Coming, was to allow God to transform him completely, replacing the natural, sinful self with a whole new life in Christ. And every human being inherits the natural, self-dominated core that Nicodemus had. Anyone who doubts this need only observe the self-centered nature of an infant!

Jesus lived the ultimate example of an exchanged life, which Paul described in Philippians 2:5–8, "Have this mind among yourselves,

We . . . relinquish our worthless . . . self in exchange for Christ's divine nature.

which is yours in Christ Jesus, who, though he was in the form of God, did not count equality with God a thing to be grasped, but made himself nothing, taking the form of a servant, being born in the likeness of men. And being found in human form, he humbled himself by becoming obedient to the point of death, even death on a cross" (ESV).

Does exchanging the self seem like an onerous requirement? Think of the exchange Christ chose for Himself in order to save us. He relinquished His position as the Divine Ruler of the universe and laid aside His immortal and omnipotent nature, exchanging it for the nature of a lowly human being. He gave up something of immeasurable value for the common life of a mortal. Of course, He did this because, as incomprehensible as it seems, He considered our salvation of even greater worth.

What if Christ had chosen to cling to self the way we do, to use His divine nature for Himself when He needed to, and simply to imitate humans while continuing with His divine self fully alive during His time on earth? He wouldn't have been human, tempted in every manner as we are. His time on earth would have been more like playacting at things; His suffering "like us," a sham. Our temptation is to let self dominate. His was to revert to His divine nature. If He had succumbed to that temptation, His mission would have failed, just as our life with Him fails when we cling to self. He lived to die for our salvation, which is only possible if we do the same—living to die, dying to live.

This comparison raises another important consideration. As we contrast our exchanged life with the one Christ chose, it should be a source of continuing dismay and shame. We are asked to relinquish our worthless, sinful self in exchange for Christ's divine nature living in us, whereas He gave up something of enormous value for something very damaged and flawed. When compared to the challenge Christ faced in His exchanged life, ours is an unbelievable bargain! In fact, it is a testimony to the seductive power of self that we so often turn down such an astonishing offer.

Death sentence—for life!

The fact that self is so seductive explains why it is so essential that we reflect on the exchanged life. The more we contemplate the life Christ is offering, the more likely we are to accept this phenomenal free gift. Understanding His offer is essential if we are to have any chance of renouncing self in order to live this life. The idea of a rebirth connotes a radical and complete shift. If we make minimal changes in our thinking rather than living the exchanged life, we are merely imitating it, something that has about as much chance of success as getting a crab apple tree to produce delicious apples. Jesus said that the only way He can live freely in and through us is for us to *die.* Self must be rooted out so that Christ can live within. " 'If you want to come with me, you must forget yourself, take up your cross every day, and follow me' " (Luke 9:23, TEV).

In the context of the life of self, the cross carries a unique meaning. We assume the Romans forced condemned criminals to carry their crosses because they were cruel and sadistic. However, the historical context illuminates the concept Christ conveyed. "After the beating, the victim was forced to bear the crossbeam to the execution site in order to signify that life was already over and [to] *break the will to live*."[3]

Taking up the cross daily is a continual renunciation of self's will to survive, reminding us the life of self is gone as we daily die with Christ. When we bear the cross, we are anticipating and accepting one inevitable conclusion—*death!* Jesus said that the price of experiencing His life in us would be death itself—and not just once, but repeatedly, over and over again. To know the exchanged life on a continuous basis requires *daily* commitment to carrying the cross on which self will repeatedly die.

This experience isn't easy because, as is true of our physical demise, dying to self is often a very painful and frightening process—remember the resistance to accepting self's hopeless condition we learned about in the last section? However, once we fully recognize self's terminal condition, we have no choice but to give up on it. And this choice is much more tolerable—even something we can embrace enthusiastically—when we consider the good news that follows: *resurrection!*

Paul reminds us of how we will be brought to life when he says, "Just as Christ was raised from the dead by the wonderful power of the Father, we also can live a *new* life. Christ died, and we have been joined with him by dying too. So we will also be joined with him by rising from the dead as he did" (Romans 6:4, 5, NCV; emphasis added). This is not about resurrecting the body, but rather the exchanged life, as Paul makes clear in the next verses. "We know that our old life died with Christ on the

A living sacrifice . . . can keep getting off the altar.

cross so that our sinful selves would have no power over us and we would not be slaves to sin. Anyone who has died is made free from sin's control" (Romans 6:6, 7, NCV).

Paul also speaks to believers about the kind of power that God offers. He says he prayed that we might "know that God's power is very great for us who believe. That power is the same as the great strength God used to raise Christ from the dead" (Ephesians 1:19, 20, NCV).

What must happen for us to receive this resurrection power? Just as was true of Christ's resurrection, ours has just one prerequisite—*death.* Resurrection power comes only to the dead! Someone who is critically ill but not yet dead needs healing power. They don't need and can't receive resurrection power until death occurs. And if this is the case physically, it is even more so spiritually. We can't receive this power when self is ill and attempting its own rehabilitation. Resurrection power is available only when self is dead with Christ on the cross. *Resurrection power comes only when we are dead to self.*

This death is also far more than a simple, one-time event, as people suggest when they say, "I am a born-again Christian." It is a terrible mistake to assume that spiritual survival requires rebirth only at the time of our conversion. We must continually—daily—be reborn in an ongoing process that is the essential challenge of the Christian life. Our having Christ continuously at work in and through us is directly related to our commitment to the constant crucifixion of self. The more we learn and live taking up our cross daily—usually many times a day—and dying to self, the more freely Christ in us determines our choices. And conversely, the more self carries the day, the more we block the resurrection power that would allow Christ to work His way in us.

We all know how resistant we are to dying physically. When terminal illnesses strike us, we do anything and everything to hang on and postpone death. Our survival instincts often drive cells and organ systems to carry on long after the mind gives up any will or desire to live. The point is that self attempts to hang on to its life with equal, if not greater, tenacity.

Paul speaks of self's survival instincts in Romans 12, saying we are to be "living sacrifices" (NIV). The problem with a living sacrifice is that it can keep getting off the altar, which is exactly what self attempts to do. Without constant vigilance to self rising, we run the risk of it becoming fully alive once again, blocking Christ from living in us. We must incorporate the life Paul called the Ephesians to embrace, when he said "Get rid of your old self, which made you live as you used to—the old self that was being destroyed by its deceitful desires. Your hearts and minds must be made completely new, and you must put on the new self, which is created in God's likeness" (Ephesians 4:22–24, TEV).

Heart transplant

The exchanged life gives us a new heart, replacing our heart of stone. But this is only the beginning. The transplant will not take hold and survive if we don't participate in ongoing spiritual treatment to prevent the self from causing rejection. If Dee Dee were fortunate enough to receive a kidney transplant, would her treatment end? Of course not. Without continued treatment, she would reject her new kidney within days. To keep the transplant viable, she would require heavy doses of immunosuppressive medication on a daily basis, blocking the antibody response. Any negligence in dosing would cause the antibody level to rise, prompting her body's natural responses to take over and destroy the lifesaving foreign kidney.

By the same token, we must always be aware that the heart transplant of Christ in our lives is foreign to our nature—and consequently, constantly at risk for rejection. Christ's nature living in us is always a threat to the survival of our sinful nature. The only way to retain this lifesaving exchange of Christ in us is to kill the antibodies of self that always threaten to set in motion natural forces of rejection. Fortunately, we are given spiritual immunosuppressants—methods to counter our natural tendency to reject Christ's heart. These offer a powerful antidote to self's dominant force that naturally rejects the foreign body of Christ in us.

Often in our spiritual journey, our experience of the excitement and hope of Christ in us is all too quickly dashed as the practical realities of our life intrude. This is usually a matter of self rising again and blocking Christ's resurrection power in us. The exchanged life is not an event; it is a process that requires ongoing maintenance if the transplant of Christ's heart is to remain fully viable. In the next five chapters, we will explore the treatment methods for maintaining this new, exchanged life—ensuring that Christ remains alive and well in us.

These crucial treatments keep the self's antibodies in check, preventing the rejection of Christ's heart. Foundational to all of them is an attribute that is integral to any successful spiritual endeavor—trust. As we learn to distrust self and accept the futility of improving it, we will invest fully in our only hope—the One who sees us not for what we are but for what He intends for us to become with His transplanted heart. Equipped with the full knowledge that Christ's heart can survive in us only as we daily die to self, we will depend only on His life-giving power—trusting His heart.

Chapter 10

Trusting His Heart

(Clarence)

*You will keep in perfect peace
him whose mind is steadfast,
because he trusts in you.
Trust in the LORD forever,
for the LORD, the LORD, is the Rock eternal.*

—*Isaiah 26:3, 4, NIV*

I was only half awake, just aware of the morning light, while still trying to catch a few more moments of shut-eye. As vague thoughts of the message I would give for church that morning ran through my mind, I flashed on the words, *I choose to trust Jesus.* The line was somewhat of a disconnect and brought me fully awake. My sermon was going to address the challenge of trusting Jesus and taking Him at His word, especially when things are difficult—those times when we want to take control.

What startled me was the way I heard the line, *I choose to trust Jesus.* It was almost as if someone were speaking to me audibly. Now let me be clear here: disembodied voices—whether from God or from anyone else—are my brother's specialty and not something I'm in the habit of experiencing! Sometimes I envy those who have this happen to them, though other times I'm skeptical. However, for me, this sense of almost audible communication was an exception.

As if this interruption weren't strange enough, I was even more taken aback by what I "almost heard" next: *Ask the congregation to learn and repeat the line several times during the sermon.* This was getting a little weird, and my immediate reaction was, *No way!*

My response was hardly surprising, since I consider most things that smack of audience manipulation to be self-serving and despicable. I've seen it done too often, usually with far more downside than upside. As I mused on the thought that invaded my consciousness that morning, it struck me as loaded with the potential for manipulation. It just wasn't me. No, God couldn't be suggesting that I initiate some hokey approach that would likely come off as staged and contrived. I could already envision the congregation dutifully chanting my slogan—likely out of pity—and it was *not* a pretty picture! I quickly dismissed the whole idea, continuing to review the sermon I planned for that morning.

"I choose to trust Jesus."

But for some reason, much to my dismay, I couldn't get that thought out of my mind. Try as I might, I was unable to shut down this idea that continued to intrude. Finally, with some trepidation, I caved, telling God, "OK, I'm going to trust that this is from You. I'll do it."

I began the sermon by setting the stage with some biblical promises as well as illustrations of trusting God in the midst of difficulties. As I completed this process, I began having second thoughts, feeling some hesitancy over what I was about to do—something that was totally out of character for me. But the call to do it was so overwhelming that I knew I had little choice, so I simply asked the church family to repeat after me the line "I choose to trust Jesus." They immediately picked up on it and quite enthusiastically learned the line, repeating it with me several times. I then asked that they say the line every time I asked them, "What are you going to say?"

I followed up with several brief scenarios. "You come home from work one day and find in the mail a large bill that was unexpected; one that you don't know how you will pay, given your financial stresses. What are you going to say?"

The congregation replied in unison, "I choose to trust Jesus."

"You are a stay-at-home mom with kids under your feet all day. Your husband comes home from work, plops himself down in his favorite chair, and begins to channel surf. You are sorely tempted to let self rise up in protest. What are you going to say?"

Again they responded, "I choose to trust Jesus."

"You go to your doctor's appointment to receive the test results from your biopsy and learn that you have cancer. What are you going to say?"

They answered back, "I choose to trust Jesus."

Throughout the sermon that morning, I returned to other scenarios, and each time they enthusiastically responded with the line. I was rather pleasantly surprised at how actively they participated in this. At the close of the message, I suggested that they make this the line of their week. I requested that they note whenever self was tempted to rise in any way and then immediately think *I choose to trust Jesus.* I also asked that they observe the changes in their attitudes when they used the line to meet the various challenges they faced in the coming week.

The feedback

I was in no way prepared for the response I received during the next few days. Our friends, Mike and Diane, called and told me the following story about using the line twice that very day:

We were driving home in one car, with our son and his wife in another car. At a stoplight, they pulled up beside us and I asked Diane to roll down her window so I could say something to my son. After I shouted through the open window, Diane immediately turned to me in irritation, saying, "You don't have to shout in my ear! I could have told him that." After a moment's pause, I said to her, "Do you think we ought to say, 'I choose to trust Jesus'?" For a fraction of a second, she paused, then we both broke out laughing, and the tension was gone.

A few minutes later, a big eighteen-wheeler, attempting to maneuver into a business, blocked the road in front of us. I began getting impatient, voicing my irritation with the delay. Diane turned to me and said, "Do you think we ought to say, 'I choose to trust Jesus'?" Again we both burst into laughter. We were amazed at how this simple line reoriented us from self to Christ. It was truly wonderful!

In the early days of that week, I received such overwhelming feedback from those who were experimenting with the line that I knew I must share it. I asked our telephone team to call the church family to encourage them to keep using the line and also to tell them that I would provide an opportunity for them to share their experiences during the next church service.

In all my years of suggesting practical applications for spiritual truths, I have never received such an outpouring of feedback. We spent half the next sermon time hearing exciting stories of how this simple statement halted the rising of self while allowing Christ's life to take charge. It has been more than two years since I first gave that line to the congregation, and I continue to hear stories of amazing changes that have come through the use of this simple acknowledgment and affirmation of trust in Jesus.

As we experimented with the line, we made two changes that have even further enhanced its effectiveness. The week after we introduced it, one of the church members told us that they were saying, "Jesus, I choose to trust You," which we have found to be an improvement since it can be seen as a direct prayer rather than a mere assertion.

Soon after this, we were discussing the power that comes with trusting Jesus' Word as well as His person, which naturally led to coupling His Word with our line of faith. The new line became "Jesus, I choose to trust You when You say _____," which would be followed by something from His Word that applied to the given situation. This adds the crucial component of constantly referencing our life situations to Scripture (something we will expand on in chapter 14). So now, whatever life throws our way, we make a habit of reminding ourselves of what He has said. This is essential, since trusting Him and His Word will have a radically different impact than does our natural inclination to trust self, as indicated in Isaiah 55:9,

"As the heavens are higher than the earth,
    so are my ways higher than your ways
    and my thoughts than your thoughts" (NIV).

Although the statement we have been using seems rather simplistic, it is loaded with meaning in four important ways: First, naming Jesus acknowledges a faith that empowers through connection with God. Second, saying the word *choose* carries surprising significance. Choosing differs from simply wishing or trying. Affirming our choice of Jesus over self immediately opens the heart, surrendering the interfering self so that Christ may freely flow through us. Third, reminding ourselves who it is that we trust helps reorient us from self to Christ. Verbally owning this orientation makes it far more difficult for us to ignore Christ's heart, something self loves to do. Affirming trust in His heart quickly brings us in line with His desires and choices. And finally, when we reference life situations to the Scriptures, we experience power as the Word directs us.

The daily habit

To effectively complete the prayer "Jesus, I choose to trust You when You say _____," we must become familiar with Scripture. As we increasingly acquaint ourselves with the Word, we will develop a repertoire of verses to complete this statement. But for those seeking immediate Word power in various situations, appendix C provides several references that many have found useful. However, regardless of the Scripture passage we choose, we can access the power of the Word only if we use the Word—spending time with God and the Bible daily.

We can access the power of the Word only if we use the Word.

I am reminded of the circumstances surrounding my father's death. He and some of my brothers were sailing a small catamaran in rather stormy seas. When it flipped, no one was wearing life preservers. They had fulfilled the Coast Guard requirement—they were carrying floatation equipment. But unfortunately, possessing the life preservers didn't save my father. The life preservers were useless when they were needed because they were attached to the boat by a hopelessly knotted, wet rope. Similarly, the Bible's lifesaving power will do us no good if we're not using it regularly. We won't even be able to complete the sentence, "Jesus, I choose to trust You when You say _____," unless we can immediately access His Word—especially when we are on the spot and self is on the prowl, looking for an opportunity to take control.

You know how inspiring it is to observe athletes at the top of their game. We love to watch them play, and we marvel at some of their achievements. Of course, we know that they built their performance upon untold hours of practice through which they developed various proficiencies. They practiced those skills until much of their performance became automatic and reflexive.

This ability to act and react reflexively is essential, since in the middle of a game, the athletes can't stop to think their way through each move. Although thought goes into their play, the action occurs so quickly that many of their responses must be completely automatic. The athletes certainly can't sit back and ignore their preparation until they are on the spot in critical games. When they've honed their movements through hours of workouts, they can call on the skills and habits they've developed to deliver the outstanding performances we love to see.

The same is true for the spiritual "athlete." If Christ's life is to shine forth with consistency in powerful ways during those times when we are on the spot in life, so to speak, we need to develop a consistent performance when we aren't on the spot. Too often, we spend little or no time alone with God and still expect Him to keep self dead and His life alive in us when we face difficulties. That simply won't happen.

Think of the level of spiritual maturity we see in Christ during His temple visit when He was just twelve years old. Talk about a spiritual athlete at the top of His game! Yet He went home and spent another eighteen years preparing for His ministry to us. Several times, the New Testament refers to times He spent alone with God. Luke 5:16 tells us that "Jesus often withdrew to lonely places and prayed" (NIV).

Christ was invested so deeply in dialogue with His Father that when He was tempted, His automatic response was, " 'It is written' " (Luke 4, NIV). Now *that's* the kind of reflex I'd like to have—to be so familiar with the Word that my knee-jerk reaction would always be to reference life to the Scripture! That is Word power! Jesus was able to give such a spiritually powerful "performance" because of His private life with His Father and the Word. We can have a similar experience if we daily remind ourselves where we must place our trust and what must be our priorities. (Appendix B provides specific suggestions for daily commitment to the exchanged life.)

Trusting His protection

Two facets of faith are essential to Christ's transplanted heart surviving in us. The first involves our trusting Christ's ability—and recognizing our own inability—to protect us. The entire exchanged life experience is predicated on this kind of trust. Will we invest our trust in self or in God? This seems rather obvious; we certainly would *say* that our trust is in God. However, the sad reality is that in this matter too, actions speak louder than words, and our actions often scream out the fact that we are reverting to our natural inclination—that of placing our trust in self.

This seemingly inevitable phenomenon can be changed only if we decide to trust God completely even when we are hurting. Such faith realizes that protecting ourselves is up to God and not us. It is faith that refuses the deception that suggests God is behind the hand we are dealt; faith that decides being under Christ's control is far more important than making sure things go our way; faith that doesn't look to the externals for its validation; faith that experiences its essence through a Christ-filled life. This faith daily proclaims, "Though he slay me, yet will I trust in him" (Job 13:15, KJV)!

This faith is evident in Philippians 4:6, 7, "Do not be anxious about anything, but in everything, by prayer and petition, with thanksgiving, present your requests to God. And the peace of God, which transcends all understanding, will guard your hearts and your minds in Christ Jesus" (NIV). Notice that this text contains the words *anything* and *everything* and that they include just

> "*The* peace of God . . . will guard your hearts and your minds."

what you would suspect—both the good and the bad. The text says that we will have such a spirit of trust even when we're in difficulty—*especially* when we're in difficulty—that we lace our prayers of petition with thanksgiving. This is a very strong promise! Yet such an experience is wonderful and brings "the peace of God, which surpasses all understanding" (NKJV). That peace will guard both our thoughts and our emotions and keep them "in Christ Jesus." What a promise!

We love to refer to the good life that Christ offers by quoting Romans 8:28, 29. Yet people often misunderstand and misinterpret this familiar text. When the two verses are read together, we learn that *His* good is not the same as *our* good. His promise is that He will work all things together for *His* good—making us more like Jesus. The text does *not* say that God will make things turn out the way *we* want in every situation—or even in most situations. He won't necessarily protect us the way we want to be protected. Remember that our ways, which are often self-based, are not His ways.

Verse 29 indicates what He wants to do for us through every circumstance—He wants to make us more Christlike. This provides the only help we need, protecting us from life's greatest threat—self. Consider the implications here: our continuous, frontline prayer should be that God keep us dead to self so that His transplanted heart may live more fully in us. I should point out that there is nothing wrong with asking Him to "fix" things so they will turn out our way. But this part of our prayer should be secondary, taking an extreme backseat (more like the back of the bus!) to what must be our primary supplication.

If this sounds rather radical, it is. However, unless this is our orientation, our praying may even raise self to a whole new level. Much of the time, the prayers of Christians are extremely self-based, seeking self-protection. "Lord, help this job interview to go well," "Help me to get a good grade," "Help me settle this account," etc. Even when we pray for noble attributes, the prayer focuses on self. "Lord, help me to be less irritable," "less selfish," "less apathetic," etc. While these are all worthwhile, the "help me" suggests that we are asking God to *help* us rather than *replace* us. Instead of protecting us, this mind-set enhances self, threatening our trust in Him and the protection that comes through Him living in us. I often advise that we need to stop trying harder—including trying harder to have Him help us—and instead work on dying more fully.

God can't assist with our miserable attempts at self-improvement any more than Jeffrey could assist with the computer reprogramming when his father was trying to control the cursor and fix things himself. This illustrates the tremendous challenge of ending our reliance on self and fully trusting in God. If you're anything like me, this is an enormous task. Even when I let go of the controls, I often have second thoughts, wondering how God will work things out and whether it will be to my liking.

Philosopher-theologian Dallas Willard says that when we are dead to self, we won't be surprised when things don't go our way, we won't be offended when things don't go our way, and we won't be controlled by the things that don't go our way.[1] Can you imagine what strength and peace will be ours when we live this way, or, more accurately, when Christ lives this way in us? It will inevitably lead to the second facet of faith.

Trust that protects His reputation

The second facet of faith focuses on our protecting the reputation of Christ's life in us, which is far more important than having things go our way. Isaiah 26:8 reads, "Your name and renown / are the desire of our hearts" (NIV). I can't overstate the importance of this perspective.

A few days before writing this section on faith, I visited with a man who was experiencing major problems with anger. He was finding dealing with his anger challenging because he felt it was so justified, due to his belief that he was being used and abused at home. I asked which was more important to him: glorifying Jesus and building His reputation, or being right and fighting for his rights—trying to get his way. The question took him aback; he hadn't thought of it that way. The way he responded initially told me he wasn't very excited about this kind of thinking. But as we talked and read Scripture together, he came to the realization that the most important agenda for followers of Christ is to glorify Him and protect His reputation through the manner in which we handle difficult situations.

When we fully embrace this concept, we experience a huge relief. How freeing to give up the unending, exhausting struggle of self-protective living! What a marvelous experience to leave our defense in God's hands! Then our primary purposes become glorifying Him by serving others in self-sacrificing love, and continually giving the Spirit control of our lives.

Furthermore, this is the most powerful witness we can make to the wonder of the gospel of Jesus Christ. It is rather overwhelming to realize that He trusts us to provide the best advertisement for adopting His transplanted heart—a trust that we are honored to justify as we protect His reputation through our attitude.

Most of us handle life quite well when things are going smoothly. What should separate Christians from others, but often doesn't, is how Christ's followers act and react when things are falling apart. Unfortunately, far too few Christians get this. Many of us equate God's blessing with having the needs of self met. This is similar to the attitude of the Pharisees, who saw misfortune such as leprosy as evidence of sin and God's curse. We consider this belief of theirs rather naive and stupid. Yet the view that we can measure spiritual blessings primarily by how well we are doing is no different than that of the Pharisees.

When things aren't going right for us Christians, typically, we may last a few seconds or even minutes longer than the nonbeliever. But then we begin to defend and protect self just as everyone else does. When that happens, the opportunity to be beautiful witnesses to God's grace passes; we lose another chance for others to see Jesus in and through us as we protect self rather than His reputation. In addition, we provide fuel to those who watch us and say that Christianity isn't all it's cracked up to be. Tragically, this is one of the reasons that organized religion has fallen into such disrepute.

When things go badly for us, the problems must be addressed. But will they be addressed by self or by Christ in us? The latter means we must be dead to self so His life in us can tackle the issues. We want to end self's tactics that either stuff or vent, and instead allow the Holy Spirit's power to effect the surrender of self. When we do this, Christ's life freely flowing in us will work on life's difficulties in a very different manner than our self would choose. Paul reminds us of this difference in the following text: "Though we live in the world, we do not wage war as the world does. The weapons we fight with are not the weapons of the world. On the contrary, they have divine power to demolish strongholds" (2 Corinthians 10:3, 4, NIV).

Our primary weapon is surrender—dying to self.

Paul said we do not fight like the world; we use different weapons. As paradoxical as it sounds, our primary weapon is surrender—dying to self. When we are crucified with Christ, His resurrection power can swing into action. With His takeover, He creates in us a totally different approach. Then, as the text says, strongholds are demolished! The stronghold of self needs to be utterly defeated and destroyed. When this happens and the Holy Spirit is in control, His limitless power will vanquish the forces of evil within us.

One of the profound implications of all we are saying in this chapter is that we need change on the inside. Who wants to buy a used car that's been wonderfully detailed on the outside, only to find that under the hood it's a piece of junk? We don't want merely to engage in behavior that merely looks good. In fact, when we focus primarily on external behavior, self (our piece of junk!) may well become even more alive while staying better hidden.

With the new spiritual paradigm, however, we are seeking a total heart change—the transplant of Christ's heart. When the heart is right, we will be done fighting for self. With the exchanged life, even at those times when things aren't going well, we will increasingly choose a positive response.

Primacy of trust

Our ability to adopt and retain Christ's heart depends absolutely on trust—trust in His life while completely distrusting the life of self. But self constantly attempts to dissuade and undermine, planting doubts and second thoughts. Wishful thinking may tempt us to reinvest in self. This ever-present threat is why retaining His heart and the treatments to prevent its rejection require daily practice, ensuring that our trust and priorities are in keeping with Christ's. He knew all too well how easily we can go off track and begin to doubt. That's why He challenged us with the following: " 'If you want to come with me, you must forget yourself, take up your cross every day, and follow me' " (Luke 9:23, TEV).

There is good reason why we began this discussion on the treatments for our exchanged life by focusing on the commitment from which these emanate—trust. This is the first of five treatments we will be addressing—one of paramount importance. The remaining four are contingent on our taking up the cross daily—dying to self as we experience that all-encompassing trust in Him. Without this trust, we run the danger of attempting to apply treatments without even having an exchanged life. This would be like Dee Dee taking immunosuppressant treatments without having a transplanted kidney—what a waste!

Our exchanged life depends on a foundation of trust that includes the following five steps:

1. Our initial tentative response to Christ's invitation depends on our willingness to take up our cross daily as we shift from trust in self to trust in Him.
2. We trust Him to show us sin in thought or action indicating that self is either alive or threatening to come alive.
3. Following this recognition, trust embraces confession, removing the barriers self raises so that Christ's life may flow through us.

4. After confession, trust is essential for a complete surrender.

5. Finally, we trust His Word to provide us power to live the abundant life. We addressed the first step of trust in this chapter and will cover the remaining four in the following chapters.

As a reminder of the daily treatments for our exchanged life and how steps two through five are tied to the foundation of trust, we have found the acronym TRUST helpful.

Take up the cross daily, trusting His heart.
Recognize the sin of allowing self to control by listening to His heart.
Unblock our hearts through confession, clearing the way for His heart.
Surrender to His heart.
Think the Word, learning His heart.

As we increasingly seek Christ's heart in us through these treatments, we will begin noticing self cropping up in all kinds of ways that we never previously considered. His transplanted heart will sensitize us to the antibodies of self that threaten to reject His heart. If we remain trusting and open in our exchanged life, this recognition of self will provide the opportunity for continuously deepening our relationship with Him. This is why the next step in dying to live is so crucial—listening to His heart.

Chapter 11

Listening to His Heart

(Clarence)

The lamp of the LORD searches the spirit of a man;
it searches out his inmost being.

—Proverbs 20:27, NIV

I always want to get my money's worth, and as we headed to the local all-you-can-eat buffet, I knew this called for a ravenous appetite. Unfortunately, at the time, all I was feeling was a knot in my stomach. The cost wasn't my concern; this wasn't exactly gourmet dining. And it wasn't that I was cheap—though, as you already know, I am! Eating at the buffet was actually Dianna's idea; she said she preferred a place like this where she could select healthful, low-fat food. However, based on years of previous experience, I knew that healthful, low-fat food wasn't the only thing on her mind.

For years, Dianna had struggled with her weight, going through several cycles of gaining and losing around sixty pounds. I struggled, too, doing everything possible to ensure that those sixty pounds stayed off—which didn't exactly help! I'm ashamed to admit that I loved conditionally when it came to Dianna's weight. I found it easy to be judgmental, since weight has never been an issue for me. But my interventions likely sabotaged Dianna's diet as much as—if not more than—her lack of discipline.

We rarely, if ever, exchanged words about her eating. We couldn't take that risk. Why would we generate a discussion that would only lead to greater conflict?

After all, when you're both right, there's really no way to resolve a conflict, and I felt I was right to be concerned with Dianna's appearance, while she felt more than justified in her anger at my attempts to control what was clearly her choice. Unfortunately, through much of that time, we hadn't learned anything of the exchanged life and were unaware that we do most of our sinning when we are right (something addressed in chapter 15).

While I said little about Dianna's weight, we had plenty of nonverbal exchanges—silent, tense communication, testifying to the fact that self was alive and well in each of us. All I needed to do was give her "the look" while we were eating. It was a look that she appeared to ignore, though we both knew that she felt as much resentment over what I communicated with that look as I felt over her eating habits. The tension was palpable, leaving us in our private cold war, and producing a climate of emotional strain that raised clouds of mistrust and hostility. Looking back, I'm amazed at how two people could feel so right and both be so very wrong. Unfortunately, it never occurred to either of us that in different ways we were both sinning and that there was any alternative.

I felt I was right to be concerned with Dianna's appearance.

Here we go again, I thought as we approached the restaurant. Dianna was in the middle of one of her cycles, which at that time involved an upswing in her weight, so I knew that she would overeat and not just the low-fat food! On her first time through the buffet line, she did reasonably well. I'd have given her a B, not that she cared. However, when she went through line the second time, she must have decided once again to bag the diet for a while. I winced as I saw her second plate of food, thinking of where all those extra calories would be deposited, and for a split second, I gave her "the look"—the one that she had become an expert at ignoring. I was clueless about my own contribution to the problem, unaware that since both of us were dominated by self, her overeating was often her declaration of independence.

We had become so accustomed to this scenario that we didn't realize how much it was hurting our relationship. We also were clueless about the devastating impact this self-empowering behavior was having on us spiritually. We did experience

Christ's presence in our lives, but all too intermittently. Unfortunately, self so dominated many of our interactions that we failed to keep His life within us. Only years later did we learn how to adopt a radically different attitude—His attitude—that allowed us to process conflicts in a different way (addressed in the next chapter). Since we did, Dianna has returned to a weight she hadn't seen in forty years and has maintained it with little of the effort she expended before.

Discovery

Like any marriage, ours has seen its ups and downs, especially during our first ten years together. Frankly, we look back on those challenging years as more work than fun. At that time, we would have rated our marriage about a two or three on a one-to-ten scale. However, through a series of providential circumstances, including a weekend Marriage Encounter seminar, God turned things around in a very few weeks. We experienced some breakthroughs in our communication, and the dramatic changes that followed made for a rich relationship—one that we would rate at a seven or eight. We even felt a bit smug about how well we were doing, especially when we observed the struggles of other couples around us.

We didn't realize, however, that we were still settling for too little—that God was offering even greater rewards in our relationship. This is so often true in our spiritual lives. We experience a religious high and then sit back and settle, never realizing that if we pushed further, we would find that God has so much more to offer. The changes that Marriage Encounter weekend brought us after ten years of marital struggles was like getting a car after traveling cross-country in a covered wagon. The difference thrilled us with the potential for the future—though we were still clueless about the option of a jet plane. Self was still alive and interfering in areas we were unaware of or were unwilling to face. Still, we thought we were doing fine, and so we continued with our more comfortable, secure relationship. It was not until twenty-nine years later that we discovered the jet-plane option in our spiritual lives—a whole new paradigm, the one presented in this book.

In the fall of 2003, insights I gained through spiritual reading and Bible study led me to the inescapable conclusion that my walk with God was woefully lacking in terms of surrender and trust. At some level, I had always known this, but with a growing sense of joy and relief, I finally knew what to do about it. I had been steeped in Christian traditions that focused primarily on performance, leaving me blind to the true nature of Christ's call. But now I began to see things in a whole new light, as though God had taken the blinders off and I was hearing the reality of His message for the first time.

The principles and methods for surrendering my self to Christ were so powerful I had to share them with Dianna. As I did so, we were both struck by the challenge of applying to our daily lives the principles we were learning. I can't tell you how often Dianna has said to me, "Don't tell me what to do. Tell me how to do it."

Applying these principles was more than something we merely aspired to; it was something we actually wanted to do. We quickly learned the first crucial key to the process of surrender—recognition of self seizing control, even in the small things.

Recognizing sin

One evening, my time with Dianna was interrupted by an unusually important phone call—one that went on for almost ninety minutes. As it was coming to a close, Dianna came into the room and, with some mild irritation, indicated that I needed to terminate the call. I was about to end it anyway, but I was hurt at her obvious irritation, especially since she had overheard enough of the conversation to know full well the importance of this call. Now, let me ask you, did self rise in her, and should her irritation with me be considered sin?

While you're reflecting on this, let me share another vignette. This one involves Dianna gently criticizing my choices to spend time with other family members rather than with our grandchildren during our weekend visits with our daughter. It wasn't that I didn't enjoy spending time with her and with our grandchildren; it was just that I spent more time with my mother and brother than Dianna thought I needed to. This disagreement clearly didn't have any moral implications, and one could certainly make a fair case for either of our views. However, as is often the case in marital disagreements, I became defensive and mildly disagreeable, with a bit of an edge to my attitude. We never did agree on the issue, and that was OK. But what about my attitude? Do you think self was rising in me? Was my response sinful, and should I have addressed it more specifically?

With our new understanding, we would both say the answer to the question in both of these scenarios is a resounding *Yes!*

If this strikes you as extreme, you're not alone. We were initially taken aback when we began examining our response to minor irritations. You know how it goes. We make comments with just a little bit of attitude, just an edge in the voice, a bit of sarcasm. Or maybe we don't even say anything—we just think it and feel it. These things happen all the time without our giving them a first, let alone a second, thought, especially when they don't escalate into major conflicts. While we're never happy with being on either the giving or the receiving end of these irritations, we seldom consider that such behaviors might involve sin in the form of self that needs to be addressed.

Should her irritation with me be considered sin?

By now you may be feeling some dismay over what seems like an expectation for perfection. But it would be a mistake to assume that this is a matter of diligently and meticulously avoiding any hint of imperfection in our behavior—a kind of obsessive trip of self-accomplishment. Rather, when we identify sin, we are talking about self—about sins of the heart and mind and not the external manifestations that may or may not accompany the rising of self. The issue is not behavior but whether in the core of our being we choose to trust Jesus rather than self.

Lest you feel somewhat put off or confused when I attach the word *sin* to such minor concerns, let me explain what I mean. In the Bible, the Greek word translated "to sin" simply means "to miss the mark." It was the same word people used when they were shooting arrows at targets and someone missed the target. People either hit the target or they missed. *Close* was not an operative word. So sin is simply missing the mark—the mark of staying dead to self and maintaining Christ's heart in us. When we hit the mark in a given situation, we are on target with dying to self and allowing Christ's attitude to shine through.

Interestingly, while no one claims to be without sin, few equate minor feelings of irritation and resentment in our day-to-day lives with sinning. Somehow, over the centuries, the meaning of sin has evolved until now people use it primarily to refer to the biggies, such as illicit sex, drugs, murder, etc. They ignore the so-called little sins, seemingly viewing them as unimportant.

While the distortion of this term seems strange, it makes sense when we see how human beings, who are wired for self, can adeptly define things in ways that protect self's image. When we define sin in such a way that it primarily means external behaviors and the major infractions that few indulge and that occur infrequently, we feel comfortable resting in the dubious assurance that we seldom sin.

Close doesn't cut it

I learned much about the importance of being on target in my quest for the college table tennis championship. For hours, I practiced to perfect my serve, to develop a killer slam, and to send a low backspin right on target as it barely cleared the net. I watched and listened to feedback from others in order to become more on target. Close just wasn't good enough. I wanted to win, so a lackluster "good" performance just wouldn't cut it. I needed to be right on target. Yet for years in my spiritual life, I was satisfied with merely being in the ballpark. I never thought of myself as really that bad, that sinful—after all, I was just barely missing the mark. Few of us would say that we are always on target. Yet when we concern ourselves only with major sins and operate under the ridiculous illusion that we are almost always on target, we can dismiss all the minor symptoms that indicate that self is fully alive.

Also, when we focus only on major sins, we negate the uniqueness of Christ's call and one of the two positions of faith previously discussed—the opportunity to glorify His reputation. Most religions and philosophies can lead to a reasonably good life in terms of avoiding the big sins. What sets the followers of Christ apart—or what is supposed to set us apart—is His heart in us, which will inevitably and dramatically affect the small sins. It's not just that *we* practice the universal golden rule; His heart living in us makes this rule the automatic choice in all things, including the small things, which is bound to leave an amazing impression on those around us.

Admittedly, some sins appear to be much more damaging than others. But this is often based on externally observable damage rather than the impact on our spiritual lives. As I perfected my table tennis game, I quickly learned to focus on the smallest aspects of my swing, recognizing that little imperfections—those that put me just off target—could spell my defeat. Since self is the greatest threat to the goal of keeping Christ's heart fully alive in us, the sins of self's rising to threaten Christ's control—even the "little" sins—will cause us to miss the mark. Given that self can best hide the fact that it's still alive when it moves us to commit only the minor sins, these are in many ways the most deserving of our concern, posing the greatest threat to the exchanged life.

Rarely do my parishioners admit an affair without recognizing that it is sinful. Yet they bombard me with minor conflicts, with hurt feelings and resentments among the believers. Few of them identify these as manifestations of self—as, in reality, sin. Any missing of the mark will interfere with our ability to experience the abundant life of Christ. We are bound to miss this if we continue to sidestep and downplay the "little" sins.

Dianna and I did exactly that for years. It never occurred to us that the smallest drifting, which threatened the rejection of Christ's heart in us, was sin—missing the mark. From the way this term had been used, we thought viewing ourselves as sinful was somehow inappropriate and over the top. Focusing on such small issues seemed rather picky, carrying the danger of letting minor concerns distract and dissuade us from our faith.

"*Well* enough" just wasn't good enough.

Why, then, did we come around to putting up with the stress of hammering ourselves over minor concerns? Why didn't we leave well enough alone? Because through prayer and study, we were increasingly convicted that "well enough" just wasn't good enough. It wasn't so much that we didn't want to be called sinful; we were fully aware of our sinful state. However, eventually we wanted to maximize the rewards of maintaining Christ's heart as fully alive within us. We had become increasingly aware and intolerant of self's tendency to rise, to take control, in a myriad of ways. With this understanding and openness to listening to His heart, we began to see sin at levels we had never noticed before. This discovery led to an awareness of how essential it is to "major in minors."

After learning of the importance of listening for the Holy Spirit's conviction of sin, we soon began questioning small interactions—seeing where self was threatening to rise up or had already come alive. We hadn't realized that we were so accustomed to and tolerant of letting self rise in little ways; we just assumed this was a normal part of life. In some ways it is. But in wanting to maintain His heart in us, we were now looking for the supranormal.

A significant aspect of our new awareness came through exposure to the power of the Word as we increasingly focused on Scripture. Listening to Christ's perspective on our plight, we became much more sin-sensitive, recognizing it as never before. And contrary to what you might expect, majoring in minors didn't make us paranoid or depressed about our numerous imperfections. Surprisingly, rather than discouraging us, it excited us because we knew that with each new discovery of sin—of self—in us, we could deepen our life in Christ.

As we move from a mind-set of trying to minimize our sense of sin—which is self attempting to protect itself—to trying to recognize it wherever it may rise, we will daily see opportunities for removing the things that block Christ's takeover in our lives. This is the second step in our treatment process, trusting Christ enough to be willing to take up the cross in order to live the exchanged life. To prevent the threat of rejecting the new heart that comes from Christ, we must become sin-sensitive. This is the *R* in TRUST—*Recognize*. It is crucial that we allow Christ's Spirit to enable us to recognize the rise of the threatening antibodies of self. When we do, we will develop an acute and painful awareness of how self interferes, blocking Christ from flowing freely through us. This recognition will call us to engage in the "unblocking" process—the next treatment for keeping His heart in us.

Chapter 12

Keeping His Heart

(Clarence)

He who conceals his sins does not prosper,
but whoever confesses and renounces them finds mercy.
Blessed is the man who always fears the LORD,
but he who hardens his heart falls into trouble.

—Proverbs 28:13, 14

Remember the lengthy phone call I received—the one about which Dianna expressed her irritation and resentment? (See chapter 11.) I found myself reflecting on that situation the following day. Dianna's and my typical responses when such frictions arose had been to say nothing. I would think she was wrong for trying to interfere with my call, and she would believe my priorities were all wrong—that I was acting as if the call were more important than time with her. Such disagreements didn't often lead to any meeting of the minds. That was true too of Dianna's resentment of how I spent my time during our weekend visits with our grandchildren.

In both scenarios, we each felt we were right. Since we could find no resolution for such issues, we typically would simply drop them. However, that didn't mean the issues were gone. Often, we continued to stroke our bruised egos while silently brooding about being misunderstood and mistreated. Even when we recognized we were wrong, we seldom addressed the matter. With self alive, we rarely discussed our wrongness about our rightness.

If this approach sounds familiar, it should. Typically, our self-driven responses tempt self to rise in others, eliciting the deception of self-justification (the third principle in chapter 5). When self is alive in us, we provoke it to rise in others, blocking trust and causing them to distance themselves from us emotionally. Unfortunately, throughout much of our marriage, Dianna and I were experts at doing this.

However, the responses that had so typified our reactions in the past didn't take place after these incidents. By the time they occurred, we were living highly atypical and unusual lives—exchanged lives in which Christ's heart was determining our choices. As a result, we immediately heard Him and recognized our sin of allowing self to rise. We were aware that self was blocking His life from flowing through us. This motivated us to confess—which "unblocks" the channels of the heart, allowing Christ's heart to work through us.

"Unblocking"

We have discovered that one of the core commitments needed for the exchanged life is a ruthless devotion to processing sin in accordance with Scripture. I'm not suggesting an obsession that has as its only purpose the removal of sin—an endeavor that will never lead to our keeping Christ's heart. Rather, this is all about having Christ in us, so toward that end, we will practice an unwavering devotion to addressing the sin that blocks our hearts.

First John 1:9 describes well the process of "unblocking." Though this verse is very familiar, we often miss one of its critical promises. The verse indicates that our confession of our sins produces two results. First, there is the forgiveness of sin, which goes far beyond just getting the books right in heaven. Unless this is a deeply relational experience, we aren't truly forgiving or forgiven and can't gain the blessing offered in the second part of this text—"and purify [cleanse] us from all unrighteousness" (NIV).

We discovered this in all the small interactions of our marriage, including the incidents previously described. Take the situation in which Dianna became impatient with me for being on the phone too long. Since we were living the exchanged life, with Christ's heart in us, our typical self-serving response could no longer dominate. Instead, Christ created unnatural, beautiful responses in us. As we were getting into bed that evening, Dianna said to me, "I'm sorry I became impatient with you. Will you forgive me?" Of course, I readily accepted, feeling very grateful for her desire to make things right. In the same vein, soon after I became irritated with her for criticizing me about not spending enough time with our grandchildren, I said to her, "I was irritated with you, and I'm sorry. Will you forgive me?" She happily accepted my apology.

Why were we making such a big deal of such small issues? Our apologies weren't motivated by a desire to get the books right or some sort of one-upmanship in which we each wanted to look like the better partner. Rather, we were concerned with what had happened to us and between us. When I confess, apologize, and ask for Dianna's forgiveness, her acceptance of me is huge, and vice versa. By the same token, God's forgiveness of our sins results in an intense relational experience. But this can happen only if we have been deeply convicted of our sins and become truly contrite. Jesus didn't die for our sins simply to get the books right. He died to bring about reconciliation between us and Him!

But this isn't the whole story. What too many readers miss in 1 John 1:9 is God's promise not only to forgive but also to purify us from all unrighteousness. When we confess our sin, something happens within us. If it doesn't happen, then we're missing some aspect of the confession process. The very act of confession involves dying to self. And when self—this entity that blocks Christ's life from flowing through us—is crucified with Christ, the blockage is removed.

Jesus didn't die . . . simply to get the books right.

I'm reminded of difficult experiences I've had with clogged drains. At times, unblocking a drain can be a rather daunting task. But when one has opened the pipe, it's a relief to see the water flowing freely. The clog of sin—self—blocks Christ from living fully in us. So, confessing sin is critical to Christ's clearing it out and sending His resurrection power flowing through us.

In a previous chapter, we noted that someone with a transplant needs continuous immunosuppressant drugs to avoid rejecting the new organ. Spiritually, the same is true when it comes to preventing self from rejecting Christ, to ensuring that we are keeping His heart. One of the most important treatments that we must administer daily is the complete confession of sin so that Christ's heart can effect our continued growth in the exchanged life experience. Based on Scripture and numerous stories from fellow Christians who are living the exchanged life, I can guarantee that if you stay committed to confessing your sins—openly admitting to missing the mark of Christlikeness—self will have less and less opportunity to reject Christ's new heart. Then you will experience the boundless joy of Christ in you that is possible only when you are freed from self. But to experience this freedom, you must understand what threatens the unblocking process.

Threats to unblocking

That verse I referred to earlier, 1 John 1:9, should be read in its context. The verses on either side of it are very significant because of what they say about the confession of sin. "If we claim to be without sin, we deceive ourselves and the truth is not in us. If we confess our sins, he is faithful and just and will forgive us our sins and purify us from all unrighteousness. If we claim we have not sinned, we make him out to be a liar and his word has no place in our lives" (1 John 1:8–10, NIV).

Two times these verses reference the claim to being without sin or to not having sinned. We previously learned how adept we are at viewing self as never wrong. We must view confession in this context of the self-deception of self-justification. When we don't confess our sin, by default we are claiming not to have sinned. Furthermore, the last thing we're willing to do when self is alive is to admit our sins. This is something we often fail to realize and even find uncomfortable.

Notice in these verses the four dangers of not confessing sin:

1. "We deceive ourselves"—something we learned about in chapter 5.
2. "The truth is not in us." This is very disconcerting and sobering, considering that Jesus is the Truth.
3. "We make him out to be a liar"—a rather preposterous proposition.
4. "His [Christ's] word has no place in our lives." Imagine where we'd be if His Word had no place in our lives—the Word that we learned has tremendous power to maintain our exchanged life.

If we wish to access this power, we must remain honestly committed to recognizing our sin and dealing with it as Scripture instructs.

Unless we understand and engage in the full process of confession, we will fail to gain the power that comes with reconciliation. While this may seem obvious, our understanding of confession and its practice is often rather limited. In fact, when we do something wrong, we generally avoid making a true apology. We let it blow over; we say, "Time heals"; we don't talk about it; we act like nothing happened; or we even say, "I'm sorry."

You may be surprised at my suggestion that saying "I'm sorry" isn't a true apology. Here's what I mean. Self is often fully alive even when we appear to apologize, which results in our assuming a self-protective mode that avoids ownership and responsibility. A classic example is the "I'm sorry, but . . ." This nonapology allows self to go through the motions of apologizing while simultaneously negating the apology by shifting blame or giving some justification. Another variant of this is the common public relations response, "I'm sorry if I offended you." This nonapology suggests that the problem is the sensitivity of the injured party. It allows someone to claim to have made an apology without really owning responsibility.

Saying "I'm sorry" isn't a true apology.

Even the simple "I'm sorry" is often inadequate. It seems better than no apology, but it is so limited that I still classify it as a nonapology. And the frequently disingenuous nature of a brief apology can often result in a whole new rise of self that actually leaves us worse off. Let me explain. The simple statement "I'm sorry" leaves the two parties relatively isolated. There has been no dialogue, no giving or responding. Compare this with an apology that is followed up with "Will you forgive me?" Here I'm asking for interaction—focusing on our relationship instead of just leaving things hanging. The question is essential to developing a shared experience.

"I need to ask your forgiveness" doesn't really cut it. This is not a request; it is a statement. We find statements very tempting because they avoid the uncomfortable vulnerability that is an essential aspect of the confessional experience.

When I ask, "Will you forgive me?" I'm not only admitting my wrong, but I'm also admitting my dependence on you to make reconciliation possible. Regretting my behavior is not enough. I am asking that you participate in this process that will unblock our relationship by removing self—something that is possible only with your active involvement. I am telling you that not only have I wronged you but now also that I need you. I've put myself in an extremely vulnerable position. This attitude is of paramount importance if we are to take the first step in the unblocking process. Only with such an attitude will we make a vulnerable, sincere supplication—one that can open the pathways of the heart and allow Christ's life to flow through us freely once more.

Beyond mere motions

The next step involves the recipient of an apology. Most of us are familiar with the common, rather lackluster responses, such as "It's OK" and "Forget it." Such responses are dismissive and diminish the importance of what is being offered. They appear to blow off the apology, and they clearly dodge the possibility for any intimacy—which is probably why we often use them. I would suggest that these responses are a kind of mild rejection. They indicate that self is alive, and they avoid the vulnerability that comes with full acknowledgment and acceptance of the confessor's plea for forgiveness.

While not always done for that reason, a dismissive acceptance can be a power play. It says to the confessor that he or she is making a big deal out of nothing—and gives the injured party an air of invincibility as he or she denies the hurt and invalidates the concern of the offending party. In essence, the injured party is refusing the tremendous gift of the other party's confession. The one responsible for the injury finds much more healing when we directly say, "Yes, I forgive you." When we do so, we will also experience the rewards that come with sharing this experience, allowing completion of the process as it comes full circle. This will remove the blocking clog of self and lead to reconciliation and healing.

We need to consider some pitfalls here. When we apologize, we need to ensure that our apology is other-centered and Christ-centered rather than self-centered. Self can rise even in our apologizing; we may be more interested in taking care of ourselves than of the other party. After we've wronged someone, we feel guilty and miserable. We're tempted to want the other party's forgiveness merely to make ourselves feel better. When this is the case, we're really focused on our feeling better rather than on what we've done to the other party and to Christ, which can lead to a new round of self rising to life and control. So, before apologizing, we must ensure that we truly have a sense of brokenness for hurting the other person and Christ.

Another issue in this process relates to the readiness of the recipient to forgive and reconcile. In major conflicts, one person may stay in their pity party much longer than the other. If the guilty party confesses while the other party is still hurting, reconciliation, if not impossible, is awkward at best. In this situation, the injured party will either feel like a hypocrite because of giving sham forgiveness or like a villain because of honestly postponing or denying forgiveness.

So what's the solution? I have learned that a helpful and sensitive approach for the guilty party is to send an e-mail or to write a note of apology and leave it for the injured party to find when the guilty party isn't around. This avoids putting the injured party on the spot by calling for an immediate response. The note should deal only with the apology, taking full ownership without referring to the transgressions of the other party. It should be very short and speak to three points: name the sin ("When I . . ."), apologize ("I'm sorry"), and ask for forgiveness ("Will you forgive me?"). As the other party reads the note, he or she can reflect without pressure and respond fully from the heart when ready, either in writing or in person.

Name the sin . . . apologize . . . and ask for forgiveness.

The above details may seem very picky, and you may be more comfortable with different wording that accomplishes that same thing. But I have found it important to be very specific about what needs to happen, since self is so very adept at short-circuiting this process. Adopting a vulnerable position of self-renunciation in confession releases major healing power that has enormous effects. Doing so supplies the antidote to self-deception. As I said early in this chapter, *when self is alive in us, we provoke it to rise in others, blocking trust and causing them to distance themselves from us emotionally.* Confession creates the opposite effect: *when we unblock our hearts through confession, we provoke trust and a corresponding unblocking in others, drawing them to us emotionally.* This kind of about-face is indicative of the radical change that will be evident in all areas of our life and relationships when Christ lives fully in us.

While the process suggested here may seem like an excessive focus on what appear to be negligible and inconsequential slights, Dianna and I have received enormous rewards from applying it. Since we have learned to major in minors, both in recognizing our sins of allowing self to rise against each other and also in engaging in the unblocking process of confession, our marriage has grown to levels of beauty we can hardly believe. At the risk of sounding sappy, I'd have to say that on a scale of one to ten, our marriage is now a twelve! This process of confession keeps us open, humble, and wonderfully gentle toward each other.

Listening to Christ's heart and recognizing the interfering self will lead to the unblocking process of confession, allowing Christ's heart to live fully in us. So, the *U* in our acronym of TRUST reminds us to *unblock* by confessing our sins. Confession is a crucial intervention that keeps self's antibodies in check, preventing our rejection of Christ's heart. And engaging in the recognition of sin and unblocking through confession lays the groundwork for the next treatment for our disease—*surrender.* Letting the sins of self go and learning to submit them to God, will lead to dependence on His life-giving power. We can keep His heart alive and well in us only by giving up on protecting and defending self—by surrendering to His heart.

Chapter 13

Surrendering to His Heart

(Clarence)

"And when you stand praying, if you hold anything against anyone, forgive him, so that your Father in heaven may forgive you your sins."

—Mark 11:25, NIV

"Have you forgiven your son's killer?"

The question cut to the core. It wasn't like Craig hadn't heard it before from the prisoners in his class. He was teaching soon-to-be released inmates about a trait that all too many of them lacked—empathy. His personal story about the murder of his son was meant to be a potent stimulus for eliciting this emotion—one these criminals desperately needed. But given that this was a mandatory class for less than motivated students, Craig had his challenges. While the prisoners often lacked empathy, they were more than adept at sensing and using the vulnerability of others to their advantage. When they learned that he was a Christian, they hit him where he was most vulnerable. They asked whether he had forgiven his son's killer.

Craig's response was always the same. "I really don't think about him," he said. "To me, he doesn't exist."

It was an answer that seldom satisfied, and one that usually led to further challenges, suggesting that he really hadn't forgiven him. For Craig, it was more than a little irritating. What right had these hardened criminals, most of whom had little regard for the rights of others, to lecture him on forgiveness? It would have been comical if it weren't for the pain involved. But no matter how often the question was asked, it invariably triggered painful thoughts—inescapable memories that repeatedly shattered Craig's fleeting moments of peace. Like a broken record, the memories kept returning, beginning with that awful call seven years before.

On September 29, 2000, the phone had rung at 4:20 A.M., waking Craig and his wife, Lois, out of a dead sleep. It brought the devastating news that is every parent's nightmare. Eric, Craig's son and Lois's stepson, had been brutally murdered. The stark pronouncement shattered their world, setting in motion repeated waves of unending pain that daily threatened to overwhelm them.

At nineteen years old, Eric had just begun to embark on his own life. He had already overcome far more obstacles than most of us face in an entire lifetime. He was deaf and also suffered from cerebral palsy. He had just begun his freshman year at Gallaudet University, a premier university for the deaf. It was indeed an exciting time as his parents anticipated the fulfillment of their dreams, while Eric set out to learn what his own dreams might entail. After all that he had already overcome, his parents had little concern for him—and certainly not for his safety. It would be difficult to imagine a safer environment than the cloistered educational community and its dormitories.

Hopes for solving the murder . . . were raised and dashed repeatedly.

Eric was busy with studies, sitting at his computer when the attack came. Taking advantage of the world of silence that hid his presence, the perpetrator snuck up behind Eric, choked him till he passed out, and then beat him to death with a chair.

Craig and Lois suffered a long and torturous journey as they struggled to understand what had taken place and why. Hopes for solving the murder and gaining some resolution were raised and dashed repeatedly. When the investigation finally resulted in an arrest, they experienced some sense of relief. But it was short lived. Months later, the murder of a second student revealed that the authorities had targeted the wrong man and botched the investigation. The killer had used Eric's debit card, but no one had thought to follow up on this. By the time that they considered robbery to be a motive, the store's surveillance videotape had been erased. If law enforcement had investigated properly, the second murder probably wouldn't have happened.

It was four long months before Joseph Mesa was arrested and confessed to both homicides. But still it didn't end. There was the five-week trial over a year later, during which Joseph attempted to plead insanity. Craig and Lois had to live and relive the horror of what had been done to Eric as they sat in the courtroom desperately hoping for justice. Six life terms plus one hundred twenty years for both murders was certainly punishment. But it brought little solace to Craig and Lois. The gnawing, unending pain, the rage, the tears that refused to stop, the emptiness that threatened to consume them—it was a gaping wound that bled daily. They were continuously dying inside.

Insatiable rage

Lois told me, their pastor, of the concern she felt for Craig because his anger seemed insatiable. She recalled the time when, with his face contorted in rage, he had repeatedly cried out, "I want to kill him!" During the first two years, her concern for him was so all-consuming that she hardly had the time or energy to process her own feelings of grief and loss.

Eventually, they joined a support group called Parents of Murdered Children (POMC). Over time, their involvement progressed to the point where Craig became a board member and began to teach inmates about empathy. That's when they forced him to confront his lack of forgiveness, something he had desperately tried to ignore but which had been interfering with his life for years. Each time the prisoners confronted him, he felt overwhelming resentment. But eventually, he realized that his unwillingness to forgive was based on his desire to hang on to his rage and the desire for vengeance he still had. He knew his feelings weren't compatible with what Christ wished for him. But the injustice his son had suffered was so extreme that no one faulted him for his unforgiving spirit—no one other than the prisoners.

Then Craig began to realize that the prisoners were right. As he prayed, "Forgive us our trespasses as we forgive those who trespass against us," he became increasingly convicted that he was blocking Christ's forgiveness toward him through his self-centered refusal to forgive. Finally, he gave up, surrendering the vengeful feelings that had been constant companions. Six years after his son was taken from him, he knelt down and prayed for a forgiving heart—Christ's heart. The transforming power was astounding; Craig told about the peace he felt when he was finally able to say honestly, "I have forgiven Joseph Mesa."

However, Lois still wasn't ready to forgive. While her rage had been far less intense, her journey to forgiveness took longer. She simply couldn't bring herself to say the words, "I forgive Joseph Mesa." For the first year, she experienced little anger, often being more preoccupied with concern for Craig. But after that year, she had a meltdown, venting her rage against the killer and what he had done to them. The experience was somewhat cathartic for her, allowing her to avoid the festering rage that plagued Craig. She understood how clinging to anger and bitterness would damage her, and was able to surrender them. Yet though she was freed from the vengeful feelings, try as she might, she couldn't forgive her son's killer.

"*Jesus* Christ gave me the power to forgive."

Lois had suffered from various ailments for years, and eventually, she felt the need for physical healing. We chose to hold a special prayer service, asking God to heal her. While we prayed, someone remembered that Lois hadn't forgiven Eric's murderer, and this person asked God to bring forgiveness to her heart.

After the service, some of those who had prayed with her had stayed to talk. Suddenly, she interrupted the conversation. "I need to say something," she said, and then she calmly stated, "I forgive Joseph Mesa." She later said, "Jesus Christ gave me the power to forgive," and related that when she was finally able to utter those words, an enormous burden was lifted off of her. She said she even felt physically lighter. Through surrender, she had allowed God's heart to live in her and to erase her unforgiving spirit.

Such forgiveness is almost inconceivable—impossible from a human standpoint. However, Christ's heart living in Craig and Lois enabled them to do unnatural things. It will in us too. Fortunately, few of us will ever face something so difficult to forgive.

Craig and Lois would say that they suffered far more and far longer than was necessary. If they had been more practiced at surrendering in the small areas of their lives, they would have been more completely dead to self, and Christ's forgiving heart would have been more fully at work in them. This would have enabled them to surrender more easily—even in the face of that great challenge.

We all struggle with seemingly minor issues that in subtle ways can jeopardize our exchanged life. The daily stresses we face threaten to bring self alive, posing challenges that call for continual surrender to Christ. While seemingly mundane, these small areas provide opportunities to surrender self's resentment to God more completely.

Called a liar

One of our editors, Jeannie, shared with me a challenge in her own life that illustrates the day-to-day offenses we all encounter. Here's the story in her own words.

A while back, I prayed an unusual prayer in the morning, telling God I knew I couldn't do it on my own that day and needed Him to carry me. Not that I didn't need Him all the time, but this day felt different. I thought at the time that it was a very strange prayer. After all, I was only going to work; I wasn't facing anything unusual.

As the day went on, our printer at work decided to malfunction. The repairman had to order a part, and we were all told to print only in black and white, since the machine would jam if we tried to print anything in color. So I carefully sent four pages to the printer—in black and white. It printed the first two pages without a problem, but then jammed, with the message indicating it needed black toner. I subsequently advised the woman in charge of the printer that it needed black toner.

After she installed the toner, it promptly jammed once again. When she unjammed it, she also noticed who had been printing when it jammed— me! She told me that the whole problem was due to the color print job I had sent. I responded by showing her the two black-and-white pages it had printed, assuring her that I had sent only black and white. I was taken aback when she replied, "Well, I know that's what you say!"

How could I let that go? Essentially, she had just called me a liar! Of course, self wanted to rise up immediately. I wanted to defend myself. I had a right to defend myself. I was more than justified. After all, I *knew* I hadn't sent a color job—and I had the first two pages of my job to prove it. But God gave me the grace to simply walk away. I began automatically saying the affirmation that had become so familiar, "I choose to trust You, Jesus," which immediately reminded me of my unusual prayer that morning. And, of course, I had learned that we are most apt to sin when we are right. I began thanking God for carrying me as I had asked, allowing me to walk away instead of having an angry confrontation. As I sat at my desk praying, God gradually moved me to a much better place, adopting Christ's attitude.

About half an hour later, when the other woman returned to her desk, I spoke up quietly. "You know, I didn't lie to you." And her response? "Oh, I know you didn't. I'm so sorry. I owe you an apology! The same part we need to print color is needed to calibrate the new black toner I put in. I am so sorry!"

Our primary concern is to avoid letting self take control.

If I had allowed self to have its way at the beginning, I would have destroyed any chance for a reasonable resolution, and tension between us would likely have persisted to this day. But by trusting Christ in me to make the choices, He gave me the victory over self that had ripple effects in my work setting.

Many people would question Jeannie's response. She obviously had a right to object to the accusation and stand up for herself. Instead, she let her coworker walk all over her. In other words, she acted like a real doormat. Or did she? It's easy to go off on a fellow worker who is making a false accusation. It's far more difficult to avoid that response. When external behavior is our only concern, confrontation seems more than reasonable. However, in the exchanged life, our primary concern is to avoid letting self take control and threaten the work of Christ's heart within us. For Jeannie—for most of us—engaging in this confrontation without self striking back would be virtually impossible. In her exchanged life, she immediately recognized this, and followed the prompting of Christ within her to make the difficult choice to ignore the natural urge to protect her self.

Often, it is the way another person treats us when self rises in them that causes self to rise in us, as Jeannie's experience illustrates. From the standpoint of the exchanged life in these situations, we won't defend self, which escalates the cycle of self-justification. Rather, we will surrender all resentment, bitterness, and desire for revenge, choosing to trust Christ instead of self to care for our needs—thus retaining His life in us. We need to surrender the sins of resentment and unwillingness to forgive the person who offended us.

Christ certainly calls us to maintain this mind-set of surrender in relating to people who have offended us. But He also calls us to surrender situations that may offend us—something Dianna experienced on a recent shopping trip.

Surrendering circumstances to God

There are only two people ahead of me, so this shouldn't take too long, Dianna thought as she got into the return line at the local department store. Two clerks were working at the customer service counter, and she expected that she would be done soon and on to her next errand. Then she noticed that one of the customers ahead of her was returning a whole shopping cart full of dishes—one at a time! *Oh well,* she thought, *at least I'll get waited on by the other clerk.* That's when she overheard the next person at the counter request a thousand dollars' worth of ten dollar gift certificates—which meant the clerk would have to process one hundred certificates one at a time! Dianna's next thought was, *Unbelievable! This is ridiculous!* Fortunately, she had been practicing the treatments for keeping Christ's heart alive in her, and she immediately recognized her response as the sin of self rising to take control. (Remember, the *R* in TRUST stands for *recognize*.) She quickly unblocked through confession, allowing Christ to flow through her as she considered her choices.

By now you have learned enough about Dianna to know the usual reactions of her old self—either to leave in absolute disgust or just to stew as she waited in line, likely with some expletives running through her mind as she joined all the others in their self-justified complaining. However, with her newfound life, she made the choice to turn to God and said, "I want to stay in Your control, and I choose to trust You to give me peace and love while waiting this out." Her temptation to be impatient and irritable totally subsided as God stayed in control of her inner spirit and self was vanquished.

In addition to surrendering self when others wrong us as well as in the day-to-day irritations of life such as Dianna encountered, there is a third kind of surrender—one that is often overlooked because of its subtlety. The manifestation of self involved in this surrender can be just as destructive, so avoiding it requires that we understand our need to surrender even self's resentment of itself!

Forgiving oneself

"Should I tell the pastor about the problem I had a few weeks ago?" Jim asked his wife, while I sat across from them. She rolled her eyes in disgust and said, "Sure. It seems like you are never going to get over this." Whereupon, Jim told me following:

> We recently purchased a new car and were going to the grocery store. In the parking lot, I got into a fender bender with another car that was totally my fault. I know it sounds crazy, but after seeing the damage to our car, I blew up—at the other driver! I was so upset, I got out of my car and really gave him a piece of my mind, telling him that his car was a piece of junk. After my tirade, I got back in my own car and sulked. My wife, who was sitting in the car all this time, gently said to me, "You need to go and apologize to that man." Of course, she was right, and after I had calmed down I agreed. He was very gracious and not only accepted my apology but even agreed that his car was a piece of junk!

I was somewhat puzzled over Jim's problem. Though self had risen, he had confessed it immediately, and I complimented him on the way he handled things after his blowup. Then he shared the crux of his problem. "Pastor, I can't let go of it. The whole thing keeps replaying in my mind, and I just can't get past what happened." This was three weeks after the incident.

Jim was struggling with the age-old problem of forgiving himself. It seemed that the only thing that would bring satisfaction was the erasure of all memory of the event. Jim simply didn't want to own what he had done, even though he had recognized his sin and had "unblocked" it—clearing it through confession.

After further discussion, I told him that his problem was one of pride. You may think I was being unfairly critical. Here he is, seeking my help, already feeling terrible about what happened, still beating himself up, and I have the nerve to tell him that he has too much pride? It does seem like I was adding insult to injury. However, let's look beyond Jim's feelings to the reality. Basically, Jim's problem was that he couldn't believe that he had behaved so badly. It shocked him, taking him totally by surprise. It was so contrary to how he viewed himself that it disturbed him to the point that he couldn't let go of it. He continued to ruminate over the incident, hoping to come to some explanation—any explanation—other than the fact that it had revealed that self was still alive and at work in him. In other words, Jim's pride just wouldn't let him admit to himself that he was indeed that bad, and sometimes worse!

I suggested that Jim simply needed to recognize how sinful he was (just as we all are), to confess this to God, and to ask forgiveness. Then trusting God's promise would lead to acceptance and moving on with Christ's exchanged life. Refusing to forgive ourselves is a matter of pride, plain and simple.

This story illustrates that in most instances in which self rises within us, pride is the culprit. In addition to surrendering other aspects of our being, we must let go of pride—that feeling that pretends we are something other than sinful human beings—and accept God's grace and forgiveness.

Surrender in all its forms is the fourth treatment for establishing Christ's heart in us—the S in TRUST. (For examples along with spiritual references, see appendix D.) Again, our complete trust lets Christ in us recognize the interfering self and allows us to unblock our hearts through confession. But as important as this is, we can allow Christ's heart to take full control only if we include the fifth treatment—one that replaces our thoughts with His. We must learn His heart.

Chapter 14

Learning His Heart

(Clarence)

"The words I have spoken to you are spirit and they are life."
—*John 6:63, NIV*

Rich organ tones provided a peaceful interlude as I took my seat in the front pew. Glancing up, I observed the shimmering silver pipes from which the soft music emanated and filled the sanctuary. As associate pastor of a vibrant, six-thousand-member university church, I had just finished my responsibilities at the podium and looked forward to relaxing as I listened to the message from our senior pastor, Lou Venden.

He had been giving a series of sermons on the life of Solomon, and the message that morning focused on the gift of wisdom Solomon had received. The story of God's offer to give the young king whatever he wanted was familiar, and I was soon reflecting on my own thoughts. *He must have already been rather astute to make such a wise choice,* I mused. The rustle of papers and a cough interrupted my brief reverie, telling me our pastor had stopped talking. I glanced up to see him looking at the congregation intently. Then he broke the silence with a question that cut to my very core: "If God invited you to ask Him for whatever you wanted, what would you ask for?"

Suddenly, I felt tears well up as, much to my dismay, I became awash in emotion. My feelings were so intense that if I had been alone I would have been sobbing.

Not wanting to distract those around me, I fought to maintain control, blinking back the tears as I struggled to understand what was happening.

This response was hardly typical. I seldom shed tears. In fact, I have often wished for the ability to cry more easily so I could experience the relief that comes from such a release. However, I had been taught in my earlier years to avoid that kind of vulnerability, which could put me at risk of further pain and insult. So, experiencing raw emotion that threatened to overwhelm me was disconcerting, to say the least.

As the sermon continued, I was only vaguely aware of Lou's voice. I had become lost in thought about this question, which had plagued me for years, one that I dared not allow into my stream of consciousness, let alone express. It threatened to reveal the truth not only about my career in pastoring, but also, and more importantly, the core assumptions of my spiritual walk.

The question shattered my facade, revealing my spiritual nakedness. I knew that the light burden that Christ offered and that I preached about was somehow unbelievably heavy in my own life. And the only abundance I experienced was an abundance of discouragement as I observed the character flaws and failings that seemed to be a permanent part of my life.

But the overwhelming sense of longing and sadness I felt was not because of my failure to be perfect. Nor was it based on what I was not receiving from God, though I did feel that something was missing. And it certainly wasn't a question of faith. I was confident that I was God's child and was sure of His saving grace. Rather, my grief was based on my own woefully inadequate response. I was ashamed because all too often, I acted like a rebellious child. I loved to sing the hymn "Be Like Jesus," but I knew full well that despite all my struggles, resolutions, and promises, I often was not like Jesus. I was grieving because I was brokenhearted over my inability to respond to His grace with a transformation of character that would be a tribute to His daily presence in my life.

If God asked me the question He asked of Solomon, I knew what I would answer. As my tears welled up, I made that request. "Lord, teach me how to return Your love with a life that is truly transformed by Your presence."

My failure

I sought healing—relief from the emotional pain that had so enveloped my life that there seemed to be little room for Christ. You will recall from my description of my childhood that from day one, I lived in constant fear of my father's anger. For decades, I woke up every morning gripped with fear as I fought the urge to pull the covers over my head, curl up in a fetal position, and hide from life. As I lay there reviewing my duties and responsibilities for the day, I knew that chronic anxiety had little to do with reality, yet I felt helpless to change my response. How I longed to find peace and healing.

Any displays of anger or aggression by others caused me to experience abject fear. This led me to stuff my anger and to avoid even any reasonable assertion that might cause conflict. As people in my brother's profession tell us, this kind of repression often causes depression, something that played out in my own life. Occasionally, I considered seeking professional help, but while my depression often left me feeling exhausted and looking for escape, it was never severe enough to move me to pursue treatment. I assumed it was something I'd have to learn to live with. How I longed to find peace and healing.

Coupled with my desire to end pain's dominance in my life was my desire to gain victory over my primary form of escape—TV. This escape was so addictive that I preferred it to spending time with Christ. The reason for my addiction was hardly obscure. We all want freedom from inner pain—that "feel good" state—even when the relief is only temporary. I was no exception.

My feelings of fear and depression kept me in such a chronic state of pain that the solace provided by that box of sounds and flickering images was irresistible. It wasn't only the entertaining stories that distracted me from my own pain. I also enjoyed the sense of relief that comes from seeing problems solved in a brief sitcom or a ninety-minute movie, no matter how contrived the story line. I remember the eagerness I felt for the day to end—anticipating escape from the reality of my own life to the pretend life of TV. If I could lose myself for just a few hours, I could forget the pain I would have to face the following day.

My Solomon prayer was not so much a request as an admission of my own sadness and sense of failure. I was totally unaware that God was about to answer my longing beyond my wildest imagination.

The first inklings of the answer came in what began as an idle conversation with my friend Ruthie during a meeting we were attending together. I was bemoaning how inadequate and relatively unsuccessful I felt in my pastoral counseling. I was tired of merely holding people's hands while they went through their pain, divorces, spiritual bankruptcies, etc., and of bringing little observable healing or growth. I felt like a pop psychologist who was spewing out platitudes and pat solutions with little ability to effect lasting changes.

Rather than sympathizing, Ruthie challenged me, suggesting that I consider attending an upcoming seminar on biblical counseling. I was hungry for any help and immediately registered for the course.

My understanding of the role of Scriptures was challenged.

I looked forward to the five-day seminar with great anticipation, expecting to hone my counseling skills. Unfortunately, I was in for a serious letdown. The first day we were told that the week would focus on biblical self-confrontation—not counseling. If I wanted to learn to do biblical counseling, I would have to attend a second seminar that built on the current one.

I was not a happy camper. I felt that I had been victimized by a bait-and-switch routine. But I wasn't about to leave—not after already having paid for the course and having arranged to take time off from work. Besides, I was still eager to take the seminar on counseling. So I decided to hunker down for the week and make the best of it. Little did I realize that the week would set in motion changes that would radically alter my spiritual perspective, leading to healing I never thought possible.

The healing began when my understanding of the role of Scriptures was challenged. I had always viewed the Bible as primarily an informational book. It was cognitive, conceptual, factual, historical, intellectual, and objective. To me, it was a book to preach from and to use in my Bible studies with others—and that was about all. I'm not saying that this perspective was completely wrong, just that it was a very limited one.

Very early in that week, my view of Scripture changed radically. I learned that the Bible is a transformational book, one that changes far more than concepts. Texts presented at the seminar supported this view.

• " 'The words I have spoken to you are spirit and they are life' " (John 6:63, NIV).

- "Humbly accept the word planted in you, which can save you" (James 1:21, NIV).
- " 'These teachings are not empty words; they are your very life' " (Deuteronomy 32:47, TEV).
- " 'Give ear and come to me; / hear me, that your soul may live' " (Isaiah 55: 3, NIV).

While I was familiar with these texts, I had never really *heard* them. Now I was struck by the realization that the uniqueness of God's Word goes far beyond its profound truths. His Word contains a wonderful power that can nurture, transform, and sustain us spiritually in a way that nothing else can. It has the power to create a mind-set that will allow Christ to live His life in us.

Gaining an understanding of how we create a thinking pattern is crucial to understanding how God's Word can transform us. My experience with a student in the university church community dramatically illustrates the importance and impact of our mind-set.

What gets the mind

I became acquainted with Kathy when she was in nursing school at the university where I served as campus chaplain. We became good friends through working together on campus spiritual activities. At first glance, one of the most notable aspects about Kathy was her stature. To say that she is a tall woman would be an understatement—she's six feet three inches tall! During the months after we met, her dating calendar was empty. This was a source of unhappiness for her, one that she talked to me about from time to time.

Now it didn't take counseling expertise to know why no one was dating this towering woman. (And since my own height is five feet six inches tall, I do mean towering!) However, during our discussions about her concerns, she never spoke of this. Finally, during one of our chats, I had the temerity to mention the obvious— few guys have the ego strength to date a woman who towers over them.

Rather than responding with the sarcastic "no kidding" reaction I expected, she expressed complete surprise over what was apparently to her a novel observation, one she had never even considered, and she quizzed me about my statement.

Shocked by her response, I found myself arguing a concept that seemed blatantly obvious to me. And I was dumbfounded when my attempts to convince her that this might be true were totally unsuccessful. Try as I might to give her the typical male perspective on this, she remained baffled as to why guys would be threatened just because she was tall.

In the midst of our conversation, Kathy shared the origin of her self-image, making the basis of our failure to connect obvious: she had been programmed with a completely different mind-set. By the time she turned two, her parents knew she would be a tall woman. So, her father took it upon himself to instill in her very positive feelings about her height. Whenever they saw a tall woman, he would point her out, tell Kathy how classy that woman was, and say that

They celebrated . . . the fact that she had reached six feet in height!

Kathy would one day be tall and have that classy look. And when Kathy turned twelve, her parents threw a party for her at which they celebrated not only her birthday but also the fact that she had reached six feet in height! She was so excited about it that she could hardly contain herself. While most girls would be self-conscious about being that tall, even stooping to diminish their height, Kathy was proud of what she believed was a powerful attribute.

Kathy's story illustrates a crucial principle that underlies the development of a mind-set for our exchanged life. Solomon stated it very succinctly: "What he thinks is what he really is" (Proverbs 23:7, TEV). I like to describe this phenomenon with the following sentence: *What gets the mind gets us, and what gets us is reported in our thoughts, attitudes, words, and actions.*

Kathy sat in my office at the age of twenty-two, absolutely convinced that it was wonderful to be a tall woman and unable to understand or accept that her height held some disadvantages. She's a living example of the power of our mind-set, which cannot only defy but even remain completely blind to conventional wisdom. Her experience clearly demonstrates that what gets the mind gets us, and what gets us is reported in our thoughts, attitudes, words, and actions. As Kathy listened to her father, with whom she had a loving, trusting relationship, she truly heard him—not just cognitively, but with emotional conviction. In the context of this relationship, her father's repeated message became permanently embedded deep in her mind and heart.

The application

God's Word, as provided in the Bible, has the potential to have an even larger influence on our minds and hearts than the words of Kathy's father had on her. Our heavenly Father is not limited in the same way as our earthly father in terms of influencing our mind-set.

When Kathy's father said positive things about being tall, he had no control over how his words would affect her. He couldn't accompany those words into her brain and influence how she would process and assimilate them. (Would that we could get inside our children's heads when we speak to them!) Once the words left his mouth, they were out of his control.

However, that's not true of the words of Scripture. In the Bible, God says there are two aspects to His communication. First, He says that while men were used as instruments to write the books of the Bible, the Holy Spirit was the true Author of Scripture. Note the following from 1 Thessalonians: "We also thank God continually because, when you received the word of God, which you heard from us, you accepted it not as the word of men, but as it actually is, the word of God, which is at work in you who believe" (2:13, NIV).

The second aspect of our reciprocal communication with God is the reality that we are the temple of the Holy Spirit. This is absolutely crucial to our spiritual understanding and experience. We are literally made to receive and house God's indwelling Spirit! "Don't you know that you yourselves are God's temple and that God's Spirit lives in you? . . . For God's temple is sacred, and you are that temple" (1 Corinthians 3:16, 17, NIV).

If we are the temple of the Holy Spirit, this means that the Author of the Scriptures is actually able to live in us. He wants to alter our hopeless self-wiring, rewiring us to make us more compatible with the exchanged life. This also means that when we take in the words of the Bible, the Author of those words is there to receive them and to give them resurrection power!

Just as Kathy was influenced by her father's words, so we are influenced by the words of God, whom we love and trust. In addition, the Holy Spirit in us is able to take these words and embed them deeply in our minds. This allows emotional conviction that facilitates the functioning of Christ's transplanted heart, effecting a miraculous transformation in our lives. *What gets the mind gets us, and what gets us is reported in our thoughts, attitudes, words, and actions.*

With these new discoveries, I embraced an entirely different biblical paradigm, adopting an attitude that opened up new horizons. During those few short days at the seminar, I became enthralled with the Bible in ways I never would have imagined. It was as though blinders had been removed, and I could now see the Scriptures as dialogical, dynamic, formational, personal, relational, and subjective. In addition to being an informational book, it had become the all-important transformational Word of life—enabling me to open myself to more and more of the work of Christ's transplanted heart.

Going through the motions

During the seminar, I had the opportunity to gain a sneak preview of the advanced course, which was taking place in another part of the same facility. At mealtimes, I questioned those in the advanced course about the techniques they were learning for scriptural counseling. I was taken aback when they told me that they were expected to quote Scripture from memory. I assumed we would need to be familiar with the texts we would use, but commit them to memory? That was a tall order! In fact, it was a challenge that blew me away. The last time I had memorized Bible verses was in childhood, when I was given ribbons or stars in Bible classes. But by now I was hooked. My new and exciting attitude about the Bible, along with my hunger to learn more about Scripture-based counseling, drove my decision. If memorizing the Word was the requirement, memorizing it was what I would do.

There was a three-month window between the first seminar and the advanced course. And, as God's timing had it, I was on a sabbatical from my teaching responsibilities during that time, which provided the perfect opportunity for me to focus on memorization of Scripture. The first seminar had provided a large syllabus on biblical self-confrontation, including numerous texts for memorization. I set my course on committing all those verses to memory.

I must confess to you that I didn't engage in this project with the most noble of motivations. In fact, it's fair to say that I was memorizing for the wrong reasons—reasons that were largely self-based. My primary motivation was the desire to look good, to demonstrate competence at the advanced seminar. I'm not proud of it, but in essence, I was back in kindergarten Bible class, performing for the stars and ribbons! Yet, amazingly, even with the wrong motivations, the principle still applied—*what gets the mind gets us, and what gets us is reported in our thoughts, attitudes, words, and actions.* Remember the cry of my heart when I was listening to Lou's sermon? I still had no idea that God was about to answer my cry in ways I never could have dreamed.

A month or so into my memorization project, I began to notice some remarkable changes in both my inner emotional state and my outward behavior. I suddenly realized I was no longer waking up with the feelings of fear and anxiety that had plagued me every morning for decades. This was an immense change that gave me an overwhelming sense of relief. Before this change, I had begun

I wasn't drawn to TV in the usual compulsive manner.

to agree with my prayer partner, Wil Alexander, who had concluded that I might never be free of my fears. He suggested that perhaps they were a bit like Paul's thorn in the flesh. Maybe God was allowing me to have this pain in order to facilitate a greater dependence on Him. The healing I experienced following immersion in the Word gave a definitive No to that suggestion.

As I internalized Scripture, new thoughts, attitudes, words, and actions relentlessly began to override patterns I had lived with for years. I still tear up when I recall the healing God worked within me during those early weeks of Bible memorization. But along with the internal changes, He also was miraculously healing my external behavior.

Remember my addiction to TV? A month or so into my Bible memorization, I suddenly realized I wasn't drawn to TV in the usual compulsive manner. Amazingly, I would often come home and not even be tempted to turn it on. I can't overemphasize the significance of this. I had fought to overcome my addiction with prayer, behavioral contracts, and renewed commitments. Yet for years, I utterly failed to gain the victory. My attempts at self-improvement had been a miserable failure—something that should come as no surprise to you now that we've learned that even God can't improve our self. Surprisingly, now that I wasn't giving particular attention to this battle, dramatic shifts were taking place. The Spirit was effecting the Word's transforming power in my life as Christ replaced my desires with His desires. He spoke of this essential heart change that is at the core of any meaningful behavioral change. " 'Out of the overflow of the heart the mouth speaks.' " He said, " 'The good man brings good things out of the good stored up in him, and the evil man brings evil things out of the evil stored up in him' " (Matthew 12:34, 35, NIV).

When we focus on heart change, behavior follows. Noted author John Piper says, "Sin is what you do when your heart is not satisfied with God."[1] As I moved through my day, eating, working, recreating, and sleeping with Scripture always on my mind, everything changed. I was freed from fear and depression. Peace came, and boredom was gone. As God promises through His Word, He was doing marvelous healing both inwardly and outwardly.

As remarkable as this change was, though, I still had not fully availed myself of the power that God offers through Scripture. For God's Word to be embedded in a manner that will lead to a transformed, exchanged life, our journey requires more than mere accurate quotation of biblical passages.

From head to heart

It is interesting to observe how words affect us, some having a major impact and others barely registering. Have you ever wondered what makes the difference? The answer lies in the two principles of learning that we have all experienced. First, if the words touch our emotions, they have a much greater impact. Second, the more time we spend with the words, the greater the likelihood they will stick in our minds.

When Kathy heard her father affirm her height, she "felt" those words. That is, she received them with a high degree of emotion. Her father's excitement at her growth was contagious, increasing her positive reaction to her height. She could hardly wait to reach six feet and have a party to celebrate it! In essence, her father's words moved from head to heart because of her relationship with him along with her emotional investment in his words.

Research has corroborated these principles of learning. Those who have studied how words influence people have discovered that if words come to us at just a cognitive, intellectual level, only about 10 percent of what we hear will stay with us. If words are accompanied by pictures, either real or imagined, about 55 percent stays with us. If they're accompanied not only by pictures but also by an emotional component, 100 percent sticks in our minds.

Now let's consider how this applies to the Christian life. When we're no longer children, at what level does most of the Word of life come to us? My experience is that for the vast majority, it is conceptual and cognitive, with little or no visual or emotional aspects accompanying it. No wonder the words of the Bible don't stick with us!

Think of how much religious life in the church takes place at the conceptual level. Sometimes I'm bored with my own sermons! I marvel at the patience of the saints as they come time after time to meetings and endure studies and messages that have very little visual or emotional content—with little power to effect real change. If we're going to experience the transforming and healing power of Scripture, we will have to take something other than a purely cognitive approach.

The script for our movie is the Bible.

In my own experience with the Scriptures, I like to include a visual component that also has an emotional impact, so it packs a more powerful punch. Toward that end, I like to use the analogy of a mini-movie production involving various aspects of our life with the Word. The script for our movie is the Bible. The Star, of course, is Jesus. And we are supporting actors.

You'll recall that I struggle with impatience. When it comes to my attitude toward my fellow drivers, I'm definitely a work in progress. God seems to give me numerous opportunities for growth in this area—I must say, more than enough! When I come across incompetent drivers—and you know how many there are—I can become quite irritated. I'm well aware that this is not exactly righteous indignation (something we'll discuss later).

I used to pray about it, asking God to give me the patience I needed to put up with those idiots. (No, I didn't call them that in prayer—I just thought it.) The prayer was better than nothing, but it didn't do much to change my feelings about the situation. Sometimes I would take the additional step of quoting Scripture—for instance, recalling lines from 1 Corinthians 13:4, 5, "Love is patient and kind. . . . [It] does not get upset with others" (NCV). I would then pray, asking God to give me patience and to remove the feelings of anger and replace them with His love. Not bad, but still very limited, as I was just repeating words I had memorized.

What if instead I were to become a mini-movie producer? My basic script is the Word. The lead Actor, as always, is Jesus, and I'm a supporting actor—supporting Him. What might happen if I were to let my imagination see Jesus sitting next to me in the car as I was ready to lean on the horn and if I were to feel His calming hand on my shoulder? Remember that words accompanied by pictures have a much deeper impact on us. As I continue playing out the movie in my mind, I respond to His calm reassurance, feeling the muscle tension dissipate and hearing more of the movie's script as Jesus speaks some very significant promises in my ear. I might hear words from James 1:20, "Man's anger does not bring about the righteous life that God desires" (NIV). Or Galatians 5:22, 23, "The fruit of the Spirit is love, joy, peace, patience, kindness, goodness, faithfulness, gentleness and self-control" (NIV).

As the movie continues, the sound track presents more scriptural lines and I stay in His presence, allowing myself to surrender my feelings of resentment and anger to Him and letting the peace that passes all understanding fill my mind and heart. Now His words have a deeply powerful healing and transforming effect on my life, allowing me to continue driving in the worst kind of traffic because I'm in a much different place internally. Furthermore, this experience will be much more likely to stay with me if I turn my mind to Him and His Word frequently throughout the day.

An emotional dimension

I realize this concept is rather novel. However, the Bible does recognize the importance of developing an immersion in the Word that includes an emotional dimension. Proverbs says,

My son, pay attention to what I say;
    listen closely to my words.

Do not let them out of your sight,
　　keep them within your heart;
for they are life to those who find them
　　and health to a man's whole body.
Above all else, guard your heart,
　　for it is the wellspring of life (4:20–23, NIV).

While developing images and emotions related to the Scriptures may seem strange, we participate in this same phenomenon in other areas of our lives. Effective learning in school always involves not only repetition but also stories, emotions, and imagery. And the media has filled our minds with thousands of images from a plethora of sources. Since our brains are increasingly conditioned to depend on images, why not incorporate this tool for learning and applying God's Word in a way that has the power to transform? (See appendix E for techniques for memorizing Scripture.)

One final word on Scripture memorization: while I have found it extremely successful in my own life, it doesn't necessarily work for everyone. The ability to memorize is highly variable, and individuals also vary in how they create a mind-set.

My wife, Dianna, does little memory work, but she is still immersed in God's Word. She experiences Word power through texts on laminated cards, which she scatters in various places—her purse, the car, the kitchen table, her makeup table, etc. This allows her to reference her life to Scripture anytime and anyplace. Others may benefit from listening to audio recordings of readings of the Word. There are also several DVDs that present the Scripture in movie form, and many songs that feature Scripture in their lyrics. Whatever method you use, incorporating the above principles of immersion, imagery, and emotional investment provides fertile ground for the Spirit's work in us.

The transforming power of Scripture is an essential defense of the exchanged life to which we will repeatedly return. As it becomes fully embedded in us, we will be far less vulnerable to the vicissitudes of self that can so easily dissuade us from living the exchanged life. Thinking the Word (the last *T* in TRUST)—viewing Scripture as transformational—influences all the other treatments for Christ's transplanted heart.

So, the treatments that support each other to the end of maintaining Christ's heart in us are summarized in our acronym, TRUST:

Take up the cross daily.
Recognize the sin of allowing self to control.
Unblock through confession.
Surrender self.
Think the Word.

Unfortunately, these treatments, which are directed at preventing our rejection of Christ's exchanged heart, don't forever vanquish self. Even as a corpse, self is only in a dormant state, ever ready to rise up. It has its own methods for attempting to undermine and destroy our new life. It may try a frontal assault on our new life, but its less-direct methods are far more difficult to resist.

One of self's strategies poses its greatest threat when we are fully committed to the exchanged life and feel the most confident about our endeavor. It is dangerous because it can precipitate a Trojan horse attack on the new heart we have received. The rejection of Christ's life-giving transplanted heart within us is so subtle that the natural self has taken over before we realize what's happening. Our spiritual survival depends on our being aware of this ominous threat and on our understanding that we are in the greatest danger when our position is the most justified—those times when being right is wrong.

Section IV

Life After Death

Although our spiritual quest has been demanding and arduous, the overwhelming rewards make it our only choice. We learned the hopelessness of dead living (section I) and then grieved and accepted the futility of allowing self to rule. Next we considered adopting the exchanged life that freed us from the tyranny of self. Learning the treatments that maintain Christ's transplanted heart has fully equipped us to celebrate this life to die for. Self continues its attempts to rise in a myriad of ways. But this presents us with daily opportunities for growth as Christ continues to reprogram our responses to be like His. This leads to victories in which we surrender ourselves and our living more fully to His heart. Our daily crucifixion with Christ allows us to be resurrected to a whole new life—life after death.

Chapter 15

When Being Right Is Wrong

(Steve)

There is a way that seems right to a man,
but in the end it leads to death.

—*Proverbs 14:12, NIV*

It was one of those Friday afternoons when everyone had the same idea: get that last-minute shopping done before the weekend. As I wended my way through the Costco parking lot looking for a space, I fumed, wondering how I had allowed myself to become like the lemmings that surrounded me. My mood brightened when I spotted the taillights of a car about to exit a space near the entrance. I waited patiently, the blinker signaling my intent, as the car backed out into my lane. I was beginning to ease forward when suddenly a red sports car in the oncoming lane darted forward and stole my prized parking space!

My initial dismay quickly turned into red-hot anger. What a selfish jerk! As my jaw clenched, I leaned on the horn, blasting my displeasure. But before I had finished, he was walking toward the entrance, not even looking in my direction. Boy, did I want to give him a piece of my mind! Wouldn't things be easier if people behaved in a reasonable, civilized manner—if life was fair?

I'm sure you can identify, having had your own share of irritating experiences. The problem is really endemic, constantly cropping up in all sorts of minor situations. These short-lived incidents challenge us numerous times a day. Someone speaks critically or with a hint of sarcasm or irritation, and we want to retort in kind. The light turns green but no one moves as the lady in the lead car puts the finishing touches on her makeup. The new clerk at the grocery store is slow, the customer in front needs a price check, or someone has the nerve to slip into the express checkout line with far more than the ten-item maximum.

You know the feeling—the irritation that wells up when the thoughtless disregard of others tramples on your rights. I even get irritated when it's no one else's fault, such as when I return from an errand only to realize that I forgot something and need to return to the store. Then there's the accident that delays my commute. Talk about inconvenience! The list goes on and on. If you take a moment to reflect on your typical day, I'm sure you can add many more situations that invite resentment.

Everyone becomes frustrated about stressful situations and the indifference, rudeness, and stupidity of others, don't they? In fact, haven't experts taught us the importance of recognizing and appropriately expressing negative feelings because otherwise they could result in depression or anxiety? Besides, what's the big deal with getting a little upset over mistreatment? As long as we keep the resentment to ourselves, no one is really hurt, right?

Unconventional wisdom

Now that I've convinced you that irritation over minor frustrations is reasonable, I must challenge this piece of conventional wisdom. There is no question that we suffer all kinds of injustices that we don't deserve. And there's also no doubt that experiencing resentment is perfectly normal—the natural reaction of self. However, with the exchanged life, we are adopting the unnatural heart of Christ, which will lead us to respond in very abnormal, unusual, and unnatural ways.

If you're feeling some resistance to this concept, you're not alone. Clarence and I have also felt it when discussing some of the irritations in our own lives. I recall some of the conversations we had on this topic soon after I had watched the "Being Right: Life That Kills" part of Clarence's DVD. For me, the message hit home in a way that was both good and bad. I appreciated the insight that knowing that I'm in the right may lessen my conviction that I need Christ to take over in my life. But since I love being right, it was also rather disconcerting and uncomfortable.

So, in one of those early conversations, I asked Clarence, "Are you saying that if I'm feeling right, I'm probably wrong?"

"Not necessarily. It depends on whether it's about self," he responded.

"But whenever I feel right or want to be right, it seems like most of the time it's based on self."

He laughed and said, "Knowing you, it probably is! Seriously, though, I think it's true for most of us much of the time that being right is all about self."

"But doesn't that make for Christian doormats?" I objected. "It seems counter-intuitive, even wrong, to question such normal emotional reactions to unfair treatment."

"It is," Clarence agreed, "but only when you look at it from a human standpoint. Christ in us would have a different response."

"The response of a Christian doormat," I responded somewhat sarcastically.

"Not at all. Christians who come across as doormats are often on their own self trip. They are frequently all about looking like good, self-deprecating Christians, which raises self to a whole new level. In addition, when there is a lack of accountability, Christians' passiveness can end up boosting self in others."

"So it's OK to get upset about how others treat us," I suggested.

"Not necessarily," Clarence answered. "It depends on the basis of our upset."

"OK, let's get specific. Remember my telling you about the stolen parking space?"

"Yeah, I remember."

"Are you saying that after being had, I'm supposed to feel bad about getting angry over it?"

"That's what I'm saying," he replied. "Actually, from my read, that's what Scripture tells us."

"Talk about adding insult to injury!"

"It does feel that way," Clarence agreed—with less sympathy than I thought was called for.

"But most people wouldn't consider our minor irritation as even wrong," I countered. "Why should we attach some moral judgment to feelings that occur naturally when we are in the right and someone's mistreating us?"

"Because of how those feelings will affect our exchanged life," Clarence answered. "Let's look at your response to the stolen parking place. You leaned on the horn angrily. Where was that coming from?"

"Anger over what he had done to me," I quickly responded.

"Exactly. *You* were first in line for *your* anticipated place near the store entrance that was going to save *you* time, and it was stolen from *you*. You'll notice that the concern is all about *you*. And if we're honest, this is the basis for most of our anger: self."

"Well, nobody's perfect," I responded defensively.

"True," Clarence conceded. "But this isn't about some perfection trip. Remember, it's all about having Christ in us. If our protest about being wronged when we're in the right is about self, then we are giving life to self and—"

"And with self alive, Christ in us in threatened." I completed his thought with a feeling of resignation. "I think I get it. To the extent that self rises in a defensive mode, Christ is unable to live in us and shape our responses like His."

"That's right," Clarence said. "And where is self under greater threat, more defensive, and more likely to rise than when we're unjustly under attack? When we are in the right but not being treated right, our bringing self to life seems so natural, reasonable, and justified that it is almost impossible to resist."

"I can't argue that," I agreed. "But it seems so hard to avoid, to do something else."

"Only if we consider it our task rather than Christ's," Clarence reminded.

Sinning when we are right

Our conversation reminded me of what Clarence talked about on the DVD—the most uncomfortable and challenging principle of the exchanged life: *we do much, if not most, of our sinning when we are right and right is not happening for us—we're not being treated right.*

Few would dispute that I was in the right while waiting for that parking space. Surely God would agree that it should have been my spot and I was unjustly treated. So, what kind of response to mistreatment does the exchanged life generate?

Christ makes clear what attitude He wants us to have when we are right and we're being mistreated. " 'Love your enemies. Do good to those who hate you, bless those who curse you, pray for those who are cruel to you' " (Luke 6:27, 28, NCV). This didn't exactly describe my attitude as I watched that sports car steal my place—not even close! On the surface, it seems rather impossible for us to have this mind-set in the face of such a blatant wrong, doesn't it? It is! I could have pretended to have that attitude, stuffed my anger, avoided blasting the horn, and perhaps even hidden all my irritation. But erasing the *feeling* of resentment calls for a completely different mind-set, one that was described in the last chapter: "Let the same mind be in you that was in Christ Jesus" (Philippians 2:5, NRSV).

If we find it hard to adopt the mind of Christ when dealing with the common, everyday irritations that challenge us, think what it is to maintain it when life throws long-term difficulties and suffering at us! This includes physical suffering, with unrelenting pain that devastates a person day after day, month after month, year after year.

Dee Dee and I know all too well the fallout from chronic pain and often have not handled it well. During the early years of her kidney failure, we hadn't yet begun to live the exchanged life. Dee Dee would often complain about her losses, feeling sorry for herself. I had my own pain and stress as her caregiver, but given her level of suffering, I could hardly complain. Instead, I

When . . . Dee Dee bled all over the bed, I would often blow.

would just shut up and stuff it—but only for so long. With self fully alive, when problems occurred during overnight dialysis, I often handled it poorly. When alarms rang, blood pressure dropped, or Dee Dee bled all over the bed, I would often blow, letting loose with a string of expletives and unfair attacks on her that still cause me shame.

Author and Christian psychologist Larry Crabb provides insight into the consequences of long-term suffering, which he calls "the problem of demandingness." "When things do not go well, especially for an extended time, when our heart is filled with more pain than joy, the temptation to let our desire for relief become a demand is strongest. And the more severe the pain, the stronger the temptation. . . . Unrelenting pain is a most suitable environment in which to grow a demanding spirit."[1]

Chronic discomfort drives our increasing investment in making things go right or at least better, inevitably altering our focus to caring for the demands of self. These demands so incessantly invade our consciousness that they risk killing the exchanged life.

Other kinds of chronic pain also raise the demanding spirit that Crabb describes. There is the disappointing, thankless job that becomes a daily and hourly source of stress and unhappiness. There is the gnawing ache that comes with the alienation of friends or family who don't want to or are unable to reconcile. There is the pain that comes from being trapped in a thankless marriage where love and trust have long since disappeared. Talk about being right and continuing to suffer in spite of it!

While the exchanged life has dramatically changed our responses for the better in recent years, the unfairness of our situation still presents some of the greatest temptations for self to rise. Such struggles pose some major challenges, but they also provide tremendous opportunities for spiritual growth. If we meet these challenges successfully, Christ's heart in us becomes ever stronger while self becomes weaker as it fails to gain a foothold. This is the silver lining of pain—and it is so crucial that it is difficult to imagine growth in the exchanged life without it.

Justifying a loser

Up to now, we have been addressing situations in life in which we are truly right—that is, those in which most observers would agree that we are in the right and are caused to suffer through no fault of our own. However, this is only a small part of how being right threatens to revive self and kill the exchanged life. As we learned in chapter 6, self is a master at justification, and given its ability to distort reality, we usually see ourselves as right and deserving in most, if not all, circumstances of life, regardless of whether we are actually right or wrong.

We've all felt that sense of rightness, often with dubious justification, in various situations. When someone else lands the promotion that was supposed to be ours, most of us feel slighted and unfairly treated. Few are likely to admit that the fellow worker was more qualified. I remember that exams in college and medical school brought me similar feelings. When I wasn't near the top, I tended to think that those who scored higher had lucked out, while I really deserved a higher grade.

This phenomenon of feeling right is something that is evident very early; I observed it in my children at a young age. They were very competitive and frequently complained that they weren't being treated fairly, and they often felt more deserving than their siblings. Their self-centered distortions were so absurd that when they complained that I was unfairly favoring a sibling, I would often jokingly respond that I loved that one more!

This self-promoting distortion that suggests we are right and deserving regardless of the reality lasts throughout our lives. It presents one of the greatest challenges of the Christian life—staying dead to self when we feel we are right but aren't being treated fairly. Its source is both our human nature and the society in which we live. As previously described, we all have self-serving, self-protective, self-centered wiring from the start. On top of this, our environment provides unending reinforcement for our championing the rightness of our self. Most media sources are constantly bombarding us with messages that we deserve better, we don't have to wait, and life should be fair. Our consumer-driven economy stays afloat by insisting that we should take better care of self, ensuring that wants become needs.

One core motivation stands behind self's fight for its rights: self-justification. Everything involved in enhancing the position of self is predicated on our acquiring a belief in the deserving nature of our self. This is the antithesis of the biblical view, which says that self is not only hopeless but also a primary impediment to the exchanged life. However, Christians of today often adopt a more "enlightened" perspective, sharing the humanistic view that suggests that the refurbishment or improvement of the self is intrinsically good.

Self is only too happy to embrace this view, which ensures its survival. We are masters at strategies that incorporate the rightness and deserving nature of self. One of the most effective of these is that of comparing ourselves with others. We can often use this to justify our sense of rightness and deservedness and enhance the position of self. After all, we're as good as anyone else and are just as deserving as they—maybe even more so—of having the advantages they possess. On the flip side, self can also justify bad behavior by finding others who behave worse, giving us the sense that we aren't really all that bad compared to others. Either way, comparison facilitates a process that leads to perceptions of a self deserving of more than it is receiving. So, self can come out on top.

Curiously, we can find reasons to be "right" and thus deserving of rewards even when we're wrong! We may admit to wrongdoing for less than noble motives, opining that we must be pretty good people to take ownership and admit our wrongdoing. Carried even further, there's the disingenuous expression of excessive guilt that demands reassurance from others, again leaving self feeling more right and more deserving than others are.

Society also colludes in maintaining self's position, endorsing commonly accepted standards that guard against offending the self through the increasingly popular political correctness. This mandates a progressively less judgmental society in which each of us can feel better about ourselves regardless of our behavior. We may be "misguided," "mistaken," or even "victims," but we're never really bad or sinful.

> *Self* can . . . justify bad behavior by finding others who behave worse.

Looking right versus being right takes precedence, as we enhance the image of our goodness while hiding the reality of our desperate condition. Sadly, the emperor has no clothes, given that preserving the lie of rightness is more important than addressing the truth of self's miserable status.

Our culture also supports self through various associations that enhance our sense of deservedness, such as involvement in religious or charitable projects and institutions or even spiritual study and prayer. These are all noble endeavors, but motivation that is based on enhancing the self will promote deserving causes at the expense of living the exchanged life. Even our legal system champions self to the point of advocating major financial benefits for those who best portray themselves as victims—whatever the reality may be.

Self is its own public relations agent; with numerous tactics, we have somehow managed to sell the view that humanity is an enlightened species that is even now evolving for the better. This shifts us from the biblical view of a hopeless self to a moral relativism that allows self to appear right and deserving of esteem, regardless of what it actually deserves.

Hopelessly unfair

So, we have an inexorable tendency to view reality through the distorted lens of self that portrays us as always deserving of more. Yet who merited more rewards but undeservedly suffered more than Christ? Even the ordeals in which we seem the most justified are rather pathetic when compared to His experience. Our misguided attempts to justify our selves give life to self. And self, in turn, kills the exchanged life by rejecting His heart, which is the only true source of justification for eternity!

It is an amazing testimony to the delusional nature of the self that we still buy into concerns over what is deserved or unfair. Intellectually, we all know self can never be satisfied and that life isn't fair. Our own experiences have taught us that no amount of effort, no government program, and no laws can ensure fairness. We are surrounded with examples of good people who, through no fault of their own, endure terrible circumstances and suffering. We also profess to believe our existence is very transient and—in terms of our physical existence and comfort—relatively meaningless, making fairness in this life irrelevant. We even teach our children that life isn't fair and that they need to learn to accept this. But when it comes to practicing what we preach amid unfairness and mistreatment, self often comes alive as we get trapped into fighting for our rights. By fighting this battle, we only lend credence to the delusion that we can obtain fairness. But feelings that focus on righting wrongs distract. Even if we are at times successful, this is only temporary. And when we win the battle for our rights, we become more invested in self, which threatens the exchanged life and leaves us the ultimate losers. Christ addressed this paradox: " 'If you try to keep your life for yourself, you will lose it. But if you give up your life for me, you will find true life [with My transplanted heart]' " (Luke 9:24 NLT).

Of course, giving up the battle for our rights is easier said than done. That is especially true when it comes to the small issues—those that involve resentments so automatic and second nature that we rarely give them a second thought. These barely register on our moral radar, eliciting little concern as to whether they are justified. I first reflected on this when I heard Clarence discuss being right. At the time, I wondered why he picked such minor irritants for his examples. If these were his biggest concerns, then either his spiritual life was a cakewalk or he was clueless! When it came to sinning, I knew I certainly had bigger fish to fry. Why would I major in minors before I had addressed the more serious concerns?

Over time, I have been given numerous painful experiences that have repeatedly answered this question. Often, with Dee Dee's suffering and my struggles with her care, we have both felt more than right in our anger and resentment, which has led to frequent conflicts. I felt far more justified about these feelings than about my petty resentment over that stolen parking space. Of course, *feeling* right and *being* right are two different things—a truth we often avoid.

When we consider the various struggles we all face, it is evident that the times of greatest suffering provide the strongest potential for self to return to life and threaten Christ's reign in us. But this is why majoring in minors is so important. If we haven't learned to invite Christ to rule over self in the small areas, we will be poorly equipped for allowing His takeover when the big stuff hits us. Clarence has repeatedly observed this, both in his own life and in the lives of those to whom he ministers. The stories he has heard from others on this journey often speak to the weakness that comes from ignoring minor concerns. Chapter 16 begins with one such story concerning a friend of his who faced a major challenge to his exchanged life. It teaches how we can give up the fight for our rights when we are wronged as we learn to choose Christ's rightness and to engage in exchanged living more effectively.

Chapter 16

Choosing His Rightness

(Clarence)

The heart is devious above all else;
it is perverse.

—*Jeremiah 17:9, NRSV*

It was a gathering like no other, as painful as it was necessary. Even the bright afternoon sun couldn't lighten our sober mood as we awkwardly took our places, anticipating the inevitable "carefrontation." Tom, a dear friend, had invited me to facilitate the process. His oldest son, Jason, had arranged this meeting just the previous day. With his marriage crumbling, Jason had called together the key players to confront his wife.

I had officiated at Jason and Kirsten's wedding just over four years before and was now here to discuss levels of betrayal seldom seen in a marriage. It was a meeting that I dreaded but could hardly refuse. After all, Tom was a close friend who often sought my counsel. He and his wife, Kathy, had only recently begun to live the exchanged life. They were now facing some challenges, and while the meeting was primarily an attempt to turn Jason's marriage around, it was also an opportunity for Tom and Kathy to learn more about dying to self.

I had just finished outlining how the meeting would proceed when Jason arrived with Kirsten. She walked in and saw her relatives and closest friends seated in a circle. But if she was shocked, her face never showed it. Her blasé attitude reminded me of what Tom had said, "She hides behind that fake smile of hers. You never know how she really feels." Given the circumstances, I worried that her smile didn't bode well for the candor we were seeking.

After I made a few opening remarks, each person in the circle gave Kirsten messages of unconditional love and affirmation. Tom was the first to speak, followed by Kathy, who told Kirsten that she loved her like a daughter. What they said sounded nice, but after what Tom had shared with me about their anger and frustration, I had to wonder whether it was really genuine. Still, at least they were providing the kind of support I knew was necessary if there was to be any hope of Kirsten risking honest, open communication. I glanced around to observe the others who were waiting their turn. There were Kirsten's two younger siblings, her parents, and two of her closest friends. As the affirmations continued, my mind wandered back to how it all had started four years before.

"Clarence." I had recognized Tom's voice on the line. "You got a minute?" Then, without waiting for me to respond, he had continued. "You're not going to believe this: I'm a grandpa!"

"You're what?" I asked incredulously, unsure how to respond to this bombshell. As far as I knew, none of his children was even dating seriously, let alone married.

"I just became a grandfather," he repeated.

"But how did . . . I mean, who . . . ?"

"You won't believe it," he said and began to explain. "Jason called me about one in the morning. Woke me out of a dead sleep. He was crying, and I was thinking he'd been in an accident or had been arrested. But then he said this girl he's been dating, Kirsten, is in the emergency room—in labor! He was at his apartment and was asking me for a ride to the hospital."

"Wow! Unbelievable!" I exclaimed. "What did Kathy say?"

"She barely woke up. I just told her that Jason had gotten stranded somewhere and needed a ride. I just wasn't up to explaining things then.

"Don't ask me how, but Jason's girlfriend hid the pregnancy from everyone. Jason was in tears when I picked him up. During the ride, I asked whether he had thought of adoption. But he just said forget it; he wasn't going to be some deadbeat dad. Clarence, he doesn't have a clue about what he's facing. I mean, he just turned nineteen!"

"I don't know what to say," I responded, not sure whether to offer congratulations or condolences. "How does Kathy feel about it?"

"How are we supposed to feel?" he responded with obvious irritation. "We're both ticked off about the whole thing. But what are we supposed to do? This is our grandson, and we just have to make the best of it. This morning we showed up at the hospital all smiles with flowers in hand. It was more than weird, Clarence. I mean, Kirsten's lying there nursing the baby, cool as a cucumber, and we've barely met her a couple times. Then her mom welcomes us, saying that we are now forever joined—to what I don't know. I mean, we'd never even met her!"

Over the next few weeks, Tom and I stayed in touch through intermittent phone calls and e-mails that kept me apprised on the latest developments. The young couple moved into Tom and Kathy's family room. They continued their studies at the community college and were soon formally engaged.

Tom shared with me his concern that Jason was simply doggedly committed to making a success of things rather than being truly in love. When I saw Jason and Kirsten in premarital counseling, I, too, became concerned. They faced tremendous hurdles, and I candidly told them that the odds were against them. But they appeared to be committed to the marriage, and nine months after Logan's birth, family and friends came together to celebrate as the young couple wed.

Troubles begin

Their troubles started soon. After two beater cars broke down within weeks of each other, Tom found a reliable used car for them, understanding they would reimburse him for the cost. However, the money order Kirsten claimed she had dropped off never materialized, even when Tom and Kathy conducted an extensive search. And when they learned that Kirsten handled all the money and had never bothered to add Jason to their new bank account, their suspicions grew.

Kirsten assured Tom and Kathy that payment would be forthcoming when she was reimbursed for the "lost" money order. Jason tried to cover for her, but by then, they knew there was no money. With growing irritation, Tom told how he pressed Jason to face reality. When Kirsten produced a financial statement that was an obvious forgery, Jason insisted on going to the bank despite her repeated objections and hysterical crying over his "controlling and badgering." At the bank,

Kirsten demanded confirmation of their nonexistent account, but the teller shook her head and rolled her eyes at Jason in dismay. And it didn't end there. Months later, Jason began receiving calls from a collection agency. Although Kirsten had assured Jason that she had taken care of the broken-down cars, she hadn't. Her negligence and lies ultimately cost them impound fees of sixteen hundred dollars!

The tone of my conversations with Tom began to change as he increasingly expressed anger and resentment. He and Kathy were committed to living the exchanged life, but, obviously, Kirsten's behavior was becoming the occasion for self to rise and challenge Christ's control in their lives. When I expressed my concern about this, Tom was rather dismissive, conveying that he felt their resentment was more than justified as they became increasingly caught up in her web of betrayal.

Her claims were totally bogus.

While the pressure was building, Kirsten was given some reprieve when the focus shifted to concerns about her health. She insisted that her diet of less than five hundred calories a day was supporting the 180 pounds she weighed. Although this was clearly impossible, Jason remained unsure, convincing his father, a physician, to call an endocrinologist. When Tom was told the obvious, that this was clearly ridiculous, he felt like a fool and vented more resentment in our conversations. Still, Jason wasn't convinced, given the minimal intake he observed, so he was supportive when Kirsten pursued an endocrinology workup.

After several weeks, Tom called, telling me that her gynecology referral was doing a diagnostic workup for a possible abdominal tumor. This time, rather than resentment, I heard genuine concern in his voice. However, this concern was short lived. A few days later, I received an urgent call from Tom. Once again, Kirsten was in the emergency room—in labor! Tom was really steamed. This repeat performance could no longer be chalked up to the stupidity of teens, and they had major concerns about Kirsten's mental stability. During an evaluation done by professionals in social work and psychiatry, Kirsten produced a calendar with extensive notations identifying the specific times and dates of all her numerous medical appointments, including a recent MRI. The psychiatrist found only one problem with her medical care—it never happened! Her claims were totally bogus. For a second time, she had neglected to obtain any prenatal care!

Understandably, Jason was beside himself, questioning whether he should even continue in the relationship. Her behavior was so bizarre that the hospital wouldn't release his baby daughter, Sally, until social services had interviewed him. I felt Jason's hurt and anger over such a betrayal—and Kathy's and Tom's pain as well. For her part, Kirsten continued to insist that she'd had no idea she was pregnant despite all the evidence to the contrary. She was so insistent that she even convinced Tom to call her doctors (those she never saw) to allow a meeting for possible recognition and confirmation of her care. After that, Tom almost lost it, telling me that she had made a fool of him for the last time!

Calm deceit

Just before our "carefrontation" meeting, Kirsten had showed Jason a bank statement, one that she claimed she had gotten at the bank that morning. At our meeting, she was confronted with irrefutable evidence that she hadn't been at the bank that day. She responded by calmly admitting her deceit over the bank account while immediately minimizing the issue. She explained that she only wanted to please Jason; he was so happy to learn of the "thousands" they had in "savings."

I was dismayed to observe her unflappable demeanor. She appeared to be oblivious to the gravity of what she had done. There was a frightening absence of remorse and of the profuse apologies that one would normally expect. Attempts to confront her about other areas of dishonesty were fruitless. Despite her parents' tearful pleadings, she vehemently insisted she knew nothing of the pregnancy until she was in labor. Her father then dropped another bombshell, alleging that she had failed out of school the previous year. She denied this heatedly, and with little more to be said, the meeting quickly ended. I recall thinking that I had never seen anyone lie with such a cool and calm demeanor.

Jason tried to put a positive spin on things, telling his parents that after we left, Kirsten broke down crying. But Tom suspected these were tears of embarrassment rather than heartfelt remorse. As you might suspect, by now Tom's attitude toward Kirsten wasn't exactly positive, and he was hardly in the mood for understanding and reconciliation. The failed intervention simply added to his and Kathy's resentment.

Tom fumed, asking how anyone could have the gall to tell lies so blatantly. What kind of fools did she take them for? With each bizarre twist in his and Kathy's relationship with Kirsten, they felt increasingly helpless, with growing hurt and anger.

In the weeks that followed, Jason was in shock. After being robbed of prenatal anticipation, he attempted to bond with the daughter he never expected. Tom told me that his son was on an emotional roller coaster with no end in sight as he struggled to grasp what he was up against. Finally, he faced reality. He would have to take on greater responsibility and control until he could trust Kirsten. After experiencing firsthand the devastating consequences of her dishonesty, he could no longer afford to take chances with their finances or the children's health and safety.

Jason shifted to a bunker mentality, hunkering down as he remained ever vigilant and guarded against all deceit. He would badger Kirsten about a lie until she would finally admit the truth. Then she would have a renewed desire to please, which laid the groundwork for the next round of lies. Given her childlike behavior, Jason seemed to have little choice but to parent her as well as their children. But, unfortunately, while it is essential to hold one's children accountable, doing so rarely works in marriages in which adults are acting like children.

Jason shifted to a bunker mentality.

With growing resentment, Tom lamented that all he and Kathy could do was sit by helplessly, knowing there was little chance that things would change. Even when Kirsten grudgingly agreed to therapy, this merely resulted in one more person being caught up in her lies. (She later said that therapy couldn't help, since she could fool any therapist.) When Jason suggested he could begin to trust her if she would go just two weeks without lying, she admitted she wasn't sure she could. Through it all, Tom and Kathy lived with the memories of what her dishonesty had taken from their son—and from them. And they lived with the pervasive fear generated by knowing that it wasn't over—that at any time they might discover another major falsehood, spelling disaster once again. No doubt about it: in just four years of marriage, Jason had been put through a gauntlet few must endure.

It doesn't seem fair, does it? As I share this, I'm sure you can feel Tom and

Kathy's pain. Imagine yourself in their position. Imagine spending hours discussing with your son all the horrors of this relationship and of the deceptions that never end—the thefts that keep on taking, especially from the innocent children. Even while writing this, I can feel the resentment Tom often shared as he relived the awful reality of the repeated betrayals. I trust that you can feel it too—the injustice of it all, those hurt feelings and the anger that rises in all of us when we are clearly in the right and yet so wrongly treated.

Exchanged life challenged

I sensed such feelings in Tom every time he spoke with me. I gently expressed concern that this ordeal was presenting a major challenge to his exchanged life. He told me that he and Kathy were asking God to show them where self was threatening His life in them and asking Him for the ability to surrender and let Him remove self. In later years, he shared with me that they really had no idea what they were praying for or the challenges that God would allow to come to them.

Have you noticed areas where self seems unwilling to let go or simply pretends it isn't running the show? You've probably experienced the gnawing awareness that something is interfering with Christ's presence and yet you know that you're just not ready to surrender in that area. That was Tom and Kathy's experience when it came to what their son was going through. They harbored intense resentment toward Kirsten, but initially, my conversations with Tom revealed that they were simply ignoring it. It was evident that through it all, they were unwittingly allowing the ongoing events to provoke self to rise at every turn.

Soon after our meeting, Tom called me again. "You won't believe the latest lie," he said with disgust. "Jason and Kirsten came over telling us that she wanted to regain our trust. I felt like telling her, 'How about being honest about the pregnancy, the stolen money, and all the other lies?' But she just handed us an e-mail that promised her a state job paying eighty thousand a year after she finishes school."

"Wow, that's pretty impressive," I observed.

"Are you kidding?" Tom said, laughing derisively. "I'm sure it's bogus. No one writes something like that in an e-mail."

"So what did she say when you confronted her?" I asked.

"We didn't. It just wasn't worth it," Tom responded. "She's supposed to finish school in a couple of months, and if I'm right and she hasn't been in school, it will all come crashing down. I'd rather just let Jason learn it for himself."

Four months after Sally's birth, Kirsten finally caved, admitting to Jason that she knew of the pregnancy from the beginning. Jason, always wanting to see the positive, thought it was a real breakthrough. But for Tom, it was too little, too late. He told me his life was becoming a nightmare of unending pain—*a perfect medium for the growth of self,* I thought.

When they asked about her graduation, sure that she was out of school, she took the bait, saying that the ceremony had been postponed until the alumni could raise money for a place to meet. If you're thinking this sounds ridiculous, Tom would definitely agree. It was so over the top that he called his son, who confirmed that she wasn't in school. A few weeks earlier, when Jason insisted on visiting what she claimed was her school work site, she had no choice but to admit that she had failed out of school the year before. He had told Kirsten to take responsibility and come clean with his parents, which, consistent with her style, she continued to avoid. With growing resentment, Tom and Kathy wondered what she had been doing all those days when she pretended to go to school while Jason worked and others cared for their children.

While Jason was increasingly angry and desperate, he was also loyal to a fault. Tom told me that even with the continuing dishonesty, he chose to forgive her, pick up the pieces, and go on—if for no other reason than for the sake of the children. Kirsten found work as a bank teller (of all places), and Jason began gaining students for private instruction in the Suzuki violin method. Tom expressed somewhat hollow support for their attempts, trying to be supportive, while remaining pessimistic, and expressing growing resentment.

Clinging to resentment

The level of injustice in the above scenario makes minor incidents like Steve's stolen parking place seem insignificant by comparison. Rather than momentary inconvenience, Tom and Kathy suffered under repeated betrayals for years. Yet through it all, despite their anger and desperation, Tom told me they never had a cross word with Kirsten; they showed her nothing but kindness and love, even when they didn't feel like it. Given all that she put them through, who could blame them if they experienced some resentment and even anger?

Most of the time, I just listened to Tom, keeping my concerns to myself. When someone is hurting like Tom, they usually aren't open to much feedback other than support for what they're going through. So I simply prayed, trusting God to do His work and use me in His own time. My patience was eventually rewarded as Tom began to share some of the struggles he was having over his resentment.

"I know I shouldn't feel this angry," Tom observed. "I just can't help it."

"Have you been praying about it?" I asked, sensing an opening.

"Yeah, I try. But I still feel angry. I mean, it seems like God Himself would feel angry about what we've been put through."

"He probably is," I observed. "But if we're really trusting Jesus, then that means letting go and trusting Him to deal with the anger."

"I know," Tom conceded. "We've prayed about it. But when I hear Kathy pray for Kirsten, it almost feels wrong, like a total disconnect. Even when we're praying, I know in my heart of hearts that I don't wish her well. I want her to suffer just like we've suffered because of her betrayals."

"It's a real challenge," I granted. "But it might really be a relief to give up the anger."

"I know. Obviously, I'm not experiencing Christ's attitude of loving my enemies and doing good to those who hurt me."

"Well, look on the positive side. At least you're recognizing the sin."

"But if I'm living the exchanged life, Christ's attitude is supposed to rule. Let's face it; self is alive and well in me."

"OK, how about the next step: confession?" I challenged.

"I've asked God's forgiveness, but it seems like I'm just going through the motions," Tom responded. "It just feels so right to be angry at her. Isn't anger sometimes justified?"

"Of course," I agreed. "But what makes it justified?"

"I'm not sure," Tom responded hesitantly. "But if any situation justifies anger, it sure seems like this one does."

"So you're saying that the more unjust the situation, the more anger is justified?"

"I'm not sure."

"By that reasoning, I guess Paul and Silas should have been beating the walls in anger rather than singing praises when they were thrown in jail," I suggested.

"OK, I see your point," Tom conceded. "But in that case, when is anger ever justified? Does anger always mean self is taking control?"

"No, but obviously when anger gives life to self, it threatens Christ's heart in us. What do you think is the main basis of your anger?" I asked.

"Well, I . . . I mean, isn't it obvious? Look what she did to Jason and the children—the lies, the stealing. Wouldn't you be angry too?"

"Yeah, I'm sure I would be. In fact I *have* been angry about it, and Jason's not even my son," I responded. "I think Christ in us will always lead to anger over the victimization of others. But is that all you're angry about?"

"What do you mean?" Tom responded somewhat evasively.

"Well, what about Kirsten? What are your feelings toward her?"

"That's harder," Tom admitted. "Like I said, I don't wish her well. And Christ in me certainly wouldn't generate what I'm feeling toward her. If I'm honest, I have to say that my concern with her is over how she hurt us and the need for her to suffer some consequences."

"And what would Christ's interest be?" I challenged.

"I guess He'd be primarily interested in her salvation," Tom grudgingly responded.

"Sounds like you have a pretty good handle on what's going on," I observed before we ended the conversation.

"Something seems wrong"

A week later, I called to see how Tom was doing.

"Something seems wrong," Tom said. "Obviously, it's Kirsten who's messing up. Why am I supposed to feel guilty about my feelings? Are we supposed to just roll over and let her do whatever she wants?"

"Of course not," I replied. "That's a major distortion that Christians come up with, often based on some notion of works-based salvation—that our salvation depends on how much we appear to be dead to self and our own interest."

"But isn't that kind of true?"

"Not really. There are several errors in that kind of thinking. First, we end up getting caught up with the *appearance* of selfless living rather than the *reality* of Christ in us. Second, when we're unable or unwilling to assert ourselves, we can hardly do the work of Christ. Think about the biblical heroes. While they weren't self-centered, they were very assertive, often causing extreme offense to others. They were anything but wimps. Third, think what the refusal to be assertive does to others."

"What do you mean?" Tom asked. "I thought we were always supposed to put the needs of others ahead of our own."

"Not necessarily," I countered. "We are to love others *as* we love ourselves, not *more than* we love ourselves. This certainly indicates that when Christ is in us, we have a healthy love for ourselves. Also, what others say they need or want may not be something we should provide them."

"Yeah, that would certainly apply to Kirsten," Tom agreed.

Christ in us [can] accomplish the unnatural and impossible.

I continued, "Jason wasn't very assertive in the early years of their relationship. He didn't expect much accountability on Kirsten's part. Some might say that his naïveté and acceptance showed a Christian attitude. In reality, however, this lack of assertiveness enabled Kirsten's theft and deceit—rather immoral behavior. But we're getting sidetracked. What about the anger you've been struggling with?"

"I'm still having a hard time with what we talked about last time. I've confessed my resentment and tried to surrender it to God. But my feelings still seem so reasonable and appropriate. And letting go of the anger—it just seems so unnatural and impossible."

"It is," I agreed. "That's the whole point of our exchanged life, to allow for Christ in us to accomplish the unnatural and impossible. This question may not seem fair, but here it is, Do you think that you're searching for truth or for a rationalization?"

"What do you mean? I've been praying like crazy about this," Tom objected.

"But whose solutions are you praying for?" I asked. "Remember how you thought that in my presentations about small things I was making a big deal about nothing?"

"Yeah. It just seemed rather obsessive to get all hyper about all the little irritations in life," Tom observed.

"You're not alone in feeling that way," I agreed. "I hear the same feedback from others. But, Tom, if it's easy for us to justify minor irritations over small injustices, how much easier is it to rationalize and justify resentment over major wrongs, such as what you've been going through?"

"Wow! I never thought about it that way," he conceded.

"I think you've come full circle in your thinking here," I said, continuing to press the point. "You've gone from asking when anger *is* justified to asking when it *isn't* justified."

"I guess you're right," Tom responded with refreshing openness. "I guess I've moved from needing to justify my feelings to accepting them until they are proven to be unjustifiable."

"And that's a tall order, given our self-serving bent," I said.

Rightness—not righteous—indignation

Even with this awareness, Tom still struggled with intense emotional resistance. The idea that his natural response to such unjust treatment was somehow wrong seemed so terribly unfair. He called a few days later. "What about righteous indignation?" he asked.

"What about *un*righteous indignation?" I countered.

"I've never heard of that," Tom responded.

Neither had I, but I decided to go with it. "Yeah, it's obviously not as popular a term. Why do you think they call it righteous indignation? *Indignation* means anger that is aroused by something that is unjust. That word doesn't necessarily include the idea of righteous. If that was part of the definition, righteous indignation would be a redundancy."

"So, what makes our indignation righteous or unrighteous?"

"I think that depends on the source of the anger. When Christ showed intense indignation in the temple marketplace, He was angry about what was being done to God and others, not about what was happening to Himself. So, here's the question for us: Is our anger based on injustice we're suffering or that others are suffering? You've told me of your resentment at how Kirsten's actions were victimizing

Jason and the children and also your indignation at the pain she's caused you."

"I have to admit, the primary source of my anger is what's been done to me. It just feels so right to be angry. Come to think of it, rather than righteous indignation, I guess my resentment is based on my *rightness* indignation."

"Hey, I like that, Tom," I observed, thinking this was something I would use in my exchanged-life sermons. " *'Rightness indignation,'* indignation over right not happening. But that's something quite unrighteous, ultimately a self trip."

Even after he had felt this uncomfortable conviction, Tom sent me an e-mail that indicated his feelings hadn't changed much. He knew that though his anger seemed justified, it was based on self and it was interfering with the exchanged life. But he continued to struggle. Even though he was convicted that his resentment was wrong, Kirsten's betrayals had hurt him so much that he continued to feel angry—only now he told me he also felt guilty about the anger, which he seemed unable to erase.

Breakthrough

Tom e-mailed me a few weeks later. There had been a breakthrough.

Hi Clarence,

With all our discussions about Christ in us and indignation and injustice, I suddenly flashed on another story—one that portrayed unbelievable injustice, making our ordeal pale in comparison. I realized that the most amazing part of the story was the response—lacking any of the expected indignation or outrage that I often feel. As I reflected on this monumental injustice, my own mistreatment suddenly felt insignificant, and, for the first time, the resentment was gone. Not that it doesn't continue to crop up at times; you know how self is always ready to rise. But whenever the stress of indignation and self-protection creeps in, contemplating this story gives me a wonderful release from the need to defend, and I experience a sense of peace once again.

Of course, you know the story that killed my indignation. My issues seem so small when I consider how Jesus was ridiculed, tortured, and finally nailed to the cross. It wasn't just the Crucifixion, since others have gone through that. But none have been so innocent and none so unbelievably empty of resentment (selflessly focusing on the needs of others while dying) than Jesus was. His is the life I want to emulate, something I know is impossible. He must do it for me, living in me through the exchanged life. Like you say, our essential task is to recognize the interfering, prideful self in order to put an end to its empowerment.

This whole experience reminds me of words that I used to somewhat thoughtlessly sing in my church school choir—words that bring tears to my eyes as I suddenly feel their truth:

When I survey the wondrous cross
On which the Prince of glory died;
My richest gain I count but loss,
And pour contempt on all my pride.

When I reflect on my resentments—now ridiculously insignificant compared to Christ's suffering—I'm beginning to understand that my struggles didn't need to be so difficult. My shift in attitude, which allows increasing acceptance of Christ's heart, gives me a different perspective on Kirsten—His perspective. Now that I've surrendered my resentment, I can more clearly see Christ's view. Let's face it; both Kirsten and I are in desperate need of His heart, and in reference to Christ's standard, comparing our relative rightness is more than ridiculous.

I end up feeling so critical of her. But really, who am I to sit in judgment over her impairments when Christ's heart has been making me painfully aware of my own, including my resentment over Kirsten? Despite all the pain her actions caused, in God's eyes—considering the varying hands we are dealt—perhaps she was doing far better than I.

I can't help but think about what feelings of inadequacies, what kind of emotional insults, what level of pain must be driving her to perpetrate such devastating dishonesty. When I surrendered my self-interest, Christ's heart in me longed for her to experience His complete acceptance, relieving her of the need to lie. His investment in Kirsten's spiritual well-being increasingly became my own. As I let His mind be in me, I've begun to actually feel pity and sympathy for her. Now, rather than worrying about my rightness, I'm invested in His rightness in me.

Also, while struggling with my anger, I began to realize that I was suffering under a burden of my own choosing rather than the light burden which Christ offers. Although I certainly didn't cause the betrayal, my response did not need to be inevitably determined by this. You know how I hate to say you were right, but you were right! If I hadn't dismissed all the minor matters you were concerned with, I would have been able to handle this much better. I was making excuses and justifying my feelings over minor stuff and getting in bad habits. Unfortunately, when it came to the major issue with Kirsten, my previous choices in the minor issues had set me up for far more struggle and failure than was needed when it came to major battles with self.

Sweating the small stuff

Remember those minor resentments we previously discussed, those that were so easy to dismiss—the stuff many think is so ridiculous to get uptight about? Tom hadn't realized that while he was concerned with major wrongs, he was giving little thought to his minor resentments—those he had so ignored that he barely considered whether they were justified. In the process, he had allowed himself to become habituated to justifying his resentments. After ignoring the small stuff, he was ill prepared to handle the major insults and responded with the familiar *rightness* indignation, desperately clinging to feelings that validated self. He hadn't developed habits of choosing Christ's rightness rather than his own.

We've all heard the expression "Don't sweat the small stuff." This is certainly good advice when it comes to the external stressors that command our attention—stuff that has little ultimate impact on our exchanged life. However, when it comes to our spiritual survival, ignoring the small stuff allows self to gain a foothold in subtle ways that we hardly notice—until we are hit with a major challenge. Unless we are daily dying to self in the small, day-to-day issues, we'll be ill prepared to resist the rising of self in larger battles. And make no mistake, when it comes to self, we are in a never-ending battle.

I recently viewed *Miracle on Ice*—a movie about the 1980 United States Olympic hockey team that defied all the odds and won the gold medal. I remember thinking at the time that they were unbelievably lucky to win against teams that were considered far superior. But after seeing their story, I realized that much more than luck went into their success. The coach studied every detail of every team they would face. He combed through every aspect of each possible recruit for his team, even testing them so he could see their psychological profiles. It had been twenty years since a U.S. hockey team had won an Olympic gold medal. The coach of the 1980 team had tried out for that earlier gold-medal team and had been the last player cut from it. With his 1980 team the overwhelming underdog,

Minor issues pose . . . the greatest opportunity in our exchanged life.

he knew this was the fight of his life—the chance to finally win a gold medal. So he spared nothing as he focused on every issue, major and minor, in preparing to face the battles at the Olympics.

He took a bunch of amateur collegiate players and drilled them, constantly pushing them to the limit and beyond, insisting that they get in the best possible shape, with the highest speed and greatest endurance possible. He constantly focused on the smallest details, knowing that his players could never measure up to the competition in skill and experience. However, by repeatedly sweating the minor issues and challenging his players at every turn, he prepared them to face the major battles that others considered insurmountable. So, they defied all the odds and won.

Minor issues pose the most ominous threat as well as the greatest opportunity in our exchanged life. When we develop habits of overlooking self's rise in minor struggles, we become spiritual lightweights, unable to battle self when challenged with larger concerns. The daily minor concerns we face afford us an endless opportunity to tackle small issues of self. When we deal with them successfully, we become habituated to the dying process, which makes us better equipped to face the major challenges of self.

As our friend Jeannie edited some of the early drafts of this book, she shared with me her experience with battles in her own life. While in the middle of our edit, she e-mailed me, mentioning that her company had just laid her off. Given the instability of our economy, a job loss is naturally a rather overwhelming stressor—especially for someone nearing retirement. Jeannie had been living the exchanged life for several years; still, considering the circumstances, I was surprised to hear that she was taking the whole thing in stride with little concern or stress.

Jeannie explained that she believed sweating the small stuff in her life had enabled her to avoid the usual stress when it came to the big stuff. She had become so habituated to trusting in Jesus while addressing those small challenges to self that when faced with the larger stress, the natural response of Christ in her took over. This left her calm and free of the usual resentment and worry that would normally accompany such a setback.

Recognizing and battling self will always be an ongoing challenge because self has an unending, constantly adapting repertoire of strategies for gaining a foothold. However, every method employed boils down to one core item—the powerhouse of self: our desires. Our selves have an entire range of desires that demand immediate satisfaction. They act as natural antibodies that can quickly overwhelm and reject the transplanted heart of Christ. If His unnatural—supernatural—heart is to remain viable and eventually to be fully assimilated within us, we must gain understanding and control of the desires of self that threaten the exchanged life.

Of all the feelings that drive self, perhaps the most seductive is anger—a feeling that ranges over a broad spectrum from mild irritation to total rage. It is a feeling that pushes self to demand satisfaction just as the gnawing pit in one's stomach demands food. Without vigilance and understanding, we may attempt to satisfy the insatiable appetite of anger and miss out on feeding Christ's heart within us.

Chapter 17

Feeding His Heart

(Clarence)

My dear brothers, take note of this: Everyone should be quick to listen, slow to speak and slow to become angry, for man's anger does not bring about the righteous life that God desires.

—James 1:19, 20, NIV

It was one of those gorgeous mornings in the Northwest when the pristine days of summer more than compensate for our damp, dreary winters. I had just finished some yard work when the phone rang. It was Tom again, this time sounding more sober than usual.

"Well, it's over," he announced. "Kirsten's leaving him."

"You mean, he's leaving her," I corrected, thinking he had misspoken.

"No, she told him she wanted a divorce. Hard to believe, I know. I felt terrible for Jason. He was in tears, saying he begged her to go to couples counseling, but she refused. I know he's hurting. I can't tell him now, but I think he's way better off without her."

"What about the kids?"

"She agreed that he'd have custody. I'm still going to meet with each of them and see if there is any way the marriage can be salvaged. But I'm not very optimistic."

Tom called me the following week, telling me of his meeting with Kirsten. "I had mixed feelings about the visit. Jason said there was no way she was going to change her mind, so I expected the only point of the meeting was for her to give me all the dirt on Jason. I have to admit, Clarence, that before we met, I really felt self rising. I prayed about it."

I said, "I'm not sure I want you to tell me what Kirsten said. Jason's a nice kid, and I don't like hearing bad stuff about people when there's really no point."

"Now you know how I felt," Tom said. "She had warned me that she was really going to give me the lowdown on Jason, so I was prepared for anything. I thought maybe she'd tell me about an affair or maybe that with all his frustration and anger he had hit her. But you wouldn't believe it. Her complaints were that he constantly badgered her about her lies; he refused to trust her; he continually rode her about her weight; and he was constantly talking about the future."

"That's it?"

"That's it," he continued. "Not exactly the stuff of most divorces. She admitted to me that she was negligent with the children during their most vulnerable time of prenatal development, and she granted that Jason would be the primary parent. And here's the good news: Jason is already past the grief. He was really mostly upset about the failure of a marriage that he'd been bound and determined to make succeed. I don't think he was really that upset about losing Kirsten. Now he's totally relieved, looking forward to the nightmare finally ending."

"I'm glad he's handling it so well," I responded.

"Yeah, it's like a huge weight has been lifted. He says that it will be great to stop parenting Kirsten and focus totally on parenting the two kids. I think he's just now realizing how his loyalty to the marriage was blinding him to the cost, especially when it came to the kids."

A seemingly amicable divorce

Tom kept me up to date, telling me of the seemingly amicable do-it-yourself divorce that limited Kirsten's involvement with the children. Understandably, Tom, Kathy, and Jason were concerned that Kirsten's dishonesty would have a destructive impact on Logan and Sally. But she readily acceded to all his requests—until her parents learned of the divorce. They were shocked, initially denying the reality and then angrily blaming Jason for hiding it, though Kirsten had assured him she had kept them fully informed. She denied knowing of the divorce and served him papers charging fraud on his part, claiming she hadn't known what she was signing.

Tom called me, distraught over the turn of events. He complained of the amoral legal system that gives rights to almost all parents regardless of their impairments or what the kids need. He expressed anger over Kirsten's refusal to pay any child support. To top it off, after they agreed to a parenting plan, she once again tried to nullify the divorce, claiming fraud in order to lay claim to their house. For Tom, this was the last straw. The house was actually Kathy and Tom's, purchased with the expectation that Jason and Kirsten would eventually pay them back and take over payments. But it never happened, and neither Jason nor Kirsten could lay any claim to it. Still, her claim that it was community property was costing Tom in legal fees. Talk about adding insult to injury! You can imagine the level of anger and vengeful feelings this elicited. Tom admitted that it was a real struggle to let Christ rather than self rule in all this.

He also had to deal with the matters of reputation and image. Self is all about image and hiding reality. Obviously, avoiding loss of face in this situation was virtually impossible. Kathy and Tom had respected Jason's choices and tried to protect him and themselves by hiding the devastating problems from family and friends. Now they had to inform them of the reality—how they had been duped and had even allowed others to be duped. Talk about embarrassing!

If this wasn't enough to cause self to rise, imagine hearing that either Kirsten or her parents were spreading lies to the effect that the marriage ended because of Jason's affairs, which was painfully ironic, since Kirsten was involved with another man at the time of the breakup. Try to envision teaching your grandchildren about morals and God's plan, only to have their mother tell them that belief in God was foolish and that sleeping with boyfriends they barely knew is OK. Imagine the feelings generated when you hear your seven-year-old grandson, who should be idolizing his parents, describe a minor incident that didn't ring true and then matter-of-factly volunteer, "Mommy lied." While I knew that vengeance belongs to the Lord, I couldn't help wishing that I might hurry His response to Tom and Kathy's pain, which was crying out for justice.

Anger's pleasure

I would like to tell you that the exchanged life freed Tom and Kathy from all resentment. But as I shared in the previous chapter, this was an ongoing struggle.

When we are so wronged, feelings of anger and revenge tend to consume us—at times to the point of obsession. I've felt the pull—that gnawing, unrelenting ache that cries out for satisfaction. The replaying of situations, the conviction about the rightness of our position and how wrongly we have been treated, lure us with an overwhelming temptation to go on a self trip. Then there's the fantasizing about options for exacting some sort of payback, the sweet anticipation of experiencing a release for the building resentment.

Noted writer Fredrick Buechner eloquently described both the pleasure and the implications of this powerful force. "Of the seven deadly sins, anger is possibly the most fun. To lick your wounds, to smack your lips over grievances long past, to roll over your tongue the prospect of bitter confrontations still to come, to savor to the last toothsome morsel both the pain you are given and the pain you are giving back—in many ways it is a feast fit for a king. The chief drawback is that what you are wolfing down is yourself. The skeleton at the feast is you."[1]

> "*Of* the seven deadly sins, anger is possibly the most fun."

Can you think of times in your life when you have been this angry, when your anger consumes you, totally dominating your thinking? In these situations, we truly have become enslaved to the cravings of anger, salivating in anticipation of its satisfaction—feasting on ourselves. I've felt it, and I have also worried about the way it consumed Jason and his parents at times.

Even when we effect some sort of justice or retribution, the resulting satisfaction is temporary at best. Whatever Kirsten might suffer, it can't give back all that she stole from Jason and her children. And even if Tom experienced the smug pleasure of knowing she got hers, the resulting temporary gratification of the insatiable self only empowers it, making its desires ever stronger and more difficult to resist. The brief release he'd gain from anger would ultimately result in increasing enslavement to it. We can't feed Christ's heart when we are dining on the feast of anger.

However, given our addiction to the quick fix and given the way our narcissistic culture constantly feeds and strengthens self, it is hardly surprising that we indulge our anger. We are increasingly intoxicated with individuality and self-expression, which results in self developing a sense of entitlement that refuses to yield or compromise. This is evident in every facet of society. Decades ago, road rage, children assaulting parents, and students plotting to bomb or shoot up schools were unthinkable. Now events of this kind have become so commonplace that we have become inured to what once was shocking.

Steve says that this is evident in his practice too. Over the past twenty-five years, he has seen a dramatic growth in the number of cases involving verbal or physical violence. He observes that patients usually come for treatment because of their emotions, with behavior being the manifestation. No other emotion is more problematic than anger. Have you ever noticed that rather than taking responsibility for it, most individuals with anger issues deny having the problem? They seldom seek treatment for themselves. Those on the receiving end of someone's anger feel far more discomfort than do those who vent the emotion. Steve tells me that when such individuals do present themselves for treatment, it's almost always because the family or the courts are forcing them to get help.

Self seeks to justify anger. It insists on retaining the option of venting hostility. It wants to hang on to this at all cost, making treatment of these individuals extremely difficult and frequently unsuccessful. Solomon described the power of this anger. "An offended brother is more unyielding than a fortified city, / and disputes are like the barred gates of a citadel" (Proverbs 18:19, NIV). The fortress of anger will remain impregnable as long as self is alive.

Anything but a doormat

By now you are probably wondering whether the exchanged life will morph us into doormats who obsequiously try to accommodate any and all people. Nothing could be further from the truth. Those who are doormats may appear extremely pleasant and accommodative on the outside, but inwardly self is stuffing things, and they are letting hidden pain and fear control them. Their fear of rejection prevents them from expressing any disagreement. So, doormat behavior is indicative of a heart still full of fear, the only cure for which is Christ's transplanted heart. And dying to self is hardly for wimps, something Aristotle understood. He observed, "I count him braver who overcomes his desires than him who conquers his enemies; for the hardest victory is over self."[2]

The exchanged life alters our usual responses to anger in ways that vary with the individual. When the resurrection life is flowing freely in us, each of us will die to our unique self, which has learned to cope with life in custom-made, self-centered ways. Passive individuals who have stuffed things will become assertive, saying No and drawing boundaries they never had the strength to do previously. When this happens, those around them, who have grown accustomed to using and abusing them, will jump to the conclusion that these

Christ and His . . . followers were anything but doormats.

passive people are now less loving and giving—less "Christian" in their attitude. In reality, however, with the death of the self that needs to please others, these people have become healthy and strong in the Lord. On the other hand, more aggressive individuals who die to self will surrender their reactive, angry ways and through Christ's strength will become softer and more gracious and loving.

Tom later admitted that he was a self-alive doormat with Kirsten at times. Remember how he was pleasant with her, even as he continued to struggle with his anger? Although he wasn't acting out angrily, he was obviously feeling resentment as self was very much alive. Eventually, he was able to see that this was causing him to reject Christ's heart—a heart that could only be fully retained when self's antibodies of anger were destroyed. When he focused on the cross and died to self, he no longer needed to control external displays of anger because with Christ in him, the anger was gone. When self is dead, its desire for anger is also dead.

It is also clear that Christ and His first followers were anything but doormats. As they uncompromisingly advocated for God, they refused to accede to the powers and conventional wisdom of the time, offending many people in positions of authority. Consequently, Christ and most of His closest companions died as martyrs—hardly the stuff of accommodative doormats! The reality is that when our choices are Christ's choices, we will neither be defensive nor worry about pleasing others. Instead, we will maintain assertive behavior in day-to-day events because Christ's choices are dominant in our lives. If Kirsten had experienced this life, her dishonesty—directed at avoiding responsibility and gaining approval— would have ended. Christ in us will end our worry about how others view us. Our only concern will be how well we represent Him. This is the life we strive for; one that I began to experience firsthand when Dianna and I first embraced the exchanged life. The power of His transforming heart in our lives is evident in the following story.

"Don't forget the casserole dish," Dianna reminded me as I straightened my tie and glanced at my watch while reviewing my responsibilities for church that day. Once again, I was reminded of the fact that as a pastor, my weekends aren't exactly the kicked-back relaxation that most others enjoy. I had to leave the house early to review some details with other people before the service, leaving Dianna to come later. I was already reviewing my lesson plan for our Bible study as I started the car. I became so caught up in my thoughts that I barely remembered the drive as I pulled into the church parking lot.

Grabbing my Bible and lesson materials, I slammed the car door. Suddenly, I stopped, wincing as reality hit. I had forgotten the casserole dish Dianna had prepared for our monthly potluck! Normally, she could have brought it, but she was still recovering from shoulder surgery, and I didn't want her to have to lift things, so I had offered to help by taking the dish. Some help I was!

Until recently, at this point I would have felt a sense of dread combined with defensiveness as I anticipated Dianna's angry, accusatory reaction. And she would have really given it to me, even after I apologized. After all, I had messed up, and her anger was fully justified since she was clearly in the right. But now I remembered the dramatic changes in Dianna. Our lives had been transformed, and I felt a sense of peace, knowing that she wouldn't respond in the old way. I was confident that I could count on her to be loving and gracious. And I was right. When I called her, apologizing for my mistake, she responded calmly, telling me that it was no problem; she already knew I had left the dish and planned on bringing it herself.

Once again, I marveled as I reflected on the dramatic change that had taken place in her life—in our life together. As we learned in our discussion on the exchanged life, this was not Dianna's "fixed-up" self acting in a new way. Self cannot be repaired, remodeled, or fixed, nor does it improve with age. Dianna had taken on a whole new life—the resurrection life of Christ. The radical nature of this change is best understood by looking at how anger became a problem for her.

Learned response

Dianna grew up in a home in which her dad's anger was a pervasive and dominant force. He was a practicing alcoholic until she was twelve years old, and even after he gave up drinking, there was little change in the level of hostility because he became a dry drunk. While his anger was rarely directed at Dianna, the exposure to his constant explosiveness and disrespect toward her mother was extremely intimidating. The pervasive hostility expressed through strings of expletives left the home in a constant state of tension.

Our parents are our teachers, often instructing with their behavior far more than through any verbal input. As Dianna observed her father's anger and profanity over the years, she learned her lessons all too well. She put into practice in our marriage the lessons she had learned growing up, both the good and the bad. While she rarely displayed outright rage or temper tantrums, the underlying pervasive resentment and hostility were still evident. Much to my dismay, she would get irritated over the smallest inconveniences. When she left home and realized that she had forgotten something, she would stew over it. If she had to wait in line at a business longer than she anticipated, she would become irritated and impatient. The level, frequency, and duration of her resentment over these irritations was more than what most would consider reasonable.

God brought resolution to her problem with anger.

Then there were those words that she had repeatedly heard her father say. As both a pastor's wife and a second-grade church school teacher, she could hardly indulge such language. The parents of the children in her classroom would be expecting them to be receiving a Christian education. Imagine what the parents would have said if their children came home spewing expletives that they had learned from their teacher! So she had to be on constant guard against any swearing and had become remarkably adept at controlling her tongue. (Self needs to look good!) But at home, she would occasionally let out some expletive, though by and large, she controlled her language even when we were alone. However, she admitted that the four-letter words reverberated in her mind.

For years, she prayed about this, asking God to remove her anger and sweep the foul language from her mind. But it didn't happen. Yet after we had come to understand the exchanged life, she quickly gained control over this problem. God brought resolution to her problem with anger while it commanded little of her attention.

Dianna and I have concluded that we spend far too much time and effort working on symptoms while ignoring the core disease of our heart. Our approach stands about the same chance of success as would our treating a raging infection with aspirin. Yet I'm sure you've observed Christians, maybe even yourself, trying to succeed in the Christian walk by bandaging flaws while overlooking the real problem.

For decades, Dianna had focused on the symptoms of anger and cursing while failing to address the destructive core that generated these symptoms—self. As long as her natural self was fully alive, it continued to infect every aspect of her life despite her futile and discouraging attempts to control the symptoms it

> *Instead* of working on symptoms, we began addressing the . . . cause.

spawned. However, once she began dying to self, the source of her anger, and gave up on *her* attempts to control her hostility, the symptoms were resolved through Christ's power working in her.

Just as Jeffrey couldn't effect the computer repair until Steve stopped trying to fix things, so Christ could erase Dianna's hostility only when she stopped trying to change herself. The major focus of our spiritual life must be on letting Christ take control as we surrendered self—all of it! Instead of working on symptoms, we began addressing the underlying cause.

With this new understanding, Dianna's prayers changed from "Lord, help me to overcome anger and cursing," to "Lord, take self away. Kill self in me. Show me any self that threatens Your heart in me, that I may surrender my self to You." She was also spending time in Scripture and prayer every day, something she had never been able to do consistently before she understood the exchanged life. Previously, she had found her devotions discouraging. The focus on self—though it was self-improvement that she sought—only strengthened its dominance, even when through her efforts she managed to gain a brief reduction in her symptoms.

In retrospect, she realized that her spiritual life was failing because her self was so alive. Remember Paul's caution in Romans 8:7 that self is hostile to God. Since self is an adversary of God, the last thing it is inclined to do is to spend time developing a relationship with Him that will threaten its existence. Therefore, the self-dominated devotional life becomes a sort of self-improvement meditation, undermining our dependence on Christ's heart in us. Given this reality, it's rather absurd to think that such devotions will enhance our spiritual life. Since genuine daily devotions are about dying to self, naturally, self will do everything possible to block them. Self's attempt at daily devotions will be directed at enhancing its image—behavior that directly negates the life we purport to seek. Talk about internal dissonance! No wonder Christians in whom self is alive are so miserable!

Pharisaical legalism

Previously, Dianna engaged in the hopeless endeavor of attempting to overlay a spiritual life on an alive self. This is the central problem of the legalism that Christ decried in the Pharisees. " 'You hypocrites! You are like whitewashed tombs, which look fine on the outside but are full of bones and decaying corpses on the inside. In the same way, on the outside you appear good to everybody, but inside you are full of hypocrisy and sins' " (Matthew 23:27, 28, TEV).

If this sounds strangely familiar to you, it should. This is the cover-up we addressed when we first discussed the problem of self having the appearance of godliness while lacking its power. Christ's words are rather harsh, and few of us would consider that they might apply to us. Yet, unfortunately, to the extent that self is alive, they fully apply. Although most of us aren't religious leaders, when self is alive, we engage in the same hypocrisy. We claim allegiance to Christ's heart in us, but it's only a cover for the fully alive self, which assures rejection of this new life. We claim trust in Jesus while hypocritically holding a secret allegiance to self.

C. S. Lewis starkly lays out the reality of our need.

> The Christian way is different: harder, and easier. Christ says . . . "I have not come to torment your natural self, but to kill it. No half-measures are

any good. I don't want to cut off a branch here and a branch there, I want to have the whole tree down. . . . Hand over the whole natural self, all the desires which you think innocent as well as the ones you think wicked— the whole outfit. I will give you a new self instead. In fact, I will give you Myself: my own will shall become yours."[3]

When Dianna's and my study convicted us that our spiritual endeavor was futile while self was alive, our devotional life changed dramatically. As Dianna became devoted to dying to self, Christ's life in her was able to carry the day—every day. Christ's heart in her so destroyed her self that she rarely experienced the resentful and hostile moments that previously had pervaded her life on a daily basis. And those pesky words no longer kept popping into her mind. This was amazing, given all the times she had tried before to terminate them and had failed. It was one thing for her to bite her lip and keep the words from coming out, but it was quite another matter to no longer even *think* the words!

However, this is actually the expected response when self is dead. We somewhat facetiously say that a corpse doesn't feel. The corollary is that if our self feels, we can rest assured that it isn't dead. Not only will a corpse not swear, but it won't even think those curse words. When self was dead, it was no longer feasting and thriving on anger. The challenge is that self is actually a corpse that keeps threatening to come to life over and over again.

Dianna had always longed to practice the life Paul advocated in his letter to the Ephesians. He wrote, "Get rid of all bitterness, passion, and anger. No more shouting or insults, no more hateful feelings of any sort. Instead, be kind and tenderhearted to one another, and forgive one another, as God has forgiven you through Christ" (Ephesians 4:31, 32, TEV). Now, with no effort on her part other than the enormous commitment to be crucified with Christ, she had undergone such a transformation that it was as though the anger and language issues had never existed.

Soon after Christ's triumph over her anger, Dianna was conversing with a friend who expressed frustration concerning her continual irritation over the smallest things. Given her own history, Dianna immediately identified with her and was about to share that she had the same problem—until she suddenly realized that this was no longer true. As she listened while her friend described to a *T* exactly what her life had been like for decades, Dianna realized with a sense of relief that virtually all of it was gone. When she returned home, she excitedly told me about the conversation and her awareness of God's transforming power in her life.

As I listened to Dianna, I was reminded of my sermon for the coming Sabbath. The timing was perfect, as I had been preaching a series on the book of James and was about to discuss verses 19 and 20 of chapter 1: "My dear brothers, take note of this: Everyone should be quick to listen, slow to speak and slow to become angry, for man's anger does not bring about the righteous life that God desires" (NIV).

I told Dianna I was going to be preaching on anger and suggested that her testimony would really enhance the message. My suggestion was more an idle musing than a proposal; I knew she would turn me down. Other than talking in front of a class of second-graders, she was adamantly opposed to doing any public speaking. So when she responded by asking what I would like her to say, I was dumbfounded! Since that time, Dianna has joined me in presenting the concept of dying to self to many audiences across the country as well as on the DVD—further evidence of the transformation in her life.

Dianna's experience demonstrates the reality of the change that Christ in us will effect. As we adopt His heart, our thoughts, feelings, desires, and motivations will become compatible with His. Then we will lose our appetite for the feast of anger, as the self that promotes this craving is dead.

However, there are other symptoms that require our vigilance. In order to keep Christ in us, we must understand them and surrender to Him again when we see these signs that self is alive.

Chapter 18

Monitoring His Heart

(Steve)

Above all else, guard your heart,
for it is the wellspring of life.

—*Proverbs 4:23, NIV*

"Uh . . . Uh . . . I—I'm sick!" Dee Dee cried, waking me from a dead sleep. "Uh . . . going to pass out!" she gasped, almost incoherent.

As I dashed to her side of the bed, I heard the thud of the dialysis machine shutting down, followed by the repetitive beeping of the alarm. I had heard Dee Dee moan like this before. It usually meant her blood pressure was low. I released the IV to pour in fluid, and then I touched the automatic blood pressure on the screen and waited for a reading. When I flipped on the light, my suspicions were confirmed. Dee Dee had passed out, the color drained from her ashen face. I caressed her forehead, noting that her skin was cool and clammy. I felt her fistula, but there was no palpable pulse. She was in shock. I was suddenly gripped with fear, my heart pounding as the adrenaline kicked in, driving out any lingering drowsiness.

The alarm rang again, this time signaling her low blood pressure. I stared at the screen, hardly believing the reading. Her systolic (the high reading) was forty-seven, and the diastolic didn't even register! I waited and watched for what seemed like hours. In reality, it was only one to two minutes before she came around.

"What happened? I was so sick," she mumbled. "Better now."

"You're OK now," I reassured, caressing her face as I breathed a sigh of relief.

But what happened? I wondered. Dee Dee rarely had a problem with blood pressure during her dialysis and had never bottomed out like this. Maybe I'd miscalculated the fluid to be taken off. Or maybe I'd entered the wrong number into the machine. But the screen showed only a pint of fluid had been removed—about a third of what was usually taken off during her overnight dialysis. The IV bag was almost empty now, and her blood pressure had risen to 85/58. Still, nothing made sense. She had to be losing fluid somewhere.

I checked the fistula, ensuring that she wasn't bleeding around the needles, and turned back to the machine. Suddenly, I saw it—a plastic filter spattered with blood. As my eyes turned down, I gasped in horror. There was a huge pool of blood on the floor, already dark purple and gelled from clotting. *How in the world?* Nothing made sense—until I followed the trail of blood. The life-sustaining fluid was seeping one drop at a time from the top of the filter, where the IV tubing was connected. I was horrified to realize that when I screwed the plastic connector on, it hadn't threaded properly and so it hadn't sealed. During the previous two hours on dialysis, the faulty seal had allowed well over a pint of blood to drip slowly to the floor. Dee Dee had lost more than 25 percent of her blood volume and could have died—all due to my negligence!

After an hour of cleaning up the mess, I was back in bed. It was 3:00 A.M., but I remained wide awake, still anxious because of the close call. I had been made acutely aware of how quickly something could go wrong. Unfortunately, after providing more than one thousand treatments entailing some six thousand hours over the years, I had come to view dialysis as routine and commonplace. It was a perspective that left me dangerously oblivious to the potential complications. As I prayed about it, I realized this minicrisis had implications for my exchanged life as well.

Symptoms of self

After experiencing the initial joy and freedom of our life in Christ, we often settle into a routine complacency, leaving us oblivious to the dangers that threaten our new life. But neglecting to attend to the details necessary to maintain Christ in us can spell disaster. The setup for Dee Dee's dialysis had become so routine that I gave it little thought, failing to check the connections carefully as I performed on automatic pilot the tasks I had done a thousand times before. My oblivious attitude resulted in negligence that imperiled Dee Dee's life. By the same token, we risk Christ's life in us when we become too complacent, assume nothing can interfere, and fail to ensure daily that our connection with Him is solid. Dee Dee's crisis reminded me of the importance of majoring in minors in my dialysis treatments, and, more importantly, in our exchanged life.

Providing Dee Dee with appropriate dialysis depends on continuous monitoring of her symptoms. If I hadn't been acutely aware of the symptoms of low blood pressure, I wouldn't have opened her IV to give her fluids, which saved precious moments that would have been lost if I would have had to take the time to measure her blood pressure first.

Maintaining the health of our exchanged life also requires frequent monitoring of symptoms—the symptoms that indicate self is alive. Recognizing the presence of this dominant force is very challenging as self is often a master at disguising its true nature and desires—not that we must then overcome it through our own efforts, but

> *Self* is often a master at disguising its true nature and desires.

that we will surrender it, ensuring that it doesn't overcome and begin rejecting Christ's transplanted heart in us.

In medicine, we don't track temperature simply to normalize it. When, on one occasion, Dee Dee ran a high fever accompanied by chills, I knew it meant trouble. I didn't just give her Tylenol to suppress the fever. Instead, I immediately took her to the hospital. I was told that further delay would likely have taken her life as the massive infection in her blood would have overwhelmed her immune system. An attempt to suppress her symptoms would have done nothing to quell the underlying disease that threatened her life. So, we track temperature and other symptoms because they serve as a barometer of underlying problems, such as infection. Similarly, we monitor our spiritual symptoms—our thoughts, motivations, behavior, and desires—not simply to control them but to gauge whether an underlying problem with self is developing, which can threaten Christ's life in us.

Early in the process, I was hung up on attempting to evaluate how I was doing by focusing on symptoms rather than on Christ in me. "Parts of your message give a wonderful hope, but other parts seem rather discouraging," I observed after hearing Clarence's presentation.

"That's true," he agreed. "Self's drive to rise to life again is often so powerful that people tend to feel disheartened. But by focusing on Jesus and trusting His power, we can avoid this pitfall. Discouragement and guilt usually indicate that self is rising. Often, we reach for the controls, attempting to take over the work that is His. Then we feel overwhelmed as we attempt the impossible task of dying to self."

"Well, it's not just feeling down about self rising. It's also about feeling that avoiding the desires of self means renouncing all pleasure."

"Yeah, that's a common distortion of this message, the notion that God calls us to a life without pleasure, one in which any gratification from a physical, emotional, or mental pursuit that isn't focused on Christ is self-based and wrong. However, Christ's life is not about perfecting an existence that denies people the normal pleasures of our physical world. Pursuing that kind of life can actually threaten His heart in us."

"So the exchanged life shouldn't be equated with the denial of pleasure?"

"Definitely not. But with Christ in us, we will no longer be drawn to the desires of self."

"How do we know whether our desires are self-based?"

"Your question takes us back to the *R* in TRUST, recognizing the sin of self rising to life. Both the Bible and Christ in us will help us see it. Let me give you an example from my life. Remember the cruise we took to Alaska?"

"Yeah, you guys had a great time."

"Well, while we were docked in port, I had an interesting experience. Dianna and I were out on deck, enjoying the gorgeous panoramic view of the stunning mountains, lakes, and forested hills and feeling overwhelmed with the beauty and grandeur of it all. An immense sense of gratitude welled up within me as I observed God's creation. Then I happened to look over the stern of the ship and saw another thing of beauty—a yacht. This wasn't just any yacht. It was huge and fully equipped; it carried a helicopter, sailboat, ski boat—the works!"

"Impressive," I observed.

"No kidding. The owner was none other than Microsoft cofounder Paul Allen. One moment I was looking at the beauty of God's creation, and the next I was seeing that magnificent yacht. But the yacht brought me a totally different feeling. It never occurred to me that I should *possess* the beautiful landscape, but when self rose within me, I longed to own that boat!"

"Yeah, sounds like some boat! But that's never been much of a temptation for me."

"Well, you were probably too young to remember it much, but I spent a lot of time on Dad's yacht, so yachts have a real draw for me, though I could never hope to afford even a small one.

"But the point is that I realized the difference between God-generated and self-generated pleasure. One brought the grateful feeling that comes from enjoying the pleasures of God's creation. That's very different from the second feeling I experienced—the urge to possess earthly objects and to find in them a sense of happiness and fulfillment. That feeling is all too transient, and when it wanes, we long to possess more, starting a cycle of pleasure seeking that never provides permanent fulfillment."

"That makes sense. But it still seems like one could get confused over interests of self versus God."

"Not if we're clear on recognizing self."

Vetting self

"What do you mean by *self*?" I asked Clarence soon after viewing his DVD.

"If you have to ask, you can rest assured that self is alive and well," he responded. "But seriously, I have to admit it's a concept that is experienced and felt more than it is dissected and parsed into an encyclopedic explanation."

"Come on! Isn't that kind of a cop-out?" I said, thinking of my miserable attempt to explain this concept to my daughter Jaclyn.

"OK. If I you want a working definition, I'd define self as any aspect of myself that interferes with Christ effecting His desires, motivations, and priorities in me. And unfortunately, I'd have to say that these interfering aspects include a lot of me."

"So the main goal is to have who I am be wiped out."

"No, the goal is to have Christ in us, which is not the same as wiping out self. If we are simply trying to erase self, we run the danger of equating this with erasing our identity, which can turn into a trip of self dying to self, ultimately subtly *raising* self."

"Still, aren't you kind of making the case that we need to become robotic automatons for Christ?" I countered.

"No, that bears no resemblance to the exchanged life. The intent is not that we turn into identical, selfless robots with no mind or identity of our own. If we merely work on becoming selfless, we've lost the battle; we'll empower self in the attempt."

"What do you mean?" I asked with growing confusion. "If I could successfully repress self and all its desires, I'd certainly be a much better person, and I'd feel pretty good about myself."

"Exactly. That's my point. If you did that, you'd have raised self to a whole new level, making you confident in your ability rather than moving you to depend on Christ in you."

"Wow, you're right," I conceded. "I guess I keep slipping into the trap of seeing this as *my* job and judging *my* efforts."

"You're not alone. We all struggle with trusting Christ to do the work, with turning it completely over to Him. That's the essential daily task—relinquishing self, including its efforts to die, so Christ can do the work."

"And when we let Him do this, what becomes of our identity and our desires? Who do we become?"

"We become what the Bible promises—adopted sons and daughters of God, each with our own identity. Do children lose their identity when people adopt them?"

"Of course not."

"It's no different with our adoption. Adoptees identify with parents who have different values and beliefs than their biological parents. Christ has no desire to erase our identity, only to replace self and its destructive desires so He can become the sole avenue through which we attain our full potential. Though we lose the desires of self, we retain those desires that are compatible with His life in us."

"So we still need to be focused on ridding ourselves of the desires of self?"

"Yes and no. We want to be rid of them, but we also have to remember that this is Christ's work, not ours. There is always the danger that we'll be distracted by the symptoms of self and consequently miss the goal of Christ in us as we become caught up in either judging or justifying our selves."

"Yeah. I find it hard to avoid the temptation to evaluate how I'm doing."

"That's the problem. Whenever we see self rising to life in us, we're tempted either to rationalize its rise or to erase it—something we can't do. If we are working on erasing such desires of self, as opposed to allowing Christ to do it, we're likely on a self trip."

"So if we can't do anything about our desires, why even bother to discuss them? It's not exactly a pleasant discussion. Why focus attention on these desires when doing so makes us feel guilty about something we can't do anything about anyway?"

"Because of our ultimate goal—living the exchanged life. It's not because I want a self-generated triumph over self that I'm concerned about my desires. Rather, my concern is with gaining the freedom that comes with Christ being the driving force of my life, a freedom that is threatened when the desires of self dominate. To keep Christ's transplanted heart, I want to know everything I can about the antibodies of self that threaten it."

Desires

As seductive as satisfying self's desires can be, we know both from experience and from what we are told in Scripture that attempting to do so is futile, because self is insatiable. Indulging these feelings only fuels the fires of self, which will ultimately lead to our defeat. The wisest man on earth gave a warning that is appropriate here. He said, "There is a way that seems right to a man, / but in the end it leads to death" (Proverbs 14:12, NIV). He wasn't referring merely to our physical death. That certainly isn't the primary concern of Scripture. He was referring to spiritual death, which we have learned results when we allow self to live. True life can never come from trusting in self. Solomon told us where to put our trust:

Trust in the LORD with all your heart
    and lean not on your own understanding;

in all your ways acknowledge him,
and he will make your paths straight (Proverbs 3:5, 6, NIV).

Paul agreed that self is hopeless and concurred that we should allow our new life in Christ to push aside self's desires. He told the Ephesians, "Get rid of your old self, which made you live as you used to—the old self that was being destroyed by its deceitful desires. Your hearts and minds must be made completely new, and you must put on the new self, which is created in God's likeness and reveals itself in the true life that is upright and holy" (Ephesians 4:22–24, TEV).

Our physical death . . . certainly isn't the primary concern of Scripture.

As usual, my discussion with Clarence regarding desires generated more questions. Given that self is such a big part of our lives and that its desires dominate us, I wondered whether the exchanged life would ultimately lead to an absence of feelings and desires outside of those we have for Christ. This notion struck me as suggesting a rather austere existence. Then Clarence referred me to a scripture that portrays a far more vibrant life than some might imagine. In the following passage, Paul clearly laid out the contrast between the self-dominated life and the exchanged life in which Christ is living in us:

I tell you: Live by following the Spirit. Then you will not do what your sinful selves want. Our sinful selves want what is against the Spirit, and the Spirit wants what is against our sinful selves. The two are against each other, so you cannot do just what you please. . . . But if the Spirit is leading you, you are not under the law. . . .

But the Spirit produces the fruit of love, joy, peace, patience, kindness, goodness, faithfulness, gentleness, self-control. There is no law that says these things are wrong. Those who belong to Christ Jesus have crucified their own sinful selves. They have given up their old selfish feelings and the evil things they wanted to do. We get our new life from the Spirit, so we should follow the Spirit (Galatians 5:16–25, NCV).

"But aren't those feelings supposed to be focused only on Christ?" I asked Clarence.

"Of course not; it doesn't say that."

"So it's acceptable to fulfill some desires in this world, even while we're living the exchanged life?"

"I should hope so. After all, we can't spend every spare moment in a monastic existence in which we focus only on our spirituality."

"Yeah, that would be pretty radical. But I thought that was kind of the idea—to live focused solely on Christ as a way to guard against the world's temptations, so self can't get a foothold."

Clarence laughed. Then he said, "That certainly doesn't sound like much fun, and I don't think that's what the Bible teaches, though some Christians have taken that view. It was a much more popular notion a century ago, when puritanical practices tended to dominate."

"But wouldn't some people argue that Christians behaved much better back then?"

"Maybe. But remember: the exchanged life isn't about behavior; it's about the heart. Denial of life's normal pleasures is likely to raise self to a whole new level."

"How?"

"Well, living a stoic life isn't Christ's plan. In fact, doing so is necessarily self-driven. So the attempt inevitably leads to the empowerment of self. When we succeed at denying ourselves pleasures, we reduce our sense of helplessness and our dependence on Christ's heart in us. In addition, refusal to experience normal life weakens our resistance to self as we are denied opportunities to challenge self in the day-to-day pleasure and pain that we normally encounter. The dominance of self is weakened when we can experience pleasure while simultaneously making Christ in us our number one priority. His presence prevents any legitimate pleasure or pursuit from becoming a self-driven obsession."

"That makes sense," I responded. "It's kind of like attempting to preserve our health by avoiding any activity that would risk physical injury and insisting on isolation to avoid exposure to infection. Without the exercise, our muscles would weaken, and without exposure to pathogens in the outside world, our immunity would be limited and would leave us vulnerable to overwhelming infection."

"Exactly! In living the exchanged life, our essential task is to engage fully in life, which opens opportunities for strengthening Christ's heart in us. The issue isn't really about the nature of the desires or pleasures. The bottom line is, How does a particular pursuit or pleasure affect Christ's heart in us?"

"OK, theoretically that sounds nice. But let's get practical and specific," I said, pushing the argument. "What pleasures are we talking about here?"

"Most of the things we enjoy, like eating, playing games, sightseeing, hobbies, or just visiting friends."

"And watching football?" I asked hopefully.

"Sure, though that depends on your perspective."

"Meaning?"

"Meaning that watching football is right or wrong based on what it does to us—or more correctly, what it does to Christ's heart in us. Does watching football cause self to rise and threaten His heart in us? Obviously, the answer will depend on our response when our team loses."

"Yeah, that says it all," I said, laughing.

"That's also a good criterion for other pursuits. All these activities are the stuff of our lives, which involves far more than sitting around praying and waiting for the Lord's coming. Enjoyable pursuits are not only permitted to those living the exchanged life, they are an essential part of it. We must engage in the real world with its pleasure as well as its pain in order to give Christ the opportunity to perfect the fruits of the Spirit in us."

Matters of the heart

Desires and the pleasure gained from fulfilling them are not intrinsically wrong—or right, for that matter. Their power for good or evil is based on what they do to our heart—more importantly, to Christ's heart in us. This in turn depends on the level of emotional investment and priority we give these desires. The secular pleasures discussed here can threaten to make self rise only when we give them a higher priority than living the exchanged life.

Notice that the fruits of the Spirit aren't actions—observable bad or good deeds. They are the character traits and feelings that underlie our actions. We aren't judged to be bad or good based on our external behavior but rather on what is in our hearts. The fruits are all about the heart—Christ's heart in us. So they provide a far more honest assessment of our character than do mere externals, which all too often are our primary focus. When we accept Christ's heart, He will create His feelings and desires in us while we engage in the daily activities of this world.

When a given desire, no matter how noble, becomes a passion over and above all others, it will resurrect the self, threatening our life in Christ. The solution to the futility of worshiping our desires is adopting the exchanged life. This will lead to a diminished need for satisfaction in the short term as we keep our eyes on the goal: Christ in us. It is a vision that is our prime source of satisfaction, in the here and now as well as for eternity.

To ensure that we are continuing to be rid of the old self every day, it is important that we recognize the desires that indicate its status. We must monitor the vital signs of our exchanged life. Symptoms that reveal that self is alive are portrayed throughout the Bible, including in the following passage:

> The wrong things the sinful self does are clear: being sexually unfaithful, not being pure, taking part in sexual sins, worshiping gods, doing witchcraft, hating, making trouble, being jealous, being angry, being selfish, making people angry with each other, causing divisions among people, feeling envy, being drunk, having wild and wasteful parties, and doing other things like these. I warn you now as I warned you before: Those who do these things will not inherit God's kingdom (Galatians 5:19–21, NCV).

When we are driven by self, we will lose out but not simply because of our evil works. Rather, our defeat will be due to the absence of Christ's saving heart, rejected by self and its evil desires. The works provide evidence that we don't have Christ's heart.

Self-based desires remain ongoing threats to our exchanged life. However, as Christ's understanding becomes our understanding, we will become increasingly aware of the dangers we will encounter. God created in us the ability to experience desire and pleasure. The question is what will we yearn for? Will we long to fulfill the insatiable needs of self, or will we have a passion for His heart?

Chapter 19

Passion for His Heart

(Steve)

Temptation comes from the lure of our own evil desires. These evil desires lead to evil actions, and evil actions lead to death.

—James 1:14, 15, NLT

I glanced out the window of our newly remodeled in-home office, taking in the beauty of our surroundings while I waited for my first patient. My eyes traveled from the lush green foliage that surrounded the hundreds of rooftops below to the glistening waters of Puget Sound, which contrasted with the dark, forested hills beyond as they merged with the snowcapped Olympic peaks, which were outlined dramatically against a cloudless blue sky. It was indeed a stunning view. But the beauty was quickly lost on me as I glanced down at the appointment book.

"Honey, we still have a couple openings for next Friday," I reminded Dee Dee, who was my receptionist and office manager. (This was years before she became ill.)

"Will you just relax?" she responded with irritation. "It always fills in. Besides, if it doesn't, you could certainly use the break."

Dee Dee was sweet, but she just didn't understand what it took to have a successful private practice. We needed to fill every slot in order to generate income for the good life I planned for us. I had recently left the military, and after a slow start, the practice was finally filling up. But no matter how busy I was, I continued to worry about whether the schedule would stay full.

"It's hard to fill the eight o'clock slots," Dee Dee observed. "No one wants to come in that early."

"Well, don't turn them down," I cautioned. "You can offer them an evening slot once in a while."

"Come on," she objected. "You can't start cutting into our time that way. We don't need the money that badly."

"But we can't count on things going this well all the time," I countered. "We need a cushion. What if business suddenly slows?"

"That's not going to happen," Dee Dee said, revealing far more confidence than I felt. "You have me filling every possible slot. You're seeing patients ten hours straight, without a break even for lunch. When are you going to stop worrying? You're being ridiculous!"

Dee Dee was right, but it would be years before I admitted it. No matter how well the practice went, I was obsessed with the possibility that it might fail. For the first five years, we never took off more than three days; it cost too much in lost income. My outlook was indeed a pathetic reflection of my insecurity and hang-ups about money. (Of course, this was prior to our adopting the exchanged life.) No matter how full the practice was, I always thought it might not continue and was obsessed with adding more patients to generate more income. Enough was never enough. *If God is not our passion, our passion is our god.*

Obsession with money doesn't end when our income increases. There's always the debate on what to do with it. I've enjoyed learning about various investments, particularly when I was into the good life. But I never really did much with this knowledge, learning just enough to know how easy it is to lose money. Clarence, however, often engaged in various moneymaking schemes. He was once in the business of renting out a motor home. Then there was a currency exchange program that guaranteed a 20 percent annual return, and a vending machine business that left him with a garage full of vending machines. He lost money on almost all his ventures; but I had to hand it to him, in his early years, he was always ready to take a risk. For him, as for most in our family, money represented security, and he was always focused on how to make a buck. *If God is not our passion, our passion is our god.*

I've always had a passion for music education, and with our encouragement (actually, we gave them no choice), all five of our children took up stringed instruments. Our oldest, Justin, was the most serious student, eventually performing at Carnegie Hall with the Tacoma Youth Symphony. He even considered making violin performance a profession. As he spoke with other musicians, he learned that most who succeed do so based far more on perspiration than inspiration, practicing countless hours daily. Indeed, practice must be the total focus of their lives. *If God is not our passion, our passion is our god.*

All [our pursuits] have the potential to sabotage our exchanged life.

For years, Dee Dee has had a passion for her *Peanuts* collection. She began it when she was ten years old. For a time, it wasn't just a hobby—it was a major focus in her life. She corresponded with and eventually met Charles Schulz, and continues to correspond occasionally with his widow. She probably has almost every book Schulz wrote, including books in Braille, Hebrew, German, and other languages. Her collection includes hundreds of figurines, music boxes, and other memorabilia. *If God is not our passion, our passion is our god.*

As I write the last part of this book, I am acutely aware of the looming deadline for sending it to the publisher. For several weeks, I've spent every spare moment working on it, rewriting the material Clarence sends for his chapters as well as writing and revising my own chapters. I e-mail myself sections of the book so that if I have a spare minute at work, I can make further reviews and revisions. It has been an all-consuming endeavor. *If God is not our passion, our passion is our god.*

Did you notice any similarities in the foregoing vignettes? Most would say that none of these passions and pursuits are really bad. Who can fault me for wanting to have a successful practice? And who can blame Clarence for wanting to supplement his modest salary as a pastor? It wasn't like he was some high stakes gambler in Vegas. Justin's passion for music is certainly something to be admired, given the less-than-noble passions of the majority of today's teens. And certainly Dee Dee's choice to celebrate the wonderful creation of Charles Schulz with a collection seems like an innocuous endeavor. Then there's my passion for writing—who could possibly fault me for assisting Clarence in putting his message on the exchanged life into written form? Yet while none of these pursuits is intrinsically wrong and some would be considered laudable, they all have the potential to sabotage our exchanged life. *If God is not our passion, our passion is our god.*

Do our passions stem from self or from our exchanged life in Christ? While we often focus on symptoms—the external manifestations, what we do rather than why we do it—the crux of our concern must be about our core desires and whether they are compatible with a passion for His heart.

Evil desires, evil actions

"How do I know which of my desires and pleasures are self based?" I asked Clarence during one of our discussions.

"God is very clear on this. Remember the text I referenced?"

"You mean the one from James about evil desires leading to evil actions?"

"Yes. You'll notice that he doesn't talk about all desires, just the evil ones. The preceding two words in the text make clear which desires are the evil ones, 'our own.' Several translations even leave out the word *evil,* since 'our own' clarifies what desires are being addressed here. When a desire is about satisfying self, the sinful self Paul wrote about, it is inevitably evil because the living self threatens Christ's heart in us.

"Remember, we focus on the symptoms of self only so that we can see what place we're giving to Christ in us. Looking at the symptoms from the standpoint of determining how we are doing will be our downfall."

"But I really want to know that I'm doing OK," I objected.

"You aren't doing OK—not with that kind of thinking. We become OK through Christ's presence and work in us. But self threatens His presence in us when we allow it to rise to life through thoughts about how *we're* doing rather than how *He's* doing in us."

"I guess you're right, but it leaves me feeling rather insecure about my salvation."

"Good! It should," Clarence shot back.

"It should?" I was really feeling confused.

"Yes, we should always feel extremely insecure when we start thinking of salvation as ours to earn rather than Christ's to give. Beyond acceptance of His heart, we can't do anything about it. In fact, the more we try, the more we'll be defeated. The notion that if we're good enough, we'll be rewarded with eternal life, is what Jesus condemned in the church leaders of His time. When we begin thinking we can do something that will help us gain salvation, we're likely to lose out because thinking like that raises self to life. There's nothing we can do to make ourselves deserving. We don't deserve salvation, and if there was any way for us to earn it, Christ wouldn't have had to come here and die for us."

"So no matter how despicable my behavior, I can be saved?"

"Absolutely! The thief on the cross certainly hadn't done anything to deserve salvation. He simply trusted Jesus and His saving power."

"I'm beginning to get it. It's all about trusting Jesus, which will have us give up on self and its ability to save."

"Yes. That will allow Christ to take over, which will improve our character and behavior. But we are saved because of His gift of salvation; the improved behavior is just an automatic by-product of His working in us. So, we do watch for the symptoms of self, but not because they determine whether or not God judges us as deserving of salvation. They don't, and we're never deserving. Instead, we watch for these symptoms to ensure that they don't threaten the primary purpose and joy in our life—Christ in us!"

Threats to His heart in us

As I reflected further on our conversation, I realized that many aspects of self could interfere with my passion for Christ more subtly than do the classic sins. Self is a master at interpreting life in such a way as to see evil as applying to others—not me! We find it easy to focus on the more blatant aspects of those sins—things that don't apply to us, allowing us to dismiss them. However, by ignoring the less obvious aspects of these sins, we may empower self in entirely new ways that will imperil our exchanged life.

The sin of gluttony is usually thought of as referring to overeating. That aspect of this sin is blatantly obvious in society today: in the United States, the incidence of obesity has tripled during the past decade. But while many of us may feel smug satisfaction because we're not among the majority who are overweight, we can still be indulging the desires of self in our eating habits. Indeed, considering Christ's reaction to the pollution of the temple in Jerusalem, I wonder what He must think of the way we treat the temple He has given us when we indulge frequently in fast food, dine out often, and wastefully consume calories that have little nutritional value.

When people give the appetites of self full rein, devastating consequences follow. Most of our illnesses and the resultant astronomical health care costs are directly related to poor personal health habits that are driven by self's desires. However, even more important than the damage we do to our physical health when we pollute God's precious creation is the impact on our spiritual health. Indulgence of these desires empowers self, threatening to substitute a passion for food for a passion for Christ. God wants us to enjoy the food He has given us, but do we eat to live or live to eat?

One of my Christian patients prided herself on living a healthy lifestyle. She was a vegan, worked out two hours daily to maintain a well-toned body, and attended a yoga class twice a week. In addition, she took a host of vitamins and dietary supplements. I used to envy that kind of discipline. However, when I consider from the perspective of the exchanged life the time and money she spent on gourmet health foods, the yoga class and health club, and all the supplements, I have my questions. When we spend a great deal of time and money in order to maintain a healthy lifestyle, I wonder whether we're caring for a body that is the temple of self rather than a temple of God.

How often have you, like me, referred to "my time"?

Time is another precious resource that God has entrusted to us. How often have you, like me, referred to "my time"? Narcissistic entitlement thinking often influences how we think of time. While most of us believe that we are extremely busy, the facts indicate that modern conveniences have freed up enormous amounts of time that we can use in service either to God or to self. How much of our time do we devote to pleasuring self with TV, movies, surfing the Web, visiting or texting on the cell phone, etc.? Remember, idle hands are the devil's workshop. Observing the way we spend our free time will give us an important reality check on the status of Christ's heart in us and whether He is truly our passion.

When enough is never enough

Years ago, an anonymous quote in a newspaper impressed me: "Why is it that we judge others by how much they give, whereas we judge ourselves by how much we have?" With some discomfort, I realized that this was certainly true of me. Envy is a rather strange phenomenon—wanting what someone else has when we are blessed with so much. But then we've already learned that self is never satisfied no matter how much we have. As Clarence noted earlier in this book, there's a difference between desiring and experiencing pleasure from the beauty that God provides on one hand, and desiring to possess things on the other.

All too often, my possessions have owned me. I recall recently needing—well, more precisely, wanting—a video camera for my son's wedding. When I shopped for it, I was overwhelmed with all the options available. What was supposed to be a simple task became daunting as I debated brands, prices, formats, and fancy options, most of which I would never use. Deciding on the camera took an inordinate amount of time because I wanted to be sure I got the best deal.

The experience made me even more aware of our consumer mentality. Greed and envy have promoted continuous longing and dissatisfaction—driving mindless, selfish, and unending procurement of more and more material possessions. Never in history have we had and wanted so much that we don't need. This mentality feeds and empowers self. It insidiously invades every aspect of our lives—lives of plenty with a plethora of choices. If you're like me, your house contains packages of things you've never opened—those things we buy because the deal was just too good to pass up and we're bound to need the item someday, only someday never comes.

As I watch the media, I realize that the messages they convey threaten my passion for Christ. Daily they tell me "you deserve it," "you don't have to wait," "you're worth it," "life is short and you only live once," meaning "get everything you can for yourself while the getting's good." We're told to make our needs, our desires, and our experiences number one. And sometimes it's a matter of making our "Christian" needs, desires, and experiences our first priority. Our consumer society entices self, suggesting that a given product is something we *must* have to make us feel better, look better, save time, save money, live longer, etc. Even though we know that most of these sales pitches are lies, we fear that we'll miss an important opportunity—it may be our one chance for more than a temporary solace or illusory solution.

Then there's the overwhelming consumer debt that many can never hope to repay as they borrow to satisfy wants that are increasingly defined as needs. Many people choose to rent a lifestyle and are left in a lifetime of bondage to things. "The borrower is the slave of the lender" (Proverbs 22:7, NRSV). Tragically, this enslavement to things will continually empower self, threatening to reject Christ's heart.

The increase in creature comforts and immediate gratification that has occurred in my short lifetime is unbelievable. Like me, you probably find it difficult to imagine life without a TV, DVD player, cell phone, computer, microwave, and MP3 player or iPod, though I've somehow managed to survive without these last two. Life has become increasingly immediate as communication that used to take days through mailed correspondence is now done instantaneously by phone or e-mail. Even this book would have taken countless more hours to write without the wonders of computer word processing. While there is much to celebrate about modern-day life, it does reduce our feelings of need and dependency. The inevitable danger is that the increasingly satisfied self will be strengthened, threatening our passion for Christ's heart.

As professed followers of Christ, we are hardly immune to the temptation of greed and envy that threatens Christ in us. As a youth and a rather immature Christian, I tended to see God as an all-powerful genie who occasionally and somewhat capriciously granted wishes—more often if you were following His teachings. I didn't develop that idea by myself. I learned about it from Christians who "testified" about how God answered their prayers.

Nowadays, in our well-heeled Western society, we even hear the needs of the self championed from some pulpits. Sermons suggest that God will give us what we want, that material success is a sign of His work in our lives. It strikes me as the height of arrogance to suggest that our lives of plenty are somehow the result of God's blessing when millions of dedicated Christians in the third world are living in abject poverty.

The issue of wants versus needs is put into perspective when Christ in us looks at the least of these. As I write, the catastrophic loss of life from a cyclone in Myanmar and an earthquake in central China are headline news. They have moved people worldwide to provide an outpouring of support. Yet isn't it puzzling that there's little publicity for the twenty-five thousand children of God who die from starvation-related diseases every day? And every thirty seconds, someone dies from malaria, which a ten-dollar mosquito net would help to prevent. Since in this global community all people are our neighbors, we must grapple with the question of whether we are loving our neighbors as ourselves. Christ in us can hardly ignore the needs of the least of these, needs to which self is able to turn a blind eye.

Vows of poverty

When I first adopted the exchanged life, the resulting change in my priorities often left me feeling confused. In the early months, I had frequent conversations with Clarence about this.

"So if the least of these are really the priority, then ideally, shouldn't we all be taking vows of poverty?" I asked.

"Not necessarily," Clarence said, "though we could certainly do far worse."

"So, just how much should we give, and how much should we keep for ourselves?"

"Everything and nothing. I know that sounds extreme, but bear with me. If we're convinced Christ in us is the only way to go, then it follows that His desires will become our desires. After His takeover, the issue isn't what we keep for self, but rather what of His we return to Him. We've admitted that all we have is His; the next step is to accept His guidance as we choose how to use what's His. I think that over time, the Holy Spirit will convict us to give increasingly of the money and time that are Christ's."

My conversation with Clarence left me scratching my head and wondering how much I could reasonably spend on creature comforts. But soon after this, I came across a quote from someone who had grappled with this dilemma far longer and at deeper levels than I. About questions regarding charity, C. S. Lewis said,

I do not believe one can settle how much we ought to give. I'm afraid that the only safe rule is to give more than we can spare. In other words, if our expenditures on comforts, luxuries, amusements, etc., is up to the standard common among those with the same income as our own, we are probably giving away too little. If our charities do not at all pinch or hamper us, I should say they are too small. There ought to be things we should like to do and cannot do because our charitable expenditure excludes them.[1]

In recent years, my charitable giving has gone up dramatically as Christ increasingly guides my spending. Yet when I read Lewis's statement, I find there is plenty to challenge me without pushing me close to vows of poverty. Augustine put it more succinctly: "Find out how much God has given you and from it take what you need; the remainder is needed by others."[2]

Our exchanged life offers the only antidote to the materially driven self. With Christ in us, we are no longer oblivious to the needs of others. In keeping with His golden rule, we might find ourselves imagining what we would say if we were one of the "least of these": *is that special vacation, that dinner out, or even that box of donuts more important than My starving child?* Not that any of these indulgences is intrinsically wrong, but we will find that inevitably, Christ in us will affect all aspects of our lives, including our spending. As we realize what He desires for others, we will need less and desire less.

Cost of security

The exchanged life also provides significant relief from the tireless search for security. I often joke about this need when I compare our present safety concerns with the risk tolerance of those who settled this country. I try to imagine what my wife would have said if we had been immigrants and, after making the long voyage to New York, I had announced, "OK, honey, we're going to get free land out west once we travel there by covered wagon and survive the wild animals, blizzards, drought, and robbers along the way." I don't know about your spouse, but I can assure you that mine would have told me I was just plain nuts!

Attempts to provide an increasing sense of security have become almost an obsession in today's culture. We're bombarded with ads and consultants advising that we need more protection, with insurance of every kind. The latest is long-term health care. But we already have the ultimate long-term health insurance policy—one that will last through eternity! We can't buy insurance that will provide the protection we need most—insurance against the ascendancy of self. Christ has already purchased this protection for us on the cross; we need only to accept His transplanted heart. Unfortunately, we often respond to our obvious vulnerability with an increasing concern about our existence. When self is alive, safety and physical survival become all important, and with this comes an aversion to any risk. Not that there's anything wrong with taking prudent measures for our physical security here on earth, but when it becomes an obsession, a passion, an end in itself, we run the danger of giving in to self.

This mind-set is also evident in concerns about our financial security—something that can become an exhausting pursuit as I discovered firsthand. Before my exchanged life, I was constantly researching how best to manage money for retirement, always seeking that elusive assurance of a sure thing. However, with the government mortgaging our future and spending our children's future to the tune of trillions of dollars in debt and entitlement obligations, the most "rock-solid" investments

The exchanged life frees us from preoccupation with finances.

provide little sense of security. The historic subprime financial crisis and government bailout of 2008 is a sobering reminder that nothing, not even T-bills, is a sure thing.

Fortunately, the exchanged life frees us from preoccupation with finances. As what we once considered to be needs become irrelevant wants, we need much less in financial resources to support our retirement. Rather than attempting to follow the ever-shifting sands of the financial markets and trying to second-guess what will be a safe haven in the future, we now realize there is no ultimate safety outside of Christ. While many find the reality painful, it also brings opportunity. With relief we can disinvest, giving up the struggle to guarantee our comfort and safety. Before my exchanged life, I had lost money in various investments. In this new life, I finally discovered the best financial investment, one with a guaranteed return—investment in that which immediately relieves the suffering of the least of these.

With this priority, caring for self also becomes increasingly irrelevant, and we discover that we need far less.

Recently deceased Nobel laureate and Soviet Siberian prison survivor Aleksandr Solzhenitsyn spoke eloquently about the reality of our needs:

> Do not pursue what is illusory . . . all [of] that is gained at the expense of your nerves decade after decade, and is confiscated in one fell night. Live with the steady superiority over life—don't be afraid of misfortune, and do not yearn after happiness; it is, after all, all the same: the bitter doesn't last forever, and the sweet never fills the cup to overflowing. It is enough if you don't freeze in the cold and if thirst and hunger don't claw at your insides. If your back isn't broken, if your feet can walk and your arms can bend, if both eyes can see, if both ears hear, then whom should you envy?[3]

Paul takes this even further:

> I am not telling you this because I need anything. I have learned to be satisfied with the things I have and with everything that happens. I know how to live when I am poor, and I know how to live when I have plenty. I have learned the secret of being happy at any time in everything that happens, when I have enough to eat and when I go hungry, when I have more than I need and when I do not have enough. I can do all things through Christ, because he gives me strength (Philippians 4:11–13, NCV).

When our attitude and desires are centered on Christ, no circumstance—not even abject poverty—can control us. What freedom, what security, what power!

The antibodies of self constantly threaten our passion for Christ's freedom, security, and power in our lives. As we seek to let Christ destroy those antibodies that fight against His heart, we must face the king of our desires, one that is in a league all its own—pride. This universal character flaw causes us to champion our standing in the world instead of protecting Christ's reputation.

Chapter 20

Protecting His Reputation

(Clarence)

Pride will destroy a person;
a proud attitude leads to ruin.

—*Proverbs 16:18, NCV*

I had just returned home from the church office when the phone rang. I was elated to hear Lorraine's voice on the other end, knowing she would be sharing news about the possibility of an all-important new church assignment. I had been an associate pastor at a university church and had enjoyed a rich and rewarding experience there. But I was ready to move to another large congregation—this time to take the reins as the lead pastor.

I was excited to learn of the position that would soon be available in a large Midwestern church. It was the perfect congregation for me—large enough to have many of the resources I had come to expect in my present church and yet young enough still to allow for innovation and change. It offered all the advantages of a large church without the usual disadvantages. And there was icing on that cake— some of our dearest friends on earth, Winton and Lorraine Beaven, were active members of this church. Winton was a mentor who'd had a dramatic impact on my life in rich and rewarding ways over the years. And, to top it all off, I knew I had the inside track. Lorraine was on the pastoral search committee and was angling for me to be their next pastor. Talk about a perfect setup! No doubt about it; I was sure the hand of God was in this. It was almost too perfect.

But then I also reasoned that it really made sense for God to give me this opportunity. I had dedicated my life to working for Him at a calling that wasn't exactly easy. Like most pastors, I had paid my dues. My early assignments involved two to three churches, making for long and exhausting weekends as I preached the same sermon two or three times. Then there was the almost impossible task of meeting the needs of all as I drove countless hours, ministering to the sick and needy among the far-flung members.

At times, it was a rather discouraging and thankless job, with tasks I could have chosen to avoid. While most pastors work hard, we have significant leeway because of limited accountability. We could work the weekends and take off the remainder of the week if we wanted to. But I seldom slacked off, often pushing myself when I felt little motivation for the tasks at hand.

My ministry at the university church had been intellectually stimulating and challenging, enriching my life as well as the lives of those with whom I worked. But after nine long years as an associate pastor, I felt that I was capable of more than continuing to play second fiddle to the lead pastor. I know that sounds rather pathetic for someone committed to serving others, but if I'm going to give you an honest understanding of my mind-set at the time, I must admit that I felt that way occasionally. I also thought that I was stagnating and needed to find other opportunities for professional growth—and yes, maybe even felt I deserved more. I had slogged along as an associate pastor long enough. Now it was time for me to move on to a different challenge.

So, I listened with bated breath as Lorraine told me of the latest developments. It was wonderful news, and I could hardly contain myself as I shared it with Dianna.

"This is fantastic!" I exclaimed as I hung up the phone.

"What? What did she say," Dianna asked impatiently.

"The church committee has narrowed it down, and," I paused, letting the anticipation build.

"And what? Come on!"

"I'm one of the three names they're considering!"

"That's great. But don't you think you're getting ahead of yourself? It's still not exactly in the bag."

"No, but it's almost a lock!" I grinned excitedly.

"What makes you so sure? You told me that the church has to submit the names to headquarters, and they decide."

"Yes, but let's face it: this isn't just any church. Given its standing and significant financial contributions, the wishes of this congregation carry considerable weight. And guess what?" I added, beaming with confidence.

"What?"

"The committee clearly indicated that I was their top choice!"

"Oh, honey, that's fantastic!" Dianna exclaimed, giving me an enthusiastic hug.

However, headquarters had other ideas. They already had their man for the position, and it wasn't me! When I heard the news a few days later, I was shocked and devastated. It was like thinking that I had the winning lotto ticket, only to notice as I went to claim the money that I had misread one number. I had already been making plans for the move and had even shared my good fortune with close friends and family. Now I felt like a fool, having to admit that I had jumped the gun and my dream position was down the tubes.

I was so sure God had been calling me to that church. Where was He in all this? I had served Him for years—and this was the thanks I got? It was so unfair. The church wanted *me;* it was *my* church, and it was taken from *me.*

My downfall

You probably have noted my perspective on the church I wanted—one that was totally self-centered and that ignored whatever designs God had for me. The god I often worshiped at the time—the one who I was so sure was calling me to that church—was obviously not the God who calls us to humble ourselves in His service. Unfortunately, I was so preoccupied with my reputation that I was clueless on how poorly I was protecting His reputation.

We can rest assured that if we think God is assisting in our self-promotion, we are worshiping a god of our own making—the god of pride. This is the most dangerous aspect of self. As C. S. Lewis puts it, "Pride leads to every other vice: it is the complete anti-God state of mind."[1] Pride also promotes behavior that is the antithesis of the golden rule. This is because pride, by its nature, is comparative and competitive. Pride is based on a deception in which we view ourselves and try to have others see us as different than we are. But how can we be invested in the well-being of others when we are all about being smarter, richer, more educated, more important, healthier, more attractive, and more popular than they are?

Another way to define pride is by its opposite—humility, a quality that is essential to the exchanged life. To the extent that we lack humility, we are operating with a prideful delusion regarding our abilities and sufficiency that blocks our awareness of our need for God's power in our life. C. S. Lewis clarifies the reason why pride is considered the most dangerous vice: "In God you come up against something which is in every respect immeasurably superior to yourself. Unless you know God as that—and, therefore, know yourself as nothing in comparison—you do not know God at all. As long as you are proud you cannot know God. A proud man is always looking down on things and people: and, of course as long as you are looking down, you cannot see something that is above you."[2]

I sought a sense of equality if not superiority.

I am ashamed to admit that at the time I was hoping to lead that church, I was very much caught up in a ladder-climbing mentality—comparing my career status as a pastor in my prime with that of others. I assiduously tracked those with a similar length of service in the ministry, such as my fellow seminarians, comparing their status and level of advancement to my own. In my pursuit of the pastoral call, I was driven by a desire for a reputable—more like "prestigious"—assignment, one that would befit my status. I sought a sense of equality if not superiority. It was indeed a pathetic and dismal testimony to how very alive self was at that time.

Looking back on it, I'm dismayed to realize that I was so caught up with self that I couldn't have heard God's call if He had shouted in my ear! Although I chose a career centered on championing and protecting Christ's reputation, this concern hardly registered as I remained completely absorbed with my own standing. In retrospect, I now know that while I may have been ready to take charge of the congregation I desired to pastor, I wasn't prepared to serve it. I was so full of self that I would have been ministering to the needs of self—both in me and in the congregation I wanted to impress. Self was so fully alive—and would have been even more so had I gained the prestige of leading a large church—that there would have been little place for Christ's heart to guide my ministry. Unfortunately, my prideful motivation at the time would have driven me to please and impress rather than to have Christ in me lead others to adopt His transforming heart.

Christian pride

Pride becomes particularly dangerous when it is tied to our Christian experience. Looking at my spiritual life in previous years, I now realize that often I prayed for my self, seeking abilities to impress others and to make me feel more secure. This made my prayer life a time when I championed self, which threatened Christ's heart in me. How often have you prayed, "Lord, help me to . . ."? The first part of the request is great; it recognizes our helplessness and dependence. But if you're like me, often the rest of the prayer undermines these attributes of our relationship with God as we pray for self's wants, which often are related to pride. We want our self to appear better than others. Even prayers for self-improvement may be bent toward our feeling self-fulfilled, prideful, and less aware of our desperate need for His heart.

Often my prayers were primarily requests for a change in life's circumstances rather than for the changes that having His heart in me brings. I had been in the habit of a type of self-improvement, self-worshiping prayer that left me full of pride as I compared myself with others. At the time, I was oblivious to this and would have been taken aback if someone had suggested I was prideful. After all, I was a pastor in God's service; how could I have a serious problem with pride? Without Christ's heart fully in me, I couldn't recognize my comparative insignificance and my desperate need for His takeover in my life. I was oblivious to the destructive power of pride—clueless that it could only be vanquished when I prayed with humility and helplessness, *Lord, let self be crucified with You so that not I, but You live in me.*

To the extent that pride is a dominant force in our life, the desires we addressed in the previous chapter are likely to be fed and strengthened. Pride is essential for self's survival, and as it decreases in power, Christ's heart in us will increase, reducing the attractiveness of the other desires of self.

Notice that James 1:14 speaks of "our *own* evil desires" (NLT; emphasis supplied). While all of us are wired for self, it is manifested in each of us in unique ways. Unfortunately, we generally are far better at seeing the manifestations of self in others than we are at seeing it in ourselves. Since what is a major temptation to others may not tempt me much at all, I can have a sense of self-satisfaction knowing that I am free of that sin. However, by indulging in this thinking, I am missing the mark by succumbing to pride.

Steve has experienced this when it comes to his choice in transportation. Others have often joked that he must not be a real doctor because he doesn't drive a fancy car or play golf. It isn't merely that he won't purchase fancy cars; his ideal buy is a car with low mileage (since he knows little about cars), one that is as old as possible and that ideally has a few dents to further lower the price. Recently, when someone ran a red light and totaled Steve's car, Steve gleefully called me about the replacement he found on Craigslist for fifteen hundred dollars. It was a 1992 Ford Tempo with sixty-seven thousand original miles on it!

Steve says his choice of cars can raise self to a whole new level—he could take smug satisfaction in the fact that he's not tied to creature comforts and status

We build walls of pride, trying to look better than we are.

in his transportation. However, in reality, his frugality is no credit to him; what he has "given up" is something that he never really desired in the first place—and all the while there's the temptation to remain blind to other areas of his life where self dominates. While Steve's decisions regarding which cars to purchase may not be influenced by greed and envy, the pride he could experience when comparing himself with others can bring self fully alive.

The prideful need to look good and protect our image is also evident in the self-assurance we often try to portray as we attempt to hide our innermost pain and vulnerability. This was evident in Christ's critical description of the pious Pharisee who prayed, " ' "God, I thank you that I am not like other men—robbers, evildoers, adulterers" ' " (Luke 18:11, NIV). Since we are all found wanting in one way or another, self must engage in a cover-up in order to benefit from such a comparison. Unfortunately, maintaining this cover-up comes at the expense of our ability to connect intimately with God and others. Instead, we build walls of pride, trying to look better than we are as we attempt to hide the reality of our core inadequacy and insecurity from ourselves and others. This avoidance of vulnerability is evident in our tendency to evade the confession process with a cursory "Sorry!" as our pride refuses the complete capitulation that ends with the words, "Will you forgive me?"

The naked emperor

The dishonesty essential for pride's success was evident in my thinking about the church call I sought. To maintain self's sense of deservedness concerning this position, I had to maintain a dishonest image of self. Although I had little knowledge of the other candidates, I had to see myself as the most qualified for that position—never mind the matter of what pastor would best facilitate Christ's working in that congregation. Such an honest evaluation would have threatened my designs to gain that position, something my pride wouldn't tolerate.

The dishonesty of pride, which supports a positive image of self, increasingly pervades every aspect of society, including the church. This has devastating consequences among believers because pride's self-promotion is the antithesis of what we need in order to succeed in our exchanged life. To the extent that we embrace pride, the resulting false confidence in self will undermine our recognition of the awesome power of Christ and our need for Him.

The dishonesty inherent in pride is seen not only in individuals but also within church organizations in which appearance is more important than reality. There is the pressure of the numbers game, with church membership, church attendance, and financial contributions used as the benchmarks of success—never mind whether these measurements have any relationship to a Christ-filled church. I sometimes wonder what church would hire Jesus today, when His résumé showed just a few converts—and some rather shaky at that—after three years of ministry!

Many people within our culture and often within the church have become like the emperor with no clothes; they regard appearance as being far more important than substance. Both our culture and many of our communities of believers are rotting with dishonesty. Little wonder that the unchurched point to pervasive hypocrisy as a reason for their cynicism about organized religion. Pride has become commonplace in and outside the church to the extent that it is an accepted way of life, leading to the perspective that all is well as long as appearances are preserved.

Too many people regard the sin to be not our nakedness but rather the failure to maintain appearances when occasional breaks in the facade reveal the painful reality. Our distorted priorities that promote pride often result in honesty being punished while the image, however hollow, is rewarded. Unless we remain on guard against the pride that brings self to life, it will indeed spell the ruin of our exchanged life.

This need to maintain constant vigilance regarding the threat of self in our lives can present a rather somber picture of life—a major downer. But that is only when we focus on self, losing sight of the goal of Christ in us. Once people experience this, the sacrifice of self becomes an increasingly minor inconvenience. And if you find yourself thinking that this life in Christ sounds like a rather boring, other-worldly existence that is too far removed from real life, think again. As the saying goes, "Don't knock it till you've tried it." Scripture puts it somewhat more eloquently. "Taste and see that the LORD is good" (Psalm 34:8, NIV). It is impossible to fully convey all the blessings of the abundant life that Christ brings. The casual observer may well view this existence as rather unappetizing, boring, and impractical, but appearances are deceiving.

As immensely rewarding as the exchanged life is, it seems impossible for us to attain, doesn't it? It is impossible for us to attain—but all things are possible with Christ! The measure of our success in approaching this ideal is the extent to which we remind ourselves of what life is about and what Christ is offering. This will inevitably lead to the recognition of the brevity of our existence in comparison to eternity. So we seek to accept His heart in our lives continually, to live each day with an eye toward the transient nature of our existence as we focus on the ultimate reality—a life to die for.

Chapter 21

A Life to Die For

(Steve)

I was put to death on the cross with Christ,
and I do not live anymore—it is Christ who lives in me.
—Galatians 2:20, NCV

"Hey, Dad, can you take a look at this mole on my back?" my son Jeffrey asked, raising his shirt.

As I saw the dark lesion in the center of his back, I felt my gut tighten and my breath catch in shock. The lesion was over an inch in diameter, raised, almost black in color, and had an irregular border. The menacing look was only surpassed by my own sense of ominous foreboding. Dermatology wasn't exactly my strong suit, but I knew this didn't look good. If Jeffrey was looking for reassurance, he was in for some serious disappointment.

"We need to have a dermatologist look at that right away," I responded, already thinking that he needed an immediate biopsy and, if positive, then surgery, and then. . . . Well, I didn't really know what came next. *Malignant melanoma:* it even sounded awful. The wife of one of my colleagues in the army had died of this type of cancer, and I recalled from med school that if it had spread, it was usually incurable.

Jeffrey had just completed the dermatology section of his anatomy and physiology class, at which point the teacher had jokingly predicted that everyone would go home and check out all their moles. After recalling that a camping buddy had told him he had a "gross-looking mole" on his back, Jeffrey returned from class determined to have a closer look. He took a behind-the-back picture with his digital camera and then looked at it on the computer monitor, comparing it to pictures of melanomas online.

Although we both had serious questions, getting the answers was going to entail a virtue that was in short supply—patience! We were relieved to get an appointment the following Monday, but the weekend seemed long as we waited and wondered. Jeffrey couldn't help doing his usual Internet research, trying to compare and grade his lesion, which only heightened his anxiety—and ours. He returned from the dermatologist with news that wasn't exactly surprising. She had confirmed that the mole looked suspicious, and subsequently removed it and sent it to pathology. We would have the report possibly by Wednesday, or Friday at the latest. Of course, we heard nothing until Friday.

I was in the middle of therapy when the call came. Dee Dee's tearful voice told me the result before she choked out the words, "It's positive." I continued with my session, trying to push back my fears and focus on the patient's concerns. Most clients seldom consider that therapists have their own struggles, which is as it should be. But at that point, I couldn't help thinking that none of the struggles that my patients were sharing in therapy could equal my own. Still, I maintained

Dee Dee's tearful voice told me the result.

my composure—the impassive demeanor that is expected regardless of what is shared or what might be on my mind—and somehow got through the last fifteen minutes.

Jeffrey was in our room in tears, already sharing the possible stage, the statistics on spread, and the worst-case scenario—a cure rate of less than 20 percent. We prayed together, though I struggled with this. While I had been living the exchanged life for only a few months, I had come to believe that God is far more interested in dealing with our spiritual well-being than our physical well-being, which, relative to eternity, is rather irrelevant. I prayed for an accepting attitude and thanked Him for the guarantee that I would have His heart in me. Beyond this, I wouldn't praise Him for a result I desired any more than I would curse Him for one I didn't want. I prayed that I might give up my will, which would assure that His heart continued to live in me regardless of our son's health. Besides, Jeffrey faced far more important issues than his physical survival.

Dee Dee's dialysis ran smoothly that night, but I couldn't sleep anyway. At 1:00 A.M., I finally gave up trying and began to write an e-mail to Jeffrey—a communication that was as much for me as for him. I prayed for the right words but had no inkling of how God would use what I wrote to change his life. Christ invites each of us to experience the same vision that I shared with Jeffrey late that night, one that made me tear up as I considered the implications.

Reality check

Dear Jeffrey,

I can't sleep, and there's only so much praying one can do, so I decided to write you. I have wanted to share and to ask about spiritual concerns for some time but have been avoiding this as I don't want to come off as preachy or laying some trip on you. I say this because I don't want you to think I'm writing only because I think you are terminal, which I certainly don't anymore than that we are all terminal. All of us live for a fairly brief time in the overall scheme of things, and as one gets older it seems a lot briefer! I also don't want you to think that I'm trying to use this vulnerable time in your life to push my own spiritual agenda; I've been planning to share these thoughts for a while. However, while I have considered sharing with you for some time, certainly the events of this week add impetus.

C. S. Lewis says that God whispers in our comfort but shouts in our pain. I don't believe that He causes or even facilitates pain. But I also seriously question whether, in this age of plenty, very many of us can come to an awareness of His presence and of our desperate need for Him to fully take over our lives without experiencing significant pain. That kind of pain reminds us of the futility of our own efforts and pursuits, which are simply a temporary distraction from our ultimate demise; it reminds us of our desperate need for something more.

I say all this because, while I know that you have been a believer, I don't know how that translates into your daily life. As you know, my dad was a deeply committed believer, yet his belief seemed to have almost no influence on his personal life, which, from anyone's perspective, was rather evil. The vast majority of Christians nowadays are unquestioning believers who are fairly willing to have Christ be a part of their lives. They hang on to the illusion of having eternal life while they continue with their own pursuits without much transformation of character. But Christ can't be a part of our lives—He wants our whole life. That's, of course, what your Uncle Clarence's DVD is all about—dying to our own natural pursuits and self-interests in order to allow for Christ's takeover. Believers rarely choose this as it is so unnatural and negates our ability to be our own gods and to pursue our own interests. I have no idea where you are in all this, though I hope that you will have a look at the DVD.

On the surface, it seems impossible to find anything positive about the devastating news of this week. But if you think about it, maybe there is. You have the luxury, albeit unenviable from a human standpoint, of facing the possibility of a premature death. You're likely saying that I'm nuts for considering that to be a luxury. But as I'm sure you observe, most people your age, and even much older, are focused on making more, gathering more, having more, and gaining more pleasurable moments each year, while they maintain some delusional sense of immortality. You, on the other hand, have now been forced to look at things that most seldom consider—certainly not at the age of twenty-one. It's an opportunity similar to what was given to me with Mommy's terminal state. And since it's about you rather than about someone you love, it hits even closer to home. Initially, when Mommy was diagnosed, I refused to admit the futility of my efforts and wouldn't consider a spiritual perspective. But Mommy continued to deteriorate, despite all my efforts to fix her, and it was when she began to consider terminating dialysis that I finally responded to God's call—one I had been drowning out for years with my own efforts and distracting pleasures.

I must tell you that with all the tears I have shed over your diagnosis, I realize that I'm certainly not dead to self. If I were, I would be less concerned with how long you live than with how you live. We have prayed continuously this week for better news, but I am increasingly convinced that while God can miraculously intervene, He seldom chooses to do so. I really don't think He's that invested in how long we live or how much we suffer—especially when you consider that human suffering is one of the few avenues He has for getting through to us. Rather, He's concerned about how we respond to what life deals us and to His offer to take over in our life.

So I am trying to pray more for acceptance of whatever happens—and even more, that you will experience some of the peace that we've had in recent months. Christ says that those who try to hang on to life—earthly life and interests—lose it, and those who lose this earthly life for His sake will find real life: spiritual life. It really is a tremendous relief to come to the awareness that our priorities, perspectives, and worries—no matter how important they seem—are futile. It truly is a freeing, unburdening joy to experience a life in Christ in which we feel no need of anything—even life itself.

This is certainly not a perspective that is easy to accept. It is especially difficult in these times when we can satisfy so many of our desires. It's also much more difficult to accept this perspective at your age, when mortality is the furthest thing from your mind. But it is something that I hope and pray you can experience. Whatever the immediate outcome of the tests and workup, you and I both know that there are no guarantees and that this cancer will be hanging over your head for a long time.

Mommy and I hope and pray that you can experience the peace that a life fully lived in Christ offers. We hope that the outcome, whatever it is, can be a rather minor irritant because your entire perspective has been transformed—though, as you know, it is certainly no minor irritant to us but something we are working to help you defeat. However, while we desperately want you to live a full life, if we had to choose between the two, we would give priority to your having a full spiritual life over your physical survival.

I hope you don't find this preachy or offensive. Mommy and I both admire the way you have handled things—continuing with your responsibilities and even helping with Mommy in this difficult week. Thank you for all the joy you bring to our lives and the love that you show us in everyday life.

Love,
Daddy

Jeffrey underwent surgery soon after this, having an eight-inch elliptical flap of skin removed from his back. We were relieved to learn that the lymph node dissection was negative. Still, while the 95 percent survival rate sounded extremely positive, it is rather disconcerting to learn at the age of twenty-one that you have a one-in-twenty chance of dying in five years.

With a sizable hole in his back, Jeffrey was laid up for a few days. But soon after his recovery, he returned to complete his quarter at school. We had dodged a bullet, and things were returning back to normal—or so it seemed. But Jeffrey was changing. He chose to move to a Christian college campus and become a dedicated follower of Jesus. While he continued his nursing studies, he met Danae, a wonderful Christian girl, and two years later they were married. It was not until twenty months after his surgery that I realized the full impact of that late-night letter I wrote. As Clarence baptized Jeffrey, I learned

We must be continually aware of our terminal condition.

of how he had been touched and challenged by Christ's message that he heard through me. The crisis in his life and the potential for a premature death had forced him to examine what his life had been and what he wanted it to be.

We must be continually aware of our terminal condition if we are to fully embrace exchanged living. While this seems obvious, if you're anything like me, you have a strong tendency to spend much of your life attempting to escape this reality. And all the distractions and transient pleasures available today certainly provide opportunities to avoid facing the brevity of life.

The life we have discussed in this book—the life to die for—makes sense only when we accept the hopelessness of self and its ultimate demise. Only with daily awareness of this will we give up on self's ability to meet our needs and satisfy our desires. Only then will we give priority to something beyond ourselves—to seek the ultimate satisfaction of Christ's heart in us, the truly abundant life. It is something most believers miss, as Clarence did throughout the majority of his ministry. Without realizing it at the time, however, he had already observed the exchanged life firsthand. It was an experience he had longed to enjoy—one that seemed all too out of reach until he learned to join those who were terminal.

Living terminally

Jody was dying. She had been diagnosed with colon cancer and had been told that she was terminal. As her former pastor, I had the opportunity to visit her during the later stages of her illness.* I found this part of my ministry—visits to the dying—always interesting and challenging. Each case offered a new experience, giving me a view of the end I may one day face. The task was also something I dreaded at times, especially when the patients were nominal believers who intensely denied their terminal condition to the end and hopelessly and desperately clung to life. I hated coming to their bedsides; there was so little to offer.

But that wasn't the case with Jody. Each time I was in town, I looked forward to seeing her. That likely sounds rather strange—looking forward to visiting with someone who was embarking on the final stages of life here on earth. After all, other than words of faith and encouragement, there really isn't much to offer someone who is dying, even when that person is a committed believer. But the pleasure exchanged during those visits wasn't something I gave to her, but rather something she gave to me.

Jody's faith was a continual source of inspiration, and she responded to her coming death as though it were a mere speed bump on her road to eternity—which it was, given her life in Christ. I constantly heard feedback from other church members on the remarkable tranquility she exhibited as she faced death. The peace and joy I saw on Jody's face and on the faces of other terminal believers I was privileged to serve left an indelible impression on me. Because these people were living terminally, their condition brought them to a stark awareness of what was truly important. The cares of this world faded to insignificance for them, and they became increasingly free to live in Christ.

> I sought the LORD, and he answered me;
>> he delivered me from all my fears.
> Those who look to him are radiant;
>> their faces are never covered with shame (Psalm 34:4, 5, NIV).

---

* Clarence is writing here and to the end of this chapter.

Before I began to live the exchanged life, when I observed the faces of believers who were dying physically but becoming more alive in Christ, I actually felt envious. *What would it be like to feel that level of tranquility?* I often wondered. It reminded me of the familiar hymn, "Peace! Peace! wonderful peace, Coming down from the Father above." The hymn brought tears to my eyes—not for the dying believer, but because of my own yearning.

You likely think it rather odd that I would envy someone who was dying. It's not that I wished for their pain, and I certainly wasn't suicidal. But I longed for that peace—the sense of abandonment and oneness with Christ that was evident in their faces. I often wondered why the rest of us so seldom experienced this. Can one have Jody's perspective only at the end of life? After coming to understand and experience the exchanged life, my answer is Yes—and No.

This is best understood by looking at the state of being terminal. Those who are dying and who can accept the reality that their life is about to end inevitably have radically different priorities. They no longer experience concern for the future. Instead, they live the life Christ recommended when He said, " 'Do not worry about tomorrow, for tomorrow will worry about itself. Each day has enough trouble of its own' " (Matthew 6: 34, NIV). The bills, the 401(k), the vacation plans, the job advancement—the imminent end of life makes all these suddenly irrelevant. When you think of all the concerns that preoccupy us, this worry-free stance sounds tempting, doesn't it? If only we didn't have to die to experience it. Yet it seems impossible to have this perspective without being terminal.

The dying believer experiences supreme peace.

It is. Let me explain.

The dying believer experiences supreme peace because, since there is no longer a point to their hanging on to the things of this earthly life (you can't take it with you), they let go. And the core of what they let go is self. The very natural tendency to defend, protect, and preserve self, which for most of us is the work of a lifetime, becomes irrelevant when we die. This was the perspective of the terminal believers that I envied. They were fully engaged in the exchanged life.

The good news is that we don't have to be facing our imminent physical death to live terminally. Christ invites us to continually live terminally—dying to self daily, losing self to gain His transplanted heart. As Paul says, "I was put to death on the cross with Christ, and I do not live anymore—it is Christ who lives in me" (Galatians 2:20, NCV). While it is easier to engage in this exchanged life when we are faced with the imminent end of self in physical death, Christ gives us the power to end the life of self much sooner. It is indeed overwhelming and inspiring to see others choose to give up on self's survival in the service of a higher cause, as seen in the sacrifice Liviu Librescu made.

No greater love

Professor Librescu had a rather remarkable life. As a child, he survived being sent to a Nazi labor camp in Romania. He became a brilliant student, earning a PhD in engineering. But his career stalled when he refused to swear allegiance to the Romanian Communist Party. Eventually, the prime minister of Israel intervened, successfully gaining permission from the Romanian government for him to emigrate to Israel. A professor of aeronautical and mechanical engineering, both in Israel and later in the United States, Librescu was a renowned researcher and teacher in his field, authoring numerous books and articles.

At seventy-six years old, with all he had accomplished and given to society, Professor Librescu certainly deserved to live out his retirement years in comfort. Yet he made a different choice on that fateful day when, in the middle of his solid mechanics class at Virginia Polytechnic Institute and State University, shots rang out down the hall. As the gunman attempted to breach classroom 204, the professor blocked the door while his students jumped out a window. He took five bullets, which killed him. But his heroic sacrifice prevented a massacre in his classroom as all but one of his twenty-three students escaped.

Professor Librescu certainly could have made other choices. No one would have faulted him if he had run for cover. After all, he had already experienced more trauma than most people do. The natural response for most of us in his position would have been escape. Yet there was something in his character that made him ignore the instinct to protect himself—that led him instead to choose to be a human shield, risking death to save his students. Such an instantaneous, selfless decision could only be the outgrowth of a character firmly oriented in terminal living. I would suggest that Professor Librescu was already so dead to self and so habituated to serving others that he automatically made the decision to protect his students rather than himself.

We are invited to engage in this same terminal living on a daily basis. Terminal living is not simply based on dying to self. Rather, this mind-set is all about having Christ in us, which brings life. Living according to our natural instincts, which aim to preserve and protect self and ultimately lead to it becoming a dominating force, is ultimately futile. Living for self results in what we have termed dead living. But when we are crucified to self daily and accept Christ's heart every day, we are spiritually resurrected to a new life in Him. Terminal living is really all about choosing to surrender self before our physical death in order that we may be brought to life in Christ. This is truly a life to celebrate.

The dying believer experiences supreme peace.

Consider Dee Dee's present life—she's suffering from the ravages of a disease that will one day kill her. Can you imagine the changes she would experience if she were to be healed? No more daily nausea, no more exhaustion, no more imbalance and the resulting falls, no more dietary restrictions, no more surgeries, and no more dialysis! She would be overwhelmed with gratitude and would be permanently wonderstruck at her new life.

Tragically, however, Dee Dee continues to suffer. Even during the year that Steve and I have worked on this book, the deterioration of her health has been painfully obvious. Her kidneys are damaged beyond repair. Her only hope would be to receive a new, fully functioning kidney. But she is one of many on the list of the United Network for Organ Sharing (UNOS). She has been on the list for ten years—along with more than eighty thousand others nationwide who are waiting for a kidney transplant. Most are waiting for someone to die—someone who will be a match. But even with a compatible match and immunosuppressive treatment, some 30 percent of those receiving cadaveric kidneys will eventually reject them. Following a successful transplant, the recipient is left with the gnawing worry that there will be a rejection crisis, requiring removal of the kidney, leaving them once again on the abominable waiting list.

However, the rest of us are also in desperate need of an organ transplant. Just as Dee Dee struggles with devastating physical disabilities, in our natural state we are saddled with overwhelming spiritual disabilities. Our self-driven heart is damaged beyond any hope of repair. It can't be cured, and no amount of wishful thinking or effort on our part can change this reality. Our only hope is to receive a new life-giving heart—one that will replace our damaged heart. But this is where our analogy breaks down—in a manner

Only [Christ's] heart can complete us.

that provides a far more optimistic prognosis for us than that given to Dee Dee and the thousands of others on the physical transplant list. Rather than a wistful hope, we are given astounding assurance regarding two crucial aspects of our transplant.

First, the transplant Jesus offers is guaranteed to be compatible! We all were created in God's image with the plan that He would live in us, so we're guaranteed that Christ's heart will be fully compatible. As long as we keep the antibodies of self in check with the treatments Christ provides, we never need worry about rejecting His heart. Commitment to the daily immunosuppressive treatments of trusting, recognizing sin, unblocking through confession, surrendering, and thinking the Word will keep His heart in us forever!

When we adopt the exchanged life, the deadness of living in our self ends as we embrace terminal living—living fully and freely—with Christ's transplanted heart in us. We have been raised from the dead! Our new life will inevitably produce an overwhelming sense of gratitude at being raised from spiritual death to life that grows more abundant in Christ each day as His heart increasingly takes over. If we are daily engaging this life, we will indeed be permanently wonderstruck—forever amazed at our new life.

The second critical difference for us is the waiting list. Thousands wait for years on the UNOS list, many dying before they move to the top of the list and are eligible to receive an organ. We are also on a list. But rather than having to wait patiently while desperately hoping against hope to receive a transplant before death strikes, we are given an astounding guarantee—there is no wait! Jesus' sacrifice on

Calvary assures a heart transplant for each of us. Only His heart can complete us, providing the solace Augustine beautifully described, "You made us for yourself, [O Lord] and our hearts are restless until they rest in you."[1]

This, then, is the life Christ offers to each of us. Admittedly, it is a challenging life—hardly for the spiritually faint of heart. But Steve and I can assure you that the radical nature of this call is surpassed only by its rewards. And those rewards are not just for some distant eternity; they are available today!

We are indeed terminal—our only hope being the inconceivable gift of Christ's heart. Jesus is patiently, longingly, waiting for us to consent to the transplant. We invite you to accept His heart, joining us in daily living in Him, which will assure us of His abundant life—a life to die for!

Continue the Experience

We invite you to continue the experience of *A Life to Die For* by visiting our Web site: alifetodiefor.com.

- Share how you feel about *A Life to Die For,* and read what others are saying about it.

- Share your insights and discuss the book with other readers.

- Communicate with the authors.

- Learn how to purchase additional copies of *A Life to Die For.*

- Learn about the DVD set *How to Die Right and Live to Tell About It* by Clarence and Dianna Schilt.

Clarence and his wife, Dianna, present a relationship-enhancement seminar centered on the theme of this book. If you would like information about arranging for them to speak to your organization or group, contact them at alifetodiefor.com.

Appendix A

Principles of the Exchanged Life

1. When self is alive, two major issues result:
   a. spiritual power in us is blocked;
   b. and spiritual power through us for others is blocked.
2. Resurrection power comes only to the dead—those who are dead to self.
3. A corpse can't be hurt, so when self is dead, its feelings can't be hurt.
4. Those who are dead to self aren't surprised when things don't go their way; they aren't offended when things don't go their way; and they aren't controlled by the things that don't go their way.
5. We do much if not most of our sinning when we are in the right but we're not being treated justly or fairly.
6. What happens *to* us is relatively inconsequential; what happens *in* and *through* us has far-reaching consequences.
7. We should be willingly surrendering to receive rather than willfully trying to achieve.
8. What gets the mind gets us, and what gets us is reported through our thoughts, attitudes, words, and actions.
9. Practice makes perfect, so we must be careful what we practice. (Are we

perfecting habits of self or of Christ in ourselves?)
10. Sin is what we do when our hearts aren't satisfied with God.

Appendix B
Daily Preparation

You shouldn't wait to think about life preservers until you're in the middle of the lake and your boat is taking on water. You should bring the life preservers with you when you get in the boat. Likewise, we shouldn't face life's daily struggles without the necessary preparation, equipping ourselves with spiritual life preservers to ensure that we are ready for any trouble that may arise. This important work involves several helpful practices. Foremost among these in our daily time with God is reaffirming the exchanged life, dying to self (putting off the old self), and receiving Christ's life (putting on the new self). This involves affirming the attitudes we seek in the exchanged life.

In what follows, we offer aids that many have found useful in daily maintaining the exchanged-life mind-set. First is prayer that focuses on receiving Christ's heart and on seeking a change in our attitude rather than in our circumstances. Next are specific steps for incorporating the mind of Christ daily. Finally, we include biblical promises that provide assurances for this new life.

An exchanged-life prayer

"Dear Lord,

"I recognize that I can't live the Christian life in my own strength or out of my own resources. Every time I try, I just get more discouraged. Depending on my own efforts has left me a self-driven failure.

"Because of my inability to live the life You want for me, I give up on my self-sufficiency and surrender my life unconditionally to You. Lord, I choose to trust You to live through me. I give up all my rights and expectations and give You permission to make me into the kind of person You want me to be.

"I believe Your Word, which says, ' "I [self] have been crucified with Christ" ' [Galatians 2:20].* I believe I was buried with Christ and have been raised with Him to a new life in which His heart works in me and through me. I thank You for Christ's sacrifice that makes me totally acceptable. I want to die daily, allowing Him to live in me so self no longer rules. I believe I have been raised to newness of life and am now seated in the heavenly places at the right hand of the Father in Christ Jesus. Father, I choose as an act of my will to claim Christ as my life, my power, and my identity.

"Do in me and with me whatever You choose. I am asking You to make Your truth a reality in my life. Let others see Your heart and Your life in me. I trust You to do what I can't do, quit what I can't quit, and, most of all, to be in me what I can't be. I thank You for giving me the mind of Christ, renewing my mind and healing damaged emotions as You transform my life and live Your life through me. I thank You for saving me from my sinful self and for the freedom from self that comes with Your takeover in my life.

"I pray in Jesus' name. Amen."

A recommended daily process for putting off the old self and putting on the new

1. Open your life to God before you do anything else.
"Lord, I am coming today in the name of Jesus to commit my life to You. I thank You continually for the sacrifice of Jesus, and I ask You to forgive my sinful heart based on all He has done for me at the cross. I ask You to reveal any part of

---

* All Scripture quotations in this appendix are from the New International Version.

self that needs to be surrendered to You today, giving me the willingness to die to any part that separates me from You. I trust what Jesus said, ' "If anyone would come after me, he must deny himself and take up his cross daily and follow me" ' [Luke 9:23]. Today, I choose to deny my self, take up my cross, and follow You. I choose to give You unrestricted access to my life."

2. Choose the exchanged life.

"Lord, You have promised, ' " 'I will give you a new heart and put a new spirit in you; I will remove from you your heart of stone and give you a heart of flesh' " ' [Ezekiel 36:26]. I choose to put off my 'old self' and to 'put on the new self, created to be like God' [Ephesians 4:22–24]. I pray that Your Holy Spirit will make this choice a reality in my life so that Your new heart, Your new nature, can live unhindered in and through me."

3. Confirm with God that you have received the exchanged life.

"Father, I would like to say with the apostle Paul, ' "I have been crucified with Christ and I no longer live, but Christ lives in me. The life I live in the body, I live by faith in the Son of God, who loved me and gave himself for me" ' [Galatians 2:20]. I trust You to reprogram me as I exercise my faith. With the promise of Your unlimited power, I can now handle gracefully all of the pressures and emergencies that I will face today."

4. Claim Bible promises.

"When your words came I ate them; / they were my joy and my heart's delight" (Jeremiah 15:16).

Bible promises to claim

"Delight yourself in the LORD / and he will give you the desires of your heart" (Psalm 37:4).

"You open your hand / and satisfy the desire of every living thing" (Psalm 145:16).

"He gives strength to the weary / and increases the power of the weak. . . . Those who hope in the LORD / will renew their strength. / They will soar on wings like eagles; / they will run and not grow weary, / they will walk and not be faint" (Isaiah 40:29, 31).

" 'Do not fear, for I am with you; / do not be dismayed, for I am your God. /

I will strengthen you and help you; / I will uphold you with my righteous right hand' " (Isaiah 41:10).

" 'I am he who will sustain you. / I have made you and I will carry you; / I will sustain you and I will rescue you' " (Isaiah 46:4). *This is a great promise for the really bad days. You can ask God to carry you.*

" 'You will seek me and find me when you seek me with all your heart. I will be found by you,' declares the LORD" (Jeremiah 29:13, 14).

" 'My grace is sufficient for you, for my power is made perfect in weakness.' Therefore, I will boast all the more gladly about my weaknesses, so that Christ's power may rest on me. That is why, for Christ's sake, I delight in weaknesses, in insults, in hardships, in persecutions, in difficulties. For when I am weak, then I am strong" (2 Corinthians 12:9, 10).

"I pray that out of his glorious riches he may strengthen you with power through his Spirit in your inner being, so that Christ may dwell in your hearts through faith. And I pray that you, being rooted and established in love, may have power, together with all the saints, to grasp how wide and long and high and deep is the love of Christ, and to know this love that surpasses knowledge—that you may be filled to the measure of all the fullness of God.

"Now to him who is able to do immeasurably more than all we ask or imagine, according to his power that is at work within us, to him be glory in the church and in Christ Jesus throughout all generations, for ever and ever! Amen" (Ephesians 3:16–21).

"My God will meet all your needs according to his glorious riches in Christ Jesus" (Philippians 4:19).

Appendix C

"Jesus, I Choose to Trust You When You Say . . ."

In chapter 10, we explained the helpfulness of the line "Jesus, I choose to trust You when You say _____." The most challenging part about using it is having verses readily at hand when needed. Below are eight things that tempt us to let self rise to life, followed by texts you can refer to when tempted. This appendix concludes with a scenario that demonstrates how you can use Scripture when you face such challenges.

Fear/anxiety

"I sought the LORD, and he answered me; / he delivered me from all my fears. / Those who look to him are radiant; / their faces are never covered with shame" (Psalm 34:4, 5).*

"Rejoice in the Lord always. I will say it again: Rejoice! Let your gentleness be evident to all. The Lord is near. Do not be anxious about anything, but in everything, by prayer and petition, with thanksgiving, present your requests to God. And the peace of God, which transcends all understanding, will guard your hearts

_____

* All Scripture quotations in this appendix are from the New International Version.

and your minds in Christ Jesus" (Philippians 4:4–7).

"There is no fear in love. But perfect love drives out fear, because fear has to do with punishment. The one who fears is not made perfect in love" (1 John 4:18).

Evil desires

"Do not let sin reign in your mortal body so that you obey its evil desires. Do not offer the parts of your body to sin, as instruments of wickedness, but rather offer yourselves to God, as those who have been brought from death to life; and offer the parts of your body to him as instruments of righteousness" (Romans 6:12, 13).

"I urge you, brothers, in view of God's mercy, to offer your bodies as living sacrifices, holy and pleasing to God—this is your spiritual act of worship. Do not conform any longer to the pattern of this world, but be transformed by the renewing of your mind. Then you will be able to test and approve what God's will is—his good, pleasing and perfect will" (Romans 12:1, 2).

"You were taught, with regard to your former way of life, to put off your old self, which is being corrupted by its deceitful desires; to be made new in the attitude of your minds; and to put on the new self, created to be like God in true righteousness and holiness" (Ephesians 4:22–24).

"Get rid of all moral filth and the evil that is so prevalent and humbly accept the word planted in you, which can save you" (James 1:21).

Anger

" 'As churning the milk produces butter, / and as twisting the nose produces blood, / so stirring up anger produces strife' " (Proverbs 30:33).

"Love is patient, love is kind. It does not envy, it does not boast, it is not proud. It is not rude, it is not self-seeking, it is not easily angered, it keeps no record of wrongs. Love does not delight in evil but rejoices with the truth. It always protects, always trusts, always hopes, always perseveres" (1 Corinthians 13:4–7).

"Therefore each of you must put off falsehood and speak truthfully to his neighbor, for we are all members of one body. 'In your anger do not sin': Do not let the sun go down while you are still angry, and do not give the devil a foothold. . . .

"Get rid of all bitterness, rage and anger, brawling and slander, along with every form of malice. Be kind and compassionate to one another, forgiving each other, just as in Christ God forgave you" (Ephesians 4:25–32).

"My dear brothers, take note of this: Everyone should be quick to listen, slow to speak and slow to become angry, for man's anger does not bring about the righteous life that God desires" (James 1:19, 20).

Depression

"Great peace have they who love your law, / and nothing can make them stumble" (Psalm 119:165).

"You will keep in perfect peace / him whose mind is steadfast, / because he trusts in you. / Trust in the LORD forever, / for the LORD, the LORD, is the Rock eternal" (Isaiah 26:3, 4).

"May the God of hope fill you with all joy and peace as you trust in him, so that you may overflow with hope by the power of the Holy Spirit" (Romans 15:13).

"Rejoice in the Lord always. I will say it again: Rejoice! Let your gentleness be evident to all. The Lord is near. Do not be anxious about anything, but in everything, by prayer and petition, with thanksgiving, present your requests to God. And the peace of God, which transcends all understanding, will guard your hearts and your minds in Christ Jesus" (Philippians 4:4–7).

Impatience

"A fool shows his annoyance at once, / but a prudent man overlooks an insult" (Proverbs 12:16).

"Love is patient, love is kind. It does not envy, it does not boast, it is not proud" (1 Corinthians 13:4).

"The fruit of the Spirit is love, joy, peace, patience, kindness, goodness, faithfulness, gentleness and self-control. Against such things there is no law. Those who belong to Christ Jesus have crucified the sinful nature with its passions and desires. Since we live by the Spirit, let us keep in step with the Spirit" (Galatians 5:22–25).

"I have learned to be content whatever the circumstances. I know what it is to be in need, and I know what it is to have plenty. I have learned the secret of being content in any and every situation, whether well fed or hungry, whether living in plenty or in want. I can do everything through him who gives me strength" (Philippians 4:11–13).

Unwillingness to forgive

" 'If you are offering your gift at the altar and there remember that your brother has something against you, leave your gift there in front of the altar. First go and be reconciled to your brother; then come and offer your gift' " (Matthew 5:23, 24).

" 'When you stand praying, if you hold anything against anyone, forgive him, so that your Father in heaven may forgive you your sins' " (Mark 11:25).

"Get rid of all bitterness, rage and anger, brawling and slander, along with every form of malice. Be kind and compassionate to one another, forgiving each other, just as in Christ God forgave you" (Ephesians 4:31, 32).

"If we confess our sins, he is faithful and just and will forgive us our sins and purify us from all unrighteousness" (1 John 1:9).

Unsuitable speech

"When words are many, sin is not absent, / but he who holds his tongue is wise" (Proverbs 10:19).

"Do you see a man who speaks in haste? / There is more hope for a fool than for him" (Proverbs 29:20).

"Do not let any unwholesome talk come out of your mouths, but only what is helpful for building others up according to their needs, that it may benefit those who listen" (Ephesians 4:29).

"If anyone considers himself religious and yet does not keep a tight rein on his tongue, he deceives himself and his religion is worthless" (James 1:26).

" 'Whoever would love life / and see good days / must keep his tongue from evil / and his lips from deceitful speech. / He must turn from evil and do good; / he must seek peace and pursue it' " (1 Peter 3:10, 11).

Difficult relationships

" 'I tell you who hear me: Love your enemies, do good to those who hate you, bless those who curse you, pray for those who mistreat you' " (Luke 6:27, 28).

"Do not take revenge, my friends, but leave room for God's wrath, for it is written: 'It is mine to avenge; I will repay,' says the Lord. On the contrary: 'If your enemy is hungry, feed him; / if he is thirsty, give him something to drink. / In doing this, you will heap burning coals on his head.' Do not be overcome by evil, but overcome evil with good" (Romans 12:19–21).

"All of you, live in harmony with one another; be sympathetic, love as brothers, be compassionate and humble. Do not repay evil with evil or insult with insult, but with blessing, because to this you were called so that you may inherit a blessing" (1 Peter 3:8, 9).

Practical application

Here's a scenario that tells how you can apply the scriptures above to situations that tempt you to allow self to rise to life: After paying your cousin Ted the price you had agreed upon for some remodeling, he reneged halfway through the project, claiming there were additional expenses, and he charged you almost double the original amount to complete the job. You and your family have to see him at family gatherings, and you're still angry and resentful.

Internalize God's Word. Accept His Word into your mind and make it your own.

- Choose a Bible text that speaks to your issue. For instance, in this case, you could choose one on forgiveness, such as " 'When you stand praying, if you hold anything against anyone, forgive him, so that your Father in heaven may forgive you your sins' " (Mark 11:25).
- Read the text aloud several times. You might also write it out, placing your name in it. As a bonus, start memorizing it.
- Ask God, "Please burn this message deep into my mind and heart."
- Tell God, "By faith I believe that You are changing me on the inside by the power of Your Word."
- Thank God, "Thank You, Lord, for giving me Your grace and power today."

Externalize God's Word. Apply the text you have chosen (in this case, on forgiveness) to the situation.

- Identify in prayer the likely challenge you will face with your given situation—in this case, having a loving and forgiving spirit toward Ted at family gatherings. Pray, "Lord, You know how I hate what Ted has done to me and my family."

- Ask God to take control of your life: "Lord, please take control of my life and give me Your forgiveness for Ted because apart from You I simply can't forgive him. I surrender my anger to You and ask for Your power to forgive."

- As you pray, use your imagination to see yourself meeting the challenge with Jesus, in His power. And when negative thoughts—for instance, vengeful thoughts toward Ted—come at you, say with the apostle Paul, "I can do everything through him who gives me strength" (Philippians 4:13).

- Thank God. Pray, "Thank You, Lord, for changing me. Thank You for beginning to transform my mind so that I reflect Jesus more and more by extending Your forgiveness to Ted."

Note: If you blow it by indulging in negative thoughts about Ted, remember that God still accounts you righteous despite your unrighteous behavior. Here's your promise: "A righteous man falls seven times, [and] he rises again" (Proverbs 24:16). Blowing it is simply an indication that self is still alive—one that leads us to seek to incorporate Christ's heart of forgiveness more fully.

Appendix D

Confession, Repentance, and Forgiveness

In chapter 12, we presented the unblocking confession process that is essential to keeping Christ's life flowing through both individual and corporate relationships. Below is a summary of this process. In addition, we have listed some of the symptoms of the rising of self that Scripture identifies (just so you won't feel left out!). These serve to alert us to the possibility that something is threatening Christ's heart in us. Finally, we've listed some important differences between proud people and humble people.

True confession

"If we claim to be without sin, we deceive ourselves and the truth is not in us. If we confess our sins, he is faithful and just and will forgive us our sins and purify us from all unrighteousness. If we claim we have not sinned, we make him out to be a liar and his word has no place in our lives" (1 John 1:8–10, NIV).

Phrases that characterize patch-up jobs, which don't provide healing

"Let it blow over; time heals." "Let's not talk about it." "Let's compromise; we're both to blame." "I've got rights too." "I'm sorry," without specific confession and request for forgiveness.

Confession and forgiveness that best comprise a healing experience

1. Name the specific sin—"I yelled at you."
2. Apologize—"I'm sorry."
3. Ask for forgiveness—"Will you forgive me?"
4. The injured party responds with forgiveness—"I forgive you."

"I'm sorry" versus "I'm sorry. Will you forgive me?"

"I'm sorry" alone is external, thing-centered, and it leaves people alone and lonely.

"I'm sorry. Will you forgive me?" is internal, involves both parties (is relationship-centered), admits I am the problem (not something), and places me at your mercy (you may or may not forgive).

"It's OK" or "Forget it" versus "I forgive you"

"It's OK" or "Forget it" puts the repentant one down, rejects them and the relationship, avoids intimacy, is thing-centered, and makes light of the repentant one's approach and apology.

"I forgive you" requires no conditions, implies a commitment ("I'm yours"), says our relationship is more important than the hurt, and centers on the repentant one.

Barriers to forgiveness

Keeping score	Needing to be right
Demanding change for forgiveness	Always placing fault on the other party
Not forgiving self	Holding the 50/50 philosophy ("It's your fault too.")

Healing builds relationship

The humility and love of the guilty party affirms the healer.

The healer's mercy, etc., overwhelms the guilty party.

Memories of the healing bring closeness.

The healing brings new depth and growth to the relationship, not just a fresh start.

Sins in Scripture
Mark 7:21–23; Romans 1:28–31; Galatians 5:19–21; Ephesians 4:25–31; 2 Timothy 3:1–5

Mind
evil thoughts	lack of thankfulness	greed
impurity of mind	selfish ambition	arrogance
love of money	pride	willfulness
self-centeredness	deceitfulness	conceit
lack of forgiveness	covetousness	haughtiness
		lust

Emotions
envy	rebelliousness	anger	loss of temper
hatred of God	hatred	bitterness	hatred of good
heartlessness	jealousy	resentment	maliciousness
			unloving attitude

Mouth
slander	backbiting	evil talk	contentiousness
malignity	quarreling	malicious remarks	disputing
whispering	lying	false accusations	blaspheming
gossip	swearing	complaining	yelling
			boasting

Behavior
adultery	fraud	witchcraft	disobedience to parents
stealing	invention of evil	drunkenness	brutality
murder	covenant breaking	carousing	lack of self-control
indecency	ruthlessness	abuse	violence
	idolatry	lack of principles	showing partiality

Characteristics of the proud and the humble

Proud, unbroken people don't think they need revival, but they know everyone else does. Humble, broken people continually sense their need for ongoing encounters with God and fresh fillings of His Spirit.

Proud people

- are quick to blame others;
- want to hide their sin;
- have a hard time saying, "I was wrong. Will you please forgive me?";
- tend to deal in generalities when confessing their sin;
- are concerned about the consequences of their sin to themselves;
- are sorry their sin was discovered;
- wait for the other party to request forgiveness when there's been a conflict;
- and don't think they have anything to repent of.

Humble, broken people

- accept personal responsibility and can see where they were wrong in a situation;
- are willing for their sins to be exposed because they have nothing to lose;
- are quick to admit their failure and to seek forgiveness;
- can acknowledge specifics when confessing their sin;
- are grieved over the cause, the root of their sin;
- are truly, genuinely repentant over their sin, which is evidenced by their forsaking that sin;
- take the initiative to be reconciled when there is a misunderstanding or a conflict in a relationship, no matter how wrong the other may have been;
- and realize they need a continual attitude of repentance.

Appendix E

Memorizing Scripture

Benefits of memorizing Scripture

Internalizing Scripture renews your mind and changes your thought life (2 Corinthians 4:16–18; Colossians 3:1–3; Hebrews 4:12).

It changes your behavior because thoughts influence behavior (Psalm 119:11; Matthew 15:18–20; Romans 13:14).

It affects how you use your tongue (Psalm 19:14; Proverbs 26:20–22; Ephesians 4:29; 1 Peter 3:10, 11).

Scripture memorization equips you to face situations biblically (Deuteronomy 6:6–8; 2 Timothy 3:16, 17).

It establishes a foundation from which to conquer temptation and overcome sin (Psalm 119:9–11; Matthew 4:1–10).

It becomes an integral part of your prayer life (Acts 4:24–31).

Living in Scripture influences how you teach and encourage others (Colossians 3:16, 17).

It provides a basis for meditation (Psalm 119:15, 16, 36, 37, 97).

Immersing yourself in Scripture stabilizes your spiritual life (Psalms 37:31; 40:8).

It enables you to extend your devotional time throughout the day (Psalm 1:2; Philippians 4:8).

It enables you to reflect on God's Word anytime and anywhere (Joshua 1:8; Psalm 63:6–8).

Memorizing deepens scriptural insights (1 Thessalonians 2:13).

It enables you to see connections between passages (2 Corinthians 4:16–18; Hebrews 11:1).

It makes you much more sensitive to and uncomfortable about sin in yourself and in others (Ephesians 4:29).

Living in Scripture deepens and broadens your prayers (Ephesians 6:17, 18).

It is Christlike (Matthew 4:1–10).

Traps in memorizing Scripture

1. Focusing on words mechanically
2. Trying to memorize too much in too short a time
3. Subtle (and not so subtle) boasting about it
4. Using verses out of context
5. Using Scripture insensitively on others (e.g., judging them)
6. Counting too much on its positive *emotional* benefits
7. Memorizing in only one or two subject areas
8. Memorizing primarily for personal benefit

Poor reasons for memorizing Scripture

1. A group you're in demands it of you
2. You're offered an external reward (e.g., a trophy or ribbon)
3. Someone else is doing it
4. It makes you feel better
5. It helps you to win arguments
6. You want to build up a spiritual scoreboard

Several suggestions

If you are feeling called to begin the journey of memorizing Scripture, I would suggest two things. First, find a time in your life when you can block out several weeks to focus on this project. I am convinced that the experience I related in chapter 14 wouldn't have happened if I had simply decided to memorize one verse a week as a new religious practice. Due to the circumstance, in a very real sense, I immersed myself in memorizing Scripture for several weeks. After that I settled into a more balanced pace of memorization, learning new verses and reviewing ones I had previously memorized. But the initial immersion is what thrust me into experiencing the huge benefits of Bible memorization.

Second, those who have studied memory processes have learned that people need to follow certain procedures. If a text is to be readily available to you once you've memorized it, you must review it daily for six weeks before laying it aside. Even then, you'll need to review it again periodically. The following steps incorporate this second suggestion:

1. Write a scripture passage on a card.
2. When you can repeat the passage by memory, write on the card the date six weeks hence.
3. Continue to repeat the passage daily for six weeks.
4. At the end of the six weeks, place the card with others to be reviewed on an occasional basis.

Scripture Memory Plan 1

1. Read the context of the verse in your Bible and meditate on it. This helps you understand the verse in its setting.
2. Thoughtfully read the verse aloud or in a whisper several times. This will help you grasp the verse as a whole.
3. Include the reference by saying it before and after the verse every time you repeat it.
4. Print your memory verse neatly on individual index cards. You may want to punch a hole in each card and use a ring clasp to keep the cards together. Place them in a packet or put an elastic band around them and carry them with you at all times.
5. Break the passage into natural phrases. Learn the reference and first phrase. Then repeat the reference, first phrase, and second phrase. Continue adding

phrases until you've memorized the verse.

6. Take advantage of your spare time during the day to pull out your packet and memorize your verses. Use the time you spend waiting in line, on the bus, doing dishes, mowing the lawn—any time your activities don't require attention to detail. A renewed thought life will emerge from this habit.

7. Review the verse every day for at least six weeks before placing it aside for periodic review.

Scripture Memory Plan 2

1. Print a verse and scripture reference on an index card. Ask God for His help in understanding and applying this portion of His Word to your life.

2. Recite the week's memory verse and reference five to ten times when you awaken in the morning and five to ten times before you go to sleep at night.

3. Carry your scripture memory card pack with you throughout the day to review the verses you've memorized. Insert your new verse into your scripture memory card pack at the end of the week.

4. Review each verse in your scripture memory card pack at least once per day for six weeks before placing it in a weekly review group of previously memorized verses.

Scripture Memory Plan 3

1. List a number of places or items that you visit regularly in your daily routine—for example, a mirror, a briefcase, a purse, the bathroom, the kitchen, a favorite book.

2. Print your memory verse and its scripture reference on as many index cards as you have places listed and post your scripture memory cards in these places.

3. Whenever you visit these places or items each day, quote the verse and the reference listed on the card.

4. At the end of the week, remove your current memory verse cards from their posted places and items and replace them with a new verse. (You can post

multiple verses while reviewing the others daily, weekly, or monthly.)

Scripture Memory Plan 4

1. Read a verse and its reference into a tape recorder, reciting it as many times as you want to repeat it.
2. At various times during each day, play back what you have recorded and recite the reference and the verse with the tape recording.
3. Recite your past memory verses and their references into your tape recorder. On a weekly basis, evaluate your retention of these verses by reciting them when you play back the verses.

Scripture Memory Plan 5

1. Get excited about what God is saying to you. This may not speed up the memorizing, but it sure makes it more fun and invigorating.
2. Allow a block of *unrushed* time for the initial memorization of a text. How well you will remember it later will be in direct proportion to the time you spend at first.
3. Read and meditate on the text and the verses and/or chapters around it to help you understand the text in its setting.
4. Begin by memorizing the key words. This helps you focus on the main thought and not on all the descriptive words or phrases, which can discourage you when first memorizing a text. Or, memorize one phrase at a time, breaking up the text into its natural phrases.
5. Look for similar sounds, rhymes, and/or repeated words.
6. Try to visualize what the words are describing as you memorize. See the place, the people, their actions, and their emotions. Put yourself in the setting being described—become a part of it. Or you can visualize by picturing the words of the text in your Bible so when you say the verse, you picture in your mind how the words are laid out in your Bible.
7. Say the text out loud with all the emotion and feeling you can put into it. This uses several of your senses, and the more senses you use, the quicker you will memorize the verse.
8. Copy the verses on cards so you can carry them around with you. If you

prefer to visualize the words as they appear in your Bible (see number 6 above), copy the text exactly as it appears in your Bible.

9. Experiment with motion: which is better for you while memorizing—walking or sitting?

10. Other things that might help you memorize more quickly:

- Highlight key words and/or phrases with different colored markers.
- Experiment with background noise—total quiet versus soft inspirational music.
- Experiment with light—bright light versus soft light.

Endnotes

Chapter 3—My Leap of Faith

1. W. Clarence Schilt, *How to Die Right and Live to Tell About It* (W. Clarence Schilt, 2005).

2. C. S. Lewis, *Mere Christianity* (San Francisco: HarperCollins, 2001), 32.

Chapter 4—Denial: The Cover-up

1. Derived from several surveys reported on at www.barna.com from 2001–2006.

2. Barna Group, "Barna Identifies Seven Paradoxes Regarding America's Faith," Barna Group, http://www.barna.org/FlexPage.aspx?Page=BarnaUpdate&BarnaUpdateID=128.

Chapter 5—Self-deception: The Lies We Believe

1. Arbinger Institute, *The Anatomy of Peace* (San Francisco: Berrett-Koehler Publishers, 2006), 229.

Chapter 6—Protest: Illusions of Self

1. David F. Wells, *God in the Wasteland* (Grand Rapids, Mich.: Eerdmans, 1994), 100, 101.

2. Think Exist.com Quotations, "Anne Lamott Quotes," ThinkExist.com, http://thinkexist.com/quotes/anne_lamott/ (accessed August 9, 2008).

Chapter 7—Despair: Solutions That Fail

1. Think Exist.com Quotations, "Benjamin Spock Quotes," ThinkExist.com, http://thinkexist.com/quotes/Benjamin_Spock/ (accessed August 9, 2008).

2. Benjamin Spock, "Interview with Dr. Spock," *Redbook,* February 1974.

Chapter 8—Acceptance: Wired for Self

1. Norman Doidge, *The Brain That Changes Itself: Stories of Personal Triumph From the Frontiers of Brain Science* (New York: Penguin Group, 2007), xvi.

Chapter 9—The Exchanged Life

1. Lewis, 191, 192.

2. Ibid., 205.

3. C. Brand, C. Draper, and A. England, eds., *Holman Illustrated Bible Dictionary* (Nashville, Tenn.: Holman Reference, 2003), s.vv. "cross," "crucifixion"; emphasis added.

Chapter 10—Trusting His Heart

1. Dallas Willard, *Renovation of the Heart* (Colorado Springs, Colo.: NavPress, 2002), 71, 72.

Chapter 14—Learning His Heart

1. John Piper, *Future Grace* (Sisters, Ore.: Multnomah, 1995), 9.

Chapter 15—When Being Right Is Wrong

1. Larry Crabb, *Inside Out* (Colorado Springs, Colo.: NavPress, 1988), 138, 141.

Chapter 17—Feeding His Heart

1. Frederick Buechner, *Wishful Thinking* (New York: Harper & Row, 1973), 2.

2. Think Exist.com Quotations, "Aristotle Quotes," ThinkExist.com, http://thinkexist.com/quotes/aristotle/2.html (accessed August 9, 2008).

3. Lewis, 196, 197.

Chapter 19—Passion for His Heart

1. Lewis, 86.

2. Best Quotes Poems.com, "Saint Augustine," Best Quotes Poems.com, http://www.best-quotes-poems.com/Saint-Augustine.html (accessed October 5, 2008).

3. Aleksandr Solzhenistsyn, *The Gulag Archipelago* (New York: Harper Collins, 1985).

Chapter 20—Protecting His Reputation

1. Lewis, 122.

2. Ibid., 124.

Chapter 21—A Life to Die For

1. Bob Stanley, "Gems From Saint Augustine," The Catholic Treasure Chest, http://home.inreach.com/bstanley/august.htm (accessed October 5, 2008).

IF YOU FOUND THIS BOOK INSPIRING AND THOUGHT-PROVOKING, YOU'LL WANT TO READ THESE BOOKS AS WELL.

Searching for a God to Love (Updated Edition)

Chris Blake

A modern classic just got better.

"God is more a poet than a police officer. He's more an acrobat than an accountant, more a midwife than an anesthetist. He values relationships more than rules. He's more interested in our nearness than in our neatness. He desires more to be loved than to be understood."

Searching for a God to Love has captivated readers for a decade and now appears in five languages. In the updated edition, author Chris Blake has added a new chapter and a series of probing study questions that can be used in small groups.

Control issues. Unloving, judgmental people. Boredom.
It had little to do with God, but it all got mixed up together.

You have questions.
You have doubts.
You've been hurt.

You ache for something more than rhetoric, preaching,
and simplistic reasoning.

Great.

You qualify to take the journey this book defines.

Paperback. 256 pages.
ISBN 13: 978-0-8163-2304-3
ISBN10: 0-8163-2304-6

3 Ways to Order
1. Local—Adventist Book Center®
2. Call—1-800-765-6955
3. Shop—AdventistBookCenter.com

© 2009 Pacific Press® Publishing Association
Please contact your ABC for pricing in Canada

Searching for the God of Grace

Stuart Tyner

THERE'S A GLORIOUS TREASURE
Free, inexhaustible, valuable beyond measure, yet refused,
ignored, trampled on, locked up, and buried . . .

SEARCHING FOR THE GOD OF GRACE explores the treasure we've struggled to accept. With a deeply hidden feeling of futility, many Christians try to take responsibility for their own salvation and blend it with Jesus' gift of atonement. Discouraged by their failures, they find no peace with God.

Stuart Tyner examines the pages of history and biblical principles of God's character to "clear away a few more obstacles, burst a few more padlocks, and unbury the spectacular riches of God's grace."

Paperback. 304 pages.
ISBN 13: 978-0-8163-2152-0
ISBN 10: 0-8163-2152-3

3 Ways to Order
1. Local—Adventist Book Center®
2. Call—1-800-765-6955
3. Shop—AdventistBookCenter.com

© 2009 Pacific Press® Publishing Association
Please contact your ABC for pricing in Canada